Microsoft® Money 2003 For Dummies®

Recording a Transaction in an Account Register

1. Open the register of the account in which you want to record a transaction.

2. Click the tab — Withdrawal, Deposit, or Transfer — that describes the transaction you intend to record.

3. In the transaction form at the bottom of the register, click the Number tab to move to the Number text box.

   You can move from box to box in a transaction form by clicking an individual box or by pressing Tab or Shift+Tab.

4. Enter a number in the Number text box, if necessary.

5. Enter the date in the Date text box.

   You can quickly enter dates by clicking the down arrow to the right of the Date text box, opening the minicalendar, and clicking a date.

6. Enter whom you paid the money to in the Pay To text box or received the money from in the From text box.

   If you've previously entered this name in the text box, simply type the first few letters to make the entire name appear.

7. Enter the transaction amount in the Amount text box.

8. In the Category text box, enter a category or subcategory.

9. If you care to, write a few words in the Memo text box to describe the transaction.

10. Click the Enter button or press the Enter key.

What to Do If You Can't Reconcile an Account

✔ Look for a transaction on the bank statement that isn't in the register. For example, if there is a difference of $25.17 between your records and the bank's, chances are you forgot to record a $25.17 transaction.

✔ Look for amounts that were entered incorrectly in the register. Transposed numbers (entering $32.41 instead of $34.21, for example) are often the culprit.

✔ Look for duplicate transactions in the register that were accidentally entered twice.

✔ See whether you entered a deposit where you meant to enter a withdrawal — or vice versa. Entering transactions on the wrong tab causes problems when you reconcile.

✔ See whether the Ending (Statement) balance is incorrect. You can't reconcile an account if you entered the ending statement balance incorrectly. Double-check the interest and service charges as well to see whether you entered them correctly.

For Dummies: Bestselling Book Series for Beginners

Microsoft® Money 2003 For Dummies®

Navigation Bar Buttons and Where They Take You

Clicking This Button	Takes You to ...
Home	The Home Page, your starting point for doing any number of tasks
Account List	The Account List window, where you see a list of your accounts and account balances
Portfolio	The Your Portfolio window, where you can monitor stocks, bonds, mutual funds, and other investment holdings
Bills & Deposits	The Bills and Deposits window, where you can record the bills you pay regularly and enlist the Money program's help in paying bills on time
MSN.com	The MSN Web portal, where you can search the Internet, read articles, and play games
Reports	The Pick a Report or Chart window, where you can generate reports and charts that show where you stand financially
Cash Flow	The Forecast Your Cash Flow window, where you can see projections about future income and spending
Budget	The Budget Planner window, where you can formulate and see whether you're meeting your budget goals
Categories	The Categories list with the names of categories that describe your income and expenses
Payees	The Payees window with a list of people to whom you've paid money and from whom you've received it

Five Things That Every Money User Should Do

- ✔ Keep your checking account, savings account, and credit card account registers up-to-date.
- ✔ Balance your bank accounts each month.
- ✔ Create categories and subcategories so that you can track your spending, income, and tax deductions.
- ✔ Back up your data file to a floppy disk or Zip drive.
- ✔ Generate a Spending by Category chart.

For Dummies: Bestselling Book Series for Beginners

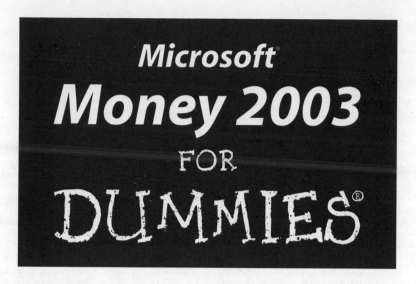

Microsoft® Money 2003 FOR DUMMIES®

by Peter Weverka

Wiley Publishing, Inc.

Microsoft® Money 2003 For Dummies®

Published by
Wiley Publishing, Inc.
909 Third Avenue
New York, NY 10022

www.wiley.com

About the Author

Peter Weverka is the bestselling author of several *For Dummies* books, including *Word 2002 For Dummies Quick Reference* and *Office XP 9 in 1 Desk Reference For Dummies,* as well as 20 other computer books about various topics. Peter's books have been translated into 16 languages and sold half a million copies. His humorous articles and stories — none related to computers, thankfully — have appeared in *Harper's, SPY,* and other magazines for grown ups.

Dedication

This book is dedicated affectionately to the intersection of 24th Street and Mission Street.

Acknowledgments

This book owes a lot to many hard-working people at the offices of John Wiley & Sons in Indianapolis, Indiana. I would like to thank Bob Woerner for giving me the opportunity to write this book and seeing it through the acquisitions stage.

I am especially grateful to Susan Christophersen for her encouragement and the long hours she worked on this book. Susan handles the editorial scalpel with great skill and is always a pleasure to work with.

Technical editor Allen Wyatt dogged me every step of the way to make sure that all the instructions in this book are indeed correct, and I want to thank him for his work. I would also like to thank TECHBOOKS Production Services for their index and proofreading, and Rich Tennant for the witty cartoons you will find in the pages of this book.

These people at John Wiley & Sons gave their all to my book, and I want to thank all of them: Laura Albert, Andy Hollandbeck, LeAndra Johnson, Stephanie Jumper, Susan Moritz, Kristin McMullan, Erin Smith, Jeremey Unger, and Erin Zeltner.

If I didn't thank the people who worked so hard on the first, second, and third editions of this book, I would be remiss, so thank you Steve Hayes, Jim McCarter, Kyle Looper, Tammy Castleman, Kathleen Dobie, Stephanie Koutek, Brian Kramer, Patricia Pan, Rev Mengle, Diane Smith, and Gareth Hancock.

Finally, thanks go to my family — Sofia, Henry, and Addie — for indulging my vampire-like work schedule and eerie demeanor at daybreak.

Peter Weverka
San Francisco
August 2002

Publisher's Acknowledgments

We're proud of this book; please send us your comments through our online registration form located at www.dummies.com/register/.

Some of the people who helped bring this book to market include the following:

Acquisitions, Editorial, and Media Development

Project Editor: Susan Christophersen

Acquisitions Editor: Bob Woerner

Technical Editor: Allen Wyatt

Editorial Manager: Carol Sheehan

Editorial Assistant: Amanda Foxworth

Production

Project Coordinator: Erin Smith

Layout and Graphics: LeAndra Johnson, Stephanie Jumper, Kristin McMullan, Jeremey Unger, Erin Zeltner

Proofreaders: Laura Albert, Andy Hollandbeck, Susan Moritz, TECHBOOKS Production Services

Indexer: TECHBOOKS Production Services

Publishing and Editorial for Technology Dummies

Richard Swadley, Vice President and Executive Group Publisher

Mary C. Corder, Editorial Director

Andy Cummings, Acquisitions Director

Publishing for Consumer Dummies

Diane Graves Steele, Vice President and Publisher

Joyce Pepple, Acquisitions Director

Composition Services

Gerry Fahey, Vice President of Production Services

Debbie Stailey, Director of Composition Services

Contents at a Glance

Table of Contents

Introduction

• •

Microsoft Money 2003 makes managing your personal finances very easy. Well, not "very easy," but close to it. With Money 2003, you don't need a bookkeeper to track your finances. You don't need an accountant or financial counselor, either. And you don't need to be a computer expert. All you need to know is how to use Money 2003.

After you start using the techniques I describe here, you will know how to record financial transactions, how much you spend in different areas, and what your net worth is. You will know what any investments you may have are worth and roughly how much you owe in taxes. You will know how to print checks, generate reports and charts that show in clear terms what your spending habits are, plan for retirement, compare mortgages and loans, and analyze different kinds of investments.

Most important, you will be able to make wise financial decisions by taking advantage of the program's numerous financial analysis tools, all of which I explain in this book. And you will also make wise decisions, because you will have the raw data on hand. After you record transactions in Money, the raw data is right there inside your computer. I show you how to analyze it, scrutinize it, dissect it, investigate it, and contemplate it. I show you how to admire it, too. After you read this book, you can start admiring what a financial wizard you have become.

Whom This Book Is For

This book is for users of Money 2003 Deluxe and Microsoft Money 2003 Standard Edition who want to get to the heart of the program without wasting time. Don't look in this book to find out how Money works. Look in this book to find out how *you* can manage *your finances* with Money.

I show you everything you need to know to stay on top of your finances — from recording checks and deposits to tracking investments. On the way, you have a laugh or two. And you can shed light on parts of your finances that have never seen the light of day before.

About This Book

This book is jam-packed with instructions, advice, shortcuts, and tips for getting the most out of Money. Here's a bare outline of the five parts of this book:

- **Part I: Setting Up and Starting Out:** Part I spells out everything you need to know to use Money wisely. It explains how to find your way around the Money windows, set up accounts, record transactions, categorize your spending and income, reconcile an account, and print checks.

- **Part II: Going Online with Money:** If your computer is connected to the Internet, you are invited to go online and take advantage of Money's online features. Among other high-tech tasks, Part II explains how to download bank statements over the Internet, pay bills online, and update your investment portfolio by getting security prices from the Internet.

- **Part III: Getting Your Money's Worth:** In Part III, you discover how to budget with Money, schedule bill payments so that you make them on time, and do the mundane chores, such as backing up your financial data, that make Money run more smoothly.

- **Part IV: Improving Your Financial Picture:** Part IV explains how to generate reports and charts so that you can see exactly where you stand financially, plan for your retirement and other future events, analyze investments and loans, track your assets and liabilities, and monitor the performance of your investments.

- **Part V: The Part of Tens:** Each of the four chapters in Part V offers 10 tidbits of advice — advice for staying on top of your finances, improving your financial health, using Money if you are self-employed, and converting from Quicken to Money.

But wait — there's more! Turn to the Appendix to find out how to install Money and to the "Glossary of Financial Terms" to look up the financial terms that appear in this book.

Foolish Assumptions

Please forgive me, but I made one or two foolish assumptions about you, the reader of this book. I assumed that

- You use a Windows operating system — Windows 95, Windows 98, Windows NT, Windows XP, or higher.

✔ You own a copy of either Microsoft Money 2003 or Microsoft Money 2003 Deluxe. (The Appendix explains how to install Money.)

✔ You are kind to foreign tourists and small animals.

Conventions Used in This Book

I want you to understand all the instructions in this book, and in that spirit, I've adopted a few conventions.

To show you how to give commands, I use the ⇨ symbol. For example, you can choose File⇨Back Up to make a backup copy of the data you store in Money. The ⇨ is just a shorthand method of saying "Choose Back Up from the File menu."

Notice how the *F* in File and the *B* in Back Up are underlined in the preceding paragraph. Those same characters are underlined in the command names in Money. Underlined letters are called *hot keys*. You can press them along with the Alt key to give commands and make selections in dialog boxes. Where a letter is underlined in a command name or in a dialog box, it is also underlined in the step-by-step instructions in this book.

Besides pressing hot keys to give commands, you can press combinations of keys. For example, you can go to the Pick a Report or Chart window by pressing Ctrl+Shift+R. In other words, hold down the Ctrl key and Shift key and press the R key at the same time. Where you see Ctrl+, Alt+, or Shift+ and a key name or key names, press the keys simultaneously.

Where you see boldface letters in this book, it means to type the letters. For example, "Type **Where Did the Money Go?** in the Report name text box" means to do exactly that: Type the words **Where Did the Money Go?**.

Icons Used in This Book

To help you get the most out of this book, I've placed icons here and there. Here's what the icons mean:

Next to the Tip icon, you can find shortcuts and tricks of the trade to make your visit to Moneyland more enjoyable.

Where you see the Warning icon, tread softly and carefully. It means that you could be about to do something that you may regret later.

When I explain a juicy little fact that bears remembering, I mark it with a Remember icon. When you see this icon, prick up your ears. You will discover something that you need to remember throughout your adventures with Money.

When I am forced to describe high-tech stuff, a Technical Stuff icon appears in the margin. Good news: Only two Technical Stuff icons appear in this entire book (I don't like reading about technical stuff any more than you do). The first reader who finds both Technical Stuff icons wins a free trip to the Happyland Desert Park in Blythe, California (just kidding!). You don't have to read what's beside the Technical Stuff icons if you don't want to.

Occasionally, Money and Money Deluxe work differently (they better work differently — the Deluxe edition costs $40 more). To mark instructions that apply only to the Deluxe edition, a Money Deluxe icon appears in the margin.

Part I
Setting Up and Starting Out

The 5th Wave   By Rich Tennant

"Since we began online shopping, I just don't know where the money's going."

In this part . . .

*H*ello, this is your captain speaking. Thank you for flying Money. In the next six chapters, you can take off, soar above the clouds, and discover the basics of tracking your finances with Microsoft Money 2003.

Please observe the "Fasten your seat belt" sign. And if I ask you to hold your breath and flap your arms to help the plane stay aloft, please do so promptly.

Chapter 1

Introducing Money

- -

- -

Chapter 1 is where you get your feet wet. Don't be shy. Walk right to the shore and sink your toes in the water. Don't worry; I won't push you from behind. Not so bad, is it?

In this chapter, you discover the various ways that Money 2003 can help you stay on top of your finances. You also discover how to start the program, find your way around the Money windows, and run Money Express, Money's sleek companion program for people who are in a hurry.

Finding Out How Money Tracks Your Finances

All the personal finance advisors agree that keeping good, accurate records is the first step toward financial security. Before you can start saving for a down payment on a house, you have to know how much you are capable of saving. Before you can tell whether your investments are doing well, you have to track them carefully. If you want to make sound financial decisions, you need to know what your spending habits are and how much income you really have.

Microsoft Money 2003 makes keeping accurate financial records very, very easy. After you use the program for a while, you will know precisely what your account balances are, what your net worth is, and how much your investments — if you have investments — are worth. To find out precisely how much you spend in different areas, all you have to do is generate a chart like the one in Figure 1-1 (Chapter 14 explains how). At tax time, you can run a report that lists and totals all your tax-deductible expenses. With Money, you can print checks, do your banking over the Internet, find out exactly what your spending habits are, compare loans and mortgages, plan for retirement, and track and analyze different kinds of investments.

Entering data correctly in Money is essential. Money can't do its job well unless you carefully and conscientiously enter financial data. If all you want to do is balance your savings and checking accounts, you've got it made, because Money offers lots of opportunities for double-checking the accuracy of transactions in savings and checking accounts. However, to track investments and loans, draw up a budget, or do a handful of other sophisticated things, you need to take care when you enter the data.

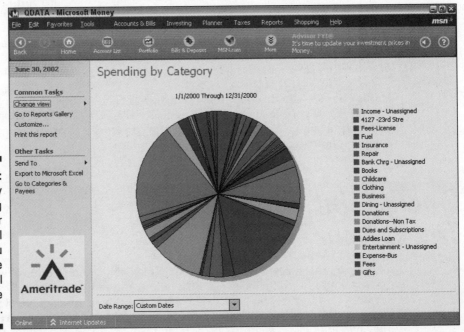

Figure 1-1:
By carefully entering your financial data, you can create meaningful charts like this one.

Starting the Program

Starting Money is as easy as falling off a log. You can start the program from the menus or by clicking the Microsoft Money shortcut icon on the desktop:

- ✔ **From the menus:** Click the Start button, choose Programs (or All Programs), and choose Microsoft Money 2003.
- ✔ **Microsoft Money shortcut icon:** Double-click the Microsoft Money 2003 shortcut icon on the desktop.

 When you install Money, the installation program asks whether you want to put a Money shortcut icon on the desktop. I hope you answered "yes," but if you didn't, you can still create a shortcut icon for starting Money. To do so, follow the standard Windows procedure for creating shortcut icons. If you don't know what those are, don't worry about a thing. Follow these steps:

1. **Click the Start button and choose Programs (or All Programs).**

2. **Locate the Microsoft Money 2003 menu command and right-click it.**

   A shortcut menu appears.

3. **Right-click Create Shortcut on the menu.**

   Another menu item called Microsoft Money 2003 (2) appears on the menu.

4. **Drag the menu command you just created onto the Windows desktop.**

   That's right — click and drag. The shortcut icon appears on the desktop.

5. **Right-click the shortcut icon, choose Rename, and enter a shorter name for the icon (I suggest "Money").**

If you have never used Money before . . .

The first time you run Money, the Setup Assistant comes on-screen and offers to help you get going. The Setup Assistant does the following:

- ✔ Creates a file for storing your financial transactions. The file is called My Money.

- ✔ Offers to Interview you about your financial plans and interests. Money will do a bit of setup work in the background on the basis of the answers you give.

- ✔ Offers to help you set up accounts in Money.

Rather than let yourself be grilled by the Setup Assistant, I recommend clicking the Skip the Setup Assistant and Start Using Money Now hyperlink. You can create bank accounts and set up categories later. Personally, I think you need to know more about Money before you get down to the nitty-gritty.

A Fast Trip around the Money Windows

When arriving in a foreign city, the first thing most people do, after finding a hotel room and taking a shower, is go for a stroll. In the following pages, you can stroll very gingerly across the Money screens. Enjoy yourself and take your sweet time. And don't forget to put film in the camera before leaving the hotel.

The Home Page

When you start Money, the first thing you see is the *Home Page,* shown in Figure 1-2. The Home Page is the starting point for all your excursions in Money. If the Home Page looks familiar, it isn't because you visited the Home Page in a past life. No, the Home Page looks familiar because it's modeled after a Web site. Notice the links that you can click and the splashy graphics. If you roll the mouse carefully just about anywhere on the Home page, you find a *hyperlink* — a link, or button, that you can click to visit a new Money window. Sometimes a little butterfly appears beside the mouse pointer when you move it over a button or hyperlink. That butterfly means that clicking the button or link takes you to a Web site on the Internet.

Notice the Home button in the upper-left corner of the screen. No matter how far you stray from the Home Page, you can always click the Home button (or press Alt+Home) to return to it. The button is always there. Click it if you get homesick.

Don't worry — the Home Page is not as complicated as it looks. It offers a look at different aspects of your finances, buttons that you can click to go to different Money windows, and links to sites on the Internet. More important, you can decide for yourself what appears on the Home Page. Later in this chapter, the section "Personalizing the Home Page" explains how to put what matters most to you on the Home Page.

The Money Help program opens when you open Money for the first time. You can see the Help program on the right side of the screen. Click the Close Money Help button (the X) to close the Help program, as shown in Figure 1-2.

Going from window to window: The Navigation bar and Navigation buttons

Besides clicking the Home button to return to the Home Page, you can also go from window to window by clicking buttons on the Navigation bar, by using the Go menu on the menu bar, or by clicking the Back or Forward button. The Navigation bar and Navigation buttons, as with the Home button, are always available and ready to be clicked. And you can open the Go menu whenever you wish.

The Navigation bar

The *Navigation bar* is the strip along the top of the screen below the menu bar. (I don't know why Microsoft chose the name Navigation bar. On most ships, the navigator sits in the wheelhouse, not in the bar.) Account List is the leftmost button on the Navigation bar; the More button is the rightmost button. By clicking one of the seven buttons — Account List, Portfolio, Bills & Deposits, MSN.com, Reports, Cash Flow, or More — you can visit other windows in Money.

Table 1-1 explains where the buttons on the Navigation bar take you. The table is here to show you what happens when you click a button and to give you a glimpse of the different tasks you can do with Money. Try clicking a button to start your own adventures in Money.

Navigation buttons · Navigation bar · Close Help Program

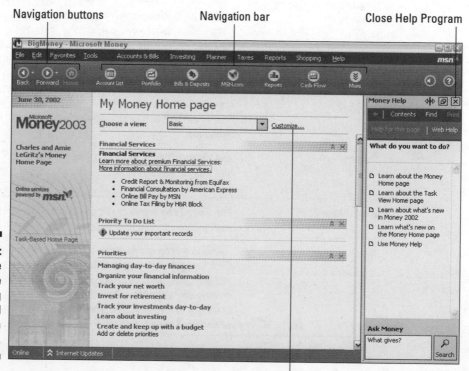

Figure 1-2:
The Home page is the starting point for all activity in Money.

Customize link

Table 1-1	Navigation Bar Buttons and Where They Take You
Clicking This Button . . .	*Takes You to . . .*
Account List	The Bank Accounts window, which lists the name of each account you set up. You can click an account name to go to its account register. Open the Bank Account window when you want to set up an account, enter account transactions, balance an account, or bank online.
Portfolio	The Portfolio window, where you can track stocks, bonds, mutual funds, and other investment holdings. Start here when you want to download security prices from the Internet.
Bills & Deposits	The Bills & Deposits window, where you can record the bills you pay regularly and enlist the Money program's help in paying those bills on time. You can also record automatic deposits in this window.
MSN.com	MSN.com, a Web portal operated by the Microsoft Corporation, where you can get the latest news, search the Internet, or read articles. You can also personalize this Web page and get financial information that pertains to securities you own. Notice that the Web page appears in the Money window, not in your Web browser window. Click the Money button (you will find it next to the Forward navigation button) to return to Money.
Reports	The Reports window, where you can generate reports and charts that show right away where you stand financially.
Cash Flow	The Cash Flow window, where you can forecast what your future income and account balances will be.
More	Displays a drop-down menu containing more choices. Click Budget on the drop-down menu to formulate a budget; Categories to create categories for tracking your income and expenses; Payees to look up the addresses of people and businesses to whom you made payments; or Money Browser to go to the MSN Web portal.

Navigation buttons: Back and Forward

The Back and Forward buttons work exactly like the Back and Forward buttons in a Web browser such as Netscape Navigator or Internet Explorer. Click the Back button to return to a window you visited; click the Forward button to revisit a window you retreated from.

Next to both the Back and Forward buttons is a little downward-pointing arrow. Click the little arrow and you see a shortcut menu that lists the windows you visited. I recommend clicking the little arrows beside the Back and Forward buttons early and often. Clicking the arrows and choosing window names is the fastest way to get from place to place in Money.

Personalizing the Home Page

When you start Money 2003, you see the Home Page (refer to Figure 1-2). The Home Page is supposed to give you a quick look at your finances, and if you play your cards right, it can do that. As shown in Figure 1-3, you can change views on the Home Page and peek into a different aspect of your finances by choosing an option on the Choose a View drop-down menu. You can, for example, see which bills are due, check account balances, and find out roughly how much in taxes you owe.

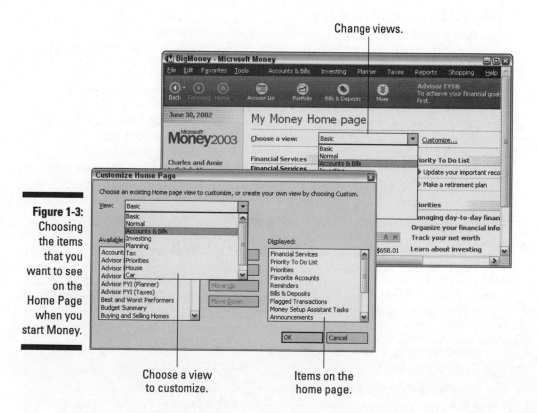

Change views.

Figure 1-3: Choosing the items that you want to see on the Home Page when you start Money.

Choose a view to customize.

Items on the home page.

Your finances, however, are yours and yours alone, so sooner or later — when you get better acquainted with Money — you need to strip the Home Page of all the stuff that Money has put on it and decide for yourself what goes there. To personalize your Home Page, start by clicking the Customize hyperlink or choosing Tools⇨Options, clicking the Feedback tab in the Options dialog box, and clicking the Customize button under Home Page Customization. Either way, you see the Customize Home Page dialog box, shown in Figure 1-3. From here, you can decide what you want to see in the different Home Page views. Choose which view you want to customize on the View drop-down menu. Then select an item from the Available box and click the Add button to move it to the Displayed box and place it on your home page. Choose Investment Performance, for example, to see at a glance how your investments are doing. Or choose Budget Summary to see whether you are sticking to a budget you prepared with Money. As you must have noticed by now, the Home Page list can get very long. To discard an item, select it in the Displayed box and click the Remove button. To put an important item at the top of the list, select it and then click the Move Up button until the item arrives in the right place.

As your adventures into Money take you deeper into the program, you will find out what all the options in the Customize Home Page dialog box are. Don't forget this very handy dialog box. You can use it to call attention to what is important in your finances each time you start Money.

The fastest way to remove an item from the Home Page is to click the X on the bar to the right of its name. I suggest doing that right away to all the advertisements for credit cards and stock-trading companies on the Home Page. Who needs another advertisement? To get rid of all the advertisements on Money screens, choose Tools⇨Options, select the General tab in the Options dialog box, and unselect the Turn Off Sponsorships and Shopping Links check box.

Choosing which window appears at startup

Suppose that you don't care to see the Home Page when you start Money. Maybe you prefer another window, an account register, or the window you were looking at when you closed the program last time around. Follow these steps to choose which window you see when you start the program:

1. **Choose Tools⇨Options to open the Options dialog box.**

2. **Click the General tab.**

3. **Under Display, click the arrow to open the Start Money with this Page Open drop-down menu, and then choose the window you would like to see.**

4. **Click OK.**

Shutting Down Money

When the time comes to close the Money program and get on with your real life, do one of the following:

- Click the Close button (the X in the far upper-right corner of the program window).
- Choose File⇨Exit.
- Press Alt+F4.

Veteran computer users are accustomed to saving files before exiting a program, but that isn't necessary with Money because the program saves data as soon as you enter it. If you look for a Save command or button in Money, you will look in vain — there isn't one.

When you shut down Money, the last thing you see is the Back Up to Floppy dialog box, as shown in Figure 1-4. This dialog box makes backing up the data you just entered in Money very easy, and I strongly recommend taking advantage of it. Chapter 10 explains everything you need to know about backing up a data file, including how to tell Money where to back up a data file. For now, click the Back Up Now button to be done with it.

Figure 1-4:
The Back Up to Floppy dialog box is your cue to make a backup copy of the Money file.

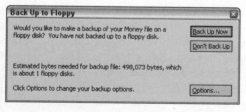

Money Express: The Fast Way to Enter Transactions

You probably didn't know it when you purchased Money 2003, but you got a second program as well. You got Money's little brother, Money Express, a program whose purpose is to keep you on your toes and help you enter transactions quickly.

When an FYI Advisor alert needs your attention (see Chapter 12) or a bill is overdue or needs to be paid soon (see Chapter 11), the Money Express program icon appears in the lower-right corner of the screen next to the clock, and Money Express opens whenever you start your computer, as shown in Figure 1-5. Simply click the Close button to dismiss Money Express. At any time, you can double-click the Money Express icon to open the Money Express window.

Choose a New Transaction option
to enter a transaction quickly.

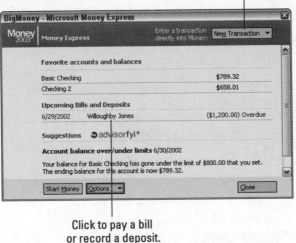

Figure 1-5:
Money
Express
warns you
when bills
are overdue
or an alert
needs your
attention.

Click to pay a bill
or record a deposit.

In the case of an upcoming or overdue bill, click the bill's name in the Money Express window to open Money to the Bills & Deposits window and pay the bill. As for the alerts, read all about 'em in the Money Express window and try not to wring your hands or sweat profusely while you are being alerted.

Personally, I like the New Transaction button in the Money Express window. Click it and choose an option on the drop-down menu that appears to quickly enter a withdrawal, deposit, or money transfer in the Rapid Transaction Entry dialog box, as Figure 1-6 shows. Whether or not you open the Money program, the transaction you enter in the dialog box is recorded in a Money register. You'll see it next time you open Money.

Some people don't like Money Express. They object to the Money Express icon crowding the corner of their computer screen. They don't care to see Money Express whenever they turn on their computer. For those people, Money offers options for deciding how much Money Express you need or want:

✔ To keep the Money Express window from appearing each time you start
   your computer, click the Options button in the Money Express window
   and choose Configure Money Express from the menu. Then, in the
   Money Express Configuration dialog box, uncheck the Run Money
   Express on Startup check box.

✔ To keep Money Express from running altogether, choose Tools➪Options,
   click the Bills and Deposits tab in the Options dialog box, and uncheck
   the Use Money Express option.

Figure 1-6:
The quick
way to
record a
transaction
in a register.

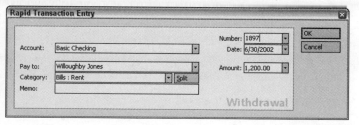

Chapter 2

Setting Up Your Accounts

· ·

In This Chapter

▶ Understanding how accounts and registers record financial activity

▶ Identifying the 17 kinds of accounts

▶ Setting up a checking and savings account

▶ Listing account numbers, contact persons, and the like

▶ Changing account names and types

▶ Setting up a credit card account

· ·

Chapter 1 gets you going with Money. In this chapter, you get down to the nitty-gritty: how to set up accounts so that you can track financial activity.

In this chapter, you discover how to set up savings, checking, and credit card accounts. You also find out about Money files, how to put an account on the Favorites menu, and how to change account names and account types.

Accounts and Registers for Recording Financial Transactions

The first step in tracking your financial activity is to set up an account for each type of item you want to track — a checking account, a savings account, or an IRA, for example. When most people hear the word *account,* they think of savings accounts, checking accounts, and other kinds of bank accounts. However, accounts in Money are a little more than that. For example, you can create a home account for tracking the value of a house. You can also create a credit card account for tracking credit card charges.

When you set up an account, you need to name the kind of account you want. Money offers 17 kinds of accounts. Table 2-1 describes the different kinds of Money accounts and mentions where you can turn to read more about them.

Table 2-1	Microsoft Money's 17 Kinds of Accounts
Account	*What the Account Is For*
Asset	Tracking the value of items that you own — real estate, a truck, a baseball card collection. Asset accounts can be useful for finding out your net worth. (See Chapter 16.)
Bank	Recording transactions made to a bank account, but not a savings account, checking account, or line of credit.
Car or Other Vehicle	Recording the equity and market value of a car, boat, or other item for which you have taken out a loan. (See Chapter 16.)
Cash	Recording cash payments and tracking petty cash accounts. (See Chapter 16.)
Checking	Recording activity in a checking account. (See "The Basics: Setting Up Checking, Savings, and Credit Card Accounts" in this chapter. Chapter 3 explains how to record transactions in checking accounts.)
Credit Card	Recording credit card purchases, finance charges, and credit card payments. (See "The Basics: Setting Up Checking, Savings, and Credit Card Accounts" in this chapter. Turn to Chapter 3, as well.)
Employee Stock Option	Tracking stock options you receive from the company you work for. (See Chapter 17.)
Home	Tracking how much equity is in a house and determining a house's market value. (See Chapter 16.)
Home Equity Line of Credit	Tracking payments and the interest portion of payments on a home equity loan. (See Chapter 3.)
Investment	Tracking the value of something you own and intend to sell later for a profit — stocks, bonds, securities, annuities, treasury bills, precious metals, real estate investment trusts (REITs), and unit trusts. (See Chapter 17.)

Account	What the Account Is For
Liability	Tracking debts for which you don't have to pay interest — income taxes that you owe and private loans, for example. (See Chapter 16.)
Line of Credit	Recording payments made with a *debit card* — a charge card that debits, or deducts money from, a bank account. (See "The Basics: Setting Up Checking, Savings, and Credit Card Accounts" in this chapter, and read Chapter 3 as well.)
Loan	Tracking debts for which you have to pay interest, such as car loans. (See Chapter 16.)
Mortgage	Tracking mortgage payments. (See Chapter 16.)
Other	Recording transactions that — you guessed it — don't fit neatly in the other 16 categories. Hmm. I've been racking my brain for an example of an account that doesn't fit into the other 16 categories, and for the life of me I can't think of one. Maybe this account is where someone would keep laundered money.
Retirement	Tracking tax-deferred retirement plans, such as 401(k)s, Keoghs, SEPs (Simplified Employee Pensions), and IRAs. (See Chapter 17.)
Savings	Recording activity in a savings account. (See "The Basics: Setting Up Checking, Savings, and Credit Card Accounts" in this chapter. Chapter 3 explains how to record transactions in a savings account.)

Each time you set up an account, Money creates a new register for recording transactions. As all bookkeepers know, a *register* is a place for recording income and expenses, withdrawals, deposits, payments, and the like. Figure 2-1 shows a checking account register for recording checks, deposits, and withdrawals in a checking account.

Registers look different, depending on the type of account you have set up, but all registers have places for recording transaction dates and transaction amounts. Registers also show balances. The *balance* is the amount of money in the account, or, in the case of an asset, liability, or investment account, the value of the thing that you're tracking.

A word about Money files

After you install Money, the program gives you the opportunity to create a file called My Money for storing your transactions. Chances are, that file is the only one you need, but some rare birds require a second file. Create more than one file if:

✔ You intend to use Money to track your personal finances and your business finances, and you want to keep the two separate. Self-employed people don't necessarily need a second file. I'm self-employed and I use the same file to track my personal and business transactions. However, if you run a small business, you absolutely need a separate file. The general rule is this: If you submit a separate tax return for your business and yourself, you need two Money files.

✔ Someone other than you uses your computer to track his or her finances with Money.

✔ You track someone else's finances.

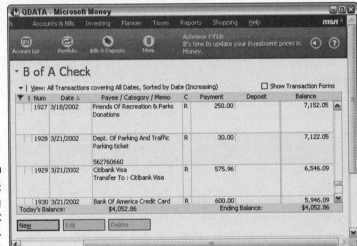

Figure 2-1: A checking account register.

The Basics: Setting Up Checking, Savings, and Credit Card Accounts

After you see the big picture and know what an account and a register are, you can create an account. In the next sections, you find out how to set up a checking account, savings account, and credit card account. Setting up the other kinds of accounts is a bit more complicated and I explain them elsewhere in this book. (Table 2-1, which appears earlier in this chapter, mentions where to turn.)

Setting up a checking or savings account

Everybody, or just about everybody, has at least one checking and one savings account. Set up an account in Money for each checking and savings account you keep with a bank. Be sure to get out the paperwork before you set up the checking or savings account. You need to know the account number and a few other details.

Follow these steps to set up the account:

1. **Choose Accounts & Bills⇨Account Setup.**

   You land in the Set Up Your Accounts window. This window is the starting point for managing accounts you have set up in Money.

2. **Click the <u>Add a New Account</u> hyperlink, the first one listed under "What do you want to do?"**

   You see the first of several New Account dialog boxes, like the one shown in Figure 2-2. Each dialog box asks a nosy question about your account.

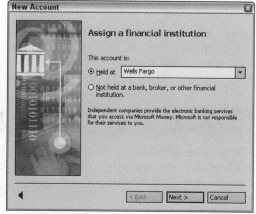

Figure 2-2: To set up a new account, fill out a bunch of dialog boxes like this one.

3. **In the <u>H</u>eld At text box, type the name of the bank or financial institution in which you keep the account; then click the Next button.**

   If you have another account with the bank and have set up an account in Money for tracking it, you can enter the bank's name by clicking the down arrow and selecting a bank name from the drop-down list.

4. In the next dialog box, choose the name of a financial institution.

Money needs the name of a bank, credit card company, brokerage house, or other financial institution in case you want to bank online. Information about the institution you choose will be stored in Money in case you want to bank over the Internet.

5. In the next dialog box, select the type of account you want to create — Checking or Savings — and then click the Next button.

Table 2-1 explains what the account types are. You can also read their descriptions in the dialog box.

6. Type a descriptive name for the account and then click the Next button.

The name you type appears in the Accounts window. Type a descriptive name so that you can distinguish this account from the others you set up in Money.

7. In the next dialog box, type the account number and click the Next button.

The dialog box you see next asks for the balance (how much money is in the account).

8. Enter a figure for the account balance, choose a currency if need be, and click the Next button.

Knowing the balance isn't as important as you may think — you can change the starting balance after you set up the account by changing the first entry in the account register.

More power to you if you know the starting balance and you have diligently kept records so that you can enter past transactions and bring the account up-to-date. If you don't know the opening balance, either enter the balance from your last bank statement or make an estimate. Chapter 3 explains the ins and outs of starting balances.

9. Select either I Have No Other Accounts at This Institution or I Have Other Accounts at This Institution and click the Next button.

This dialog box wants to know whether you keep other accounts at the same bank where you keep this account.

Clicking I Have No Other Accounts at This Institution takes you to the Finish dialog box.

Clicking I Have Other Accounts at This Institution takes you to the dialog box for selecting an account type. Follow Steps 5 through 9 again to give Money the lowdown on the next account.

10. **Click the Finish button.**

    The last dialog box offers a button called Go to Online Setup for setting up online bank accounts, but you don't have to click it just yet. Take a peek at Chapter 7 if online banking is your cup of tea.

At the end of the ordeal, you go to the Online Services Manager window. Money, it seems, will do anything to get you to bank online. You can visit this window whenever you please by choosing Accounts & Bills⇨Online Services Manager. Chapter 7 explains how to complete the setup work for going online.

Listing contact names, phone numbers, and other account details

Before you put away the paperwork and say good-bye to the account you set up, take a moment to acquaint Money with the details. As Figure 2-3 shows, the program has a special Update Details window for entering a bank's telephone number, an account's minimum balance, and anything else you care to enter.

The Update Details window is a handy place to store bank telephone numbers and other information. If you lose your passbook, ATM card, or credit card and need to call the bank, for example, you can get the number from the Update Details window. The window also has a check box for making an account appear on the Favorites menu.

Follow these steps to get to the Update Details window and enter the pertinent information or view information about an account you already set up:

1. **Click the Account List button on the Navigation bar to go to the Accounts window.**

   You can also get there by choosing Accounts & Bills⇨Account List.

2. **Click the name of the account whose details you want to enter or see.**

   You go to the account register where activity in the account is recorded.

3. **Click the <u>Change Account Details</u> hyperlink.**

   You can find it on the left side of the window, under "Common Tasks."

   The fastest way to get to the Update Details window is to right-click an account name in the Accounts window and choose See Account Details from the shortcut menu.

4. Enter or view information about your account in the window.

In Figure 2-3, I entered a contact name and a telephone number, for example.

5. Click the Done button if you entered information in the Update Details window.

Where is the Done button? It's at the bottom of the window. You have to scroll to get there. After you click the Done button, you return to the account register.

Enter information about the account.

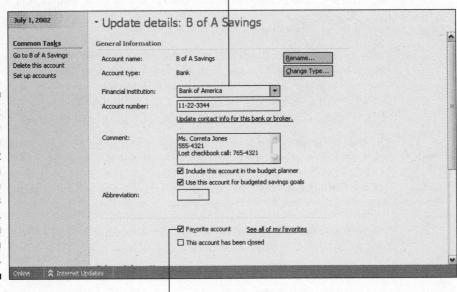

Figure 2-3:
Keep
information
about
accounts on
the Update
Details
window,
where you
can get it in
a hurry.

Click to put the account on the Favorites menu.

Changing an account's name or type

Suppose that you got it wrong. Suppose that you gave the account the wrong name or told Money that a checking account was a savings account. All is not lost. You can fix these grievous errors by returning to the Account Details window and clicking the Change Account Details button.

Selecting your "favorite" accounts

Checking accounts, credit card accounts, and other accounts that you have to dig into on a regular basis are good candidates for "favorite" status. The names of favorite accounts appear on the Favorites menu. All you have to do to open a favorite account is choose Favorites⇨ Favorite Accounts and the name of the account. As Chapter 1 explains, you can also make your "favorite" accounts appear on the Home Page so that account balances stare you in the face, for good or ill, whenever you start Money. By clicking an account name on the Home Page, you can view the account's register and enter transactions.

Follow these instructions to make an account a favorite account:

✔ Right-click an account name in the Accounts window and choose Favorite (click the Account List button to open the Accounts window).

✔ Choose Favorites⇨Organize Favorites⇨ Accounts and, in the Select Your Favorite Accounts window, check the names of accounts.

✔ Click the Favorite Account check box on the Update Details window (refer to Figure 2-3).

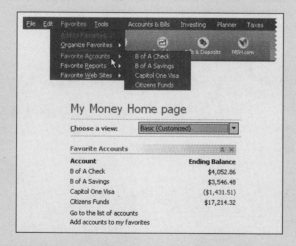

Follow these steps to change the name and other information about an account:

1. Go to the Accounts window.

To get there, click the Account List button on the Navigation bar or choose Accounts & Bills⇨Account List.

2. Click the name of the account that needs an overhaul.

This action opens the account register.

3. **Click the <u>Change Account Details</u> hyperlink.**

   You land in the Update Details window (refer to Figure 2-3). From here, you can change the account number, the minimum balance, and more trivial things as well. You can also rename an account or change its type.

4. **Rename the account or change the account type.**

   Click the Rename or Change Type button.

   • **Rename an account:** Click the Rename button, type a new name in the Modify Account dialog box, and click OK.

   • **Change an account type:** Click the Change Type button. As shown in Figure 2-4, you see the Modify Account dialog box. Choose a new account type from the Account Type list and click OK.

If you want to change account types but can't find a radio button on the list for the account type you want, you're out of luck. In its wisdom, Money puts radio buttons in the Modify Account dialog box only for accounts to which your account can be changed. Camels can't fly, and credit card accounts can't, for example, be changed into investment accounts.

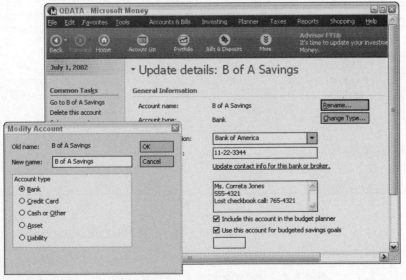

Figure 2-4:
To change the account type, choose a new account type in this dialog box and click OK.

If all you want to do is change the name of an account, here's the fastest way: Right-click the name of the account in the Accounts window, choose Rename from the shortcut menu, enter a new name, and click OK.

Setting Up an Account to Track Credit Card and Line of Credit Transactions

Except for filling out an extra dialog box or two, setting up a credit card or line of credit account works the same way as setting up a checking or savings account. Set up a credit card or line of credit account for each credit card and each line of credit you have. When you set up the account, Money asks how much you owe and whether you want a reminder when the credit card bill or line of credit bill is due.

Get out your last credit card or line of credit statement and follow these steps to set up a credit card or line of credit account:

1. **Place a finger of your right hand on this page and, with your left hand, turn back several pages to the "Setting up a checking or savings account" section.**

2. **Follow Steps 1 through 7 (but not Step 5) of the instructions for setting up a checking or savings account.**

   In other words, go to the Set Up Accounts window, click the <u>Add a New Account</u> hyperlink, enter the name of the bank or credit card issuer, select Credit Card or Line of Credit as the account type, enter a descriptive name for the account, and enter the account number.

   Those steps bring you to the dialog box shown in Figure 2-5, where Money asks how much you owe. I hope that you are all paid up and owe nothing, but if you resemble the average citizen, you owe the bank or credit card issuer some money.

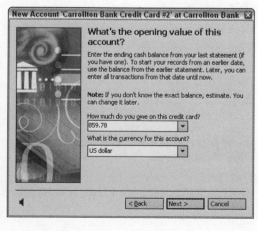

Figure 2-5:
In this dialog box, tell Money how much you owe the bank or credit card issuer.

 3. **Type 0 if the credit card or line of credit is paid in full; otherwise, type how much your last statement says that you owe; then click the Next button.**

 4. **Select the <u>C</u>redit Card or C<u>h</u>arge Card option and click the Next button.**

    This dialog box asks whether your account will track a credit card or charge card. As the dialog box explains, charge cards have to be paid in full each month, but you can carry debt from month to month with a credit card.

    Select the Credit Card option if the account tracks credit card spending or a line of credit. Otherwise, select Charge Card. If yours is a credit card that you don't need to pay in full but you intend to pay off each month, click the Always Pay Entire Balance Each Month check box.

    What happens next depends on whether the account tracks a credit card or charge card.

    If the account tracks a charge card, skip ahead to Step 6.

    If the account tracks a credit card or line of credit, the dialog box that appears asks you to list the interest rate you get charged for carrying debt, as Figure 2-6 shows.

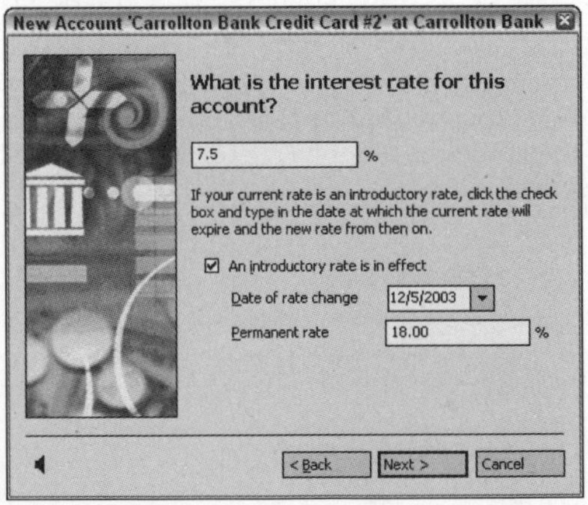

Figure 2-6:
In this dialog box, list the interest rate you get charged for carrying debt on a credit card.

 5. **Tell Money what rate of interest you are charged for using the credit card and then click the Next button.**

    List the interest rate in the first % box. If the rate is a temporary, introductory rate, click the An Introductory Rate Is in Effect check box and enter the permanent rate and the date that the temporary rate expires. Money needs this information for the Debt Reduction Planner and other features designed to help you manage debt.

6. **In the dialog box that follows, type the maximum amount that you can charge on your credit or charge card; then click the Next button.**

Your credit card statement lists the most you can borrow on your credit card. Get the figure from your statement.

7. **Make sure that the first option button, No, Don't AutoBalance This Account, is selected, and then click the Next button.**

This dialog box is kind of misleading. It seems to say that if you pay your credit card bill in full each month, you should click the second radio button, Yes, AutoBalance This Account. But you should do no such thing. Click the second radio button only if you *don't* want to track the charges you run up on your credit card.

8. **If you want the bill to appear on the Bills and Deposits window, make sure that you check the Yes, Remind Me When the Bill Is Due check box. Enter an estimate of how much you owe in an average month; also, enter a date in the Bill Is Due Next On box. Then click the Next button.**

As shown in Figure 2-7, the next dialog box asks whether you want to put the monthly credit card or line of credit payment on the Bill Calendar. If you click Yes, a reminder to pay the bill appears in the Manage Scheduled Bills and Deposits window and in Money Express. Chapter 11 explains how to schedule bills and deposits. For now, all you need to know is that the Manage Scheduled Bills and Deposits window reminds you when bills are due. If you want, the notice can also appear on the Home Page, where you can see it each time you start Money.

Figure 2-7:
From this dialog box, you can add the credit card or line of credit payment to the Bill Calendar and maybe pay the bill on time.

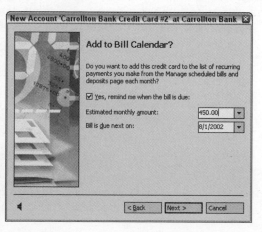

I strongly recommend placing a check mark in the Yes, Remind Me When the Bill Is Due check box. Credit cards and lines of credit can get very, very expensive if you don't work to pay them off or if you forget to pay them on time. Banks charge outrageous interest rates on lines of credit and credit cards. A reminder to pay the bill can help keep you from being squeezed by creditors.

Credit card and line of credit bills fall due on the same day each month. Each month, Money reminds you five days before each payment is due.

9. **Click Next in the following dialog box, which asks whether you can earn frequent flyer miles with your credit or charge card.**

   Chapter 11 explains how to track frequent flyer miles. Don't worry about it for now.

10. **Select either the I Have No Other Accounts at This Institution button or the I Have Other Accounts at This Institution; then click the Next button.**

    Selecting I Have No Other Accounts at This Institution takes you to the last dialog box, where you can click the Finish button and be done with it. Selecting I Have Other Accounts at This Institution takes you back to the dialog box for choosing an account type.

11. **Click the Finish button.**

    You can ignore the Go to Online Setup button for now. As Part II of this book explains, you can download credit card transaction records over the Internet. See Chapter 7 if that subject interests you.

After you set up your credit card or line of credit account, go to the Update Details window and enter the phone number of the credit card issuer or bank You may need the number, for example, if you must report a lost credit card. The "Listing contact names, phone numbers, and other account details" section in this chapter explains how the Update Details window works.

Chapter 3

Recording Your Financial Activity

∙∙∙

In This Chapter

▶ Opening an account register

▶ Recording transactions in registers

▶ Recording credit card transactions and payments

▶ Locating and fixing errors in registers

▶ Deleting and voiding transactions

▶ Printing an account register

∙∙∙

his chapter tackles the four or five things you have to do each time you run the Money program. It explains how to open an account register and how to record deposits, withdrawals, payments, and charges in registers. You also find out how to record a transfer of money between accounts, how to move around in a register, and how to find transactions in large registers. This chapter describes how to delete and void transactions. Finally, for the person who likes to leave behind a wide paper trail, this chapter explains how to print a register.

Accomplish the tasks described in this chapter and you are well on your way to becoming an ace user of the Money program.

The Basics: Recording Transactions in Savings and Checking Registers

After you set up an account (the subject of Chapter 2), you're ready to start recording transactions in the account's register. A *register* is the place where checks, payments, deposits, charges, and withdrawals are recorded. Figure 3-1 shows a checking account register. As with all registers, this one has places for numbering transactions, recording transaction dates, and viewing balances.

Check numbers

Date of transaction

Running balance

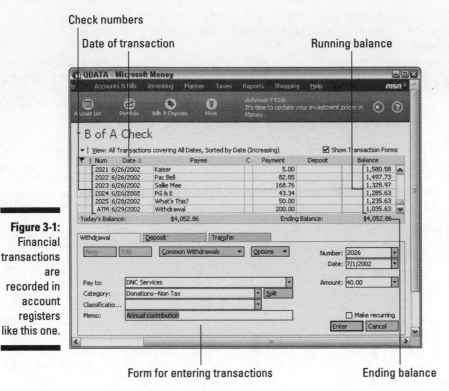

Figure 3-1:
Financial
transactions
are
recorded in
account
registers
like this one.

Form for entering transactions

Ending balance

The following sections explain how to record transactions in savings and checking account registers. Everybody, or almost everybody, has a savings or checking account, so these accounts are a good place to start. These sections explain how to open an account register and view it in different ways. You also find out how to record deposits, withdrawals, and checks, as well as how to record a transfer of money from one account to another. The basic techniques for recording transactions that you discover here apply to all the accounts you set up in Money — investment accounts, cash accounts, asset accounts, you name it.

Opening an account register

The first step to opening an account register is to go to the Accounts window. You can get there in one of three ways:

- ✔ Click the Account List button on the Navigation bar.
- ✔ Choose Accounts & Bills➪Account List.
- ✔ Press Ctrl+Shift+A.

The Accounts window, shown in Figure 3-2, is Account Central as far as Money is concerned. The window lists each account you have and how much money is in each account. Negative balances — credit card balances are usually negative because they represent money that you owe — are shown in red and surrounded by parentheses. At the bottom of the window is your total account balance, the sum of your savings, debts, assets, and liabilities, also known as your *net worth*. The sidebar "Reading the Accounts window" describes ways of viewing account names in the window.

The Accounts window shows you at a glance what your account balances are and where you stand financially. It's a nice place to visit, but when you're in a hurry, you can open an account register without going to the Accounts window first. Here are the various and sundry ways to open an account register:

- ✔ Click an account name in the Accounts window.

- ✔ Right-click an account name and choose See Account <u>R</u>egister on the shortcut menu.

- ✔ Choose F<u>a</u>vorites➪Favorite A<u>c</u>counts on the menu bar and then click the name of an account, assuming that you opted to make it a favorite. Favorite accounts can also be reached by choosing Accounts & Bills➪ Favorite Accounts. As Chapter 2 explains, you can also list favorite accounts on the Home Page and open them from there.

Click an account name to
open an account register.

Account balances.

Figure 3-2:
You can
open any
account
register
from the
Accounts
window.

Click to display accounts
in different ways.

Your net worth.

Reading the Accounts window

To begin with, accounts in the Accounts window are arranged by type, but you can change that. You can arrange accounts by name or by bank or brokerage firm. To do so, click the Sort account list by hyperlink and choose an option from the drop-down menu:

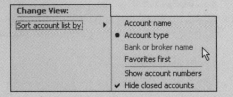

The menu also offers options for hiding closed accounts, showing account numbers,

and displaying favorite accounts at the top of the list. (Chapter 10 explains how to handle accounts you have closed.)

Click the plus (+) or minus sign (-) next to a subheading in the Accounts window to display or hide the account names under the subheading. When accounts are arranged by type, for example, clicking the minus (–) sign next to the "Bank Accounts" subheading removes all bank account names from the window.

Similarly, you can click the plus (+) or minus sign (–) next to an account name to see or hide the last handful of transactions that were recorded in the account.

Suppose that you're in one account register and you want to see a different register? Money provides a shortcut for skipping merrily from one register to the next. As shown in Figure 3-3, click the arrow beside the name of the account you are working with. You see a menu for going from register to register. Favorite accounts are listed at the top.

Which of these methods for opening an account register works best? How should I know? All I know is, you shouldn't try them all at one time.

Click here to open the account menu.

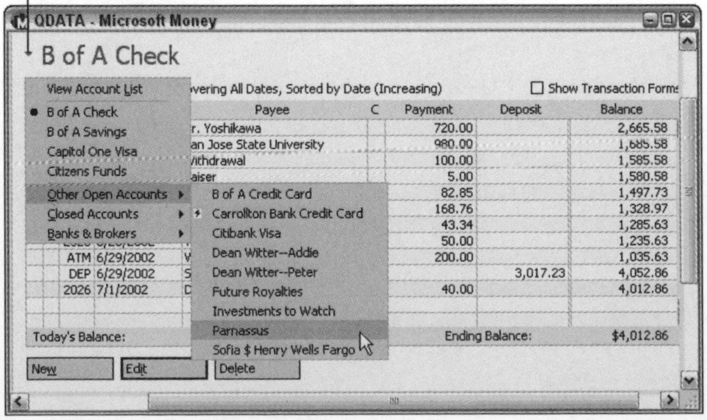

Figure 3-3:
Going from one register to the next.

Recording checks, deposits, withdrawals, and debit card purchases in registers

At the bottom of the Account Register window is a form for entering transactions in the register, as shown in Figure 3-4. (If you don't see the form, click the Show Transaction Forms check box in the upper-right corner of the window.) To enter a transaction, click a tab — Withdrawal, Deposit, or Transfer — and then fill in the transaction form.

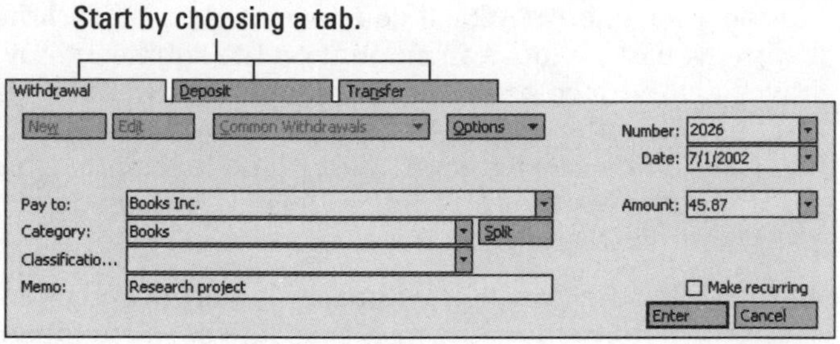

Start by choosing a tab.

Figure 3-4: Recording a transaction in an account register.

Which tab you click depends on which type of transaction you want to enter:

- ✔ **Withdrawal tab:** Taking money out of an account? Stealing from yourself isn't really stealing, but so that you don't feel guilty, let Money know how much you're taking out on this tab. Use this tab when you record check payments and cash withdrawals — any transaction in which money leaves an account.

- ✔ **Deposit tab:** When you put money into an account, record the transaction on this tab. Record all deposits to an account on this tab. That includes check deposits and deposits made at a cash machine.

- ✔ **Transfer tab:** Shifting money from one account to another? Click the Transfer tab.

Follow these steps to record a check, deposit, withdrawal, cash-machine withdrawal, or debit card purchase in a register:

1. **Open the register of the account in which you want to record a transaction (see the "Opening an account register" section, earlier in this chapter).**

2. **Click the Withdrawal or Deposit tab.**

   Is money going in or going out of the account? Outgoing money is recorded on the Withdrawal tab; incoming money is recorded on the Deposit tab.

3. **Tell Money what kind of transaction you want to record.**

   In some cases, you have to click the Common Withdrawals or Common Deposits button to describe a transaction.

   - **Cash withdrawal:** Do nothing. You're all set.

   - **ATM cash-machine withdrawal:** Click the Common Withdrawals button, then choose ATM. If you have made cash withdrawals before, you can choose an amount on the submenu, but if you haven't withdrawn before or the amount you want to withdraw isn't listed, choose Other Amount. When you are done recording the transaction, the letters ATM (automatic teller machine) will appear in the Number box of the register so that you know that the withdrawal was made at a cash machine.

   - **Check:** Click the Common Withdrawals button and choose Write a Check. Money enters the next available check number in the Number box. If this number is incorrect, enter the correct number.

   - **Check to a credit card issuer:** Click the Common Withdrawals button, choose Credit Card Payment, and choose the name of the credit card issuer from the drop-down menu. Later in this chapter, the section "Recording a credit card payment" explains this kind of transaction in detail.

   - **Debit card purchase:** Click the Common Withdrawals button and choose Debit Card Purchase. (If you got cash back with your purchase, see "Recording a deposit or debit card purchase with cash back," later in this chapter.)

   - **Cash deposit:** You're all set. Do nothing.

   - **Deposit of a check or checks:** You're all set, unless you want to record a deposit of more than one check or you got cash back after the deposit. See "Splitting deposits and withdrawals that don't fit in one category" and "Recording a deposit or debit card purchase with cash back," later in this chapter.

4. **Enter a number in the Number text box, if necessary.**

   To move from place to place on a transaction form, click elsewhere, or press Tab or Shift+Tab.

Only checks require a number, but you can enter deposit slip and withdrawal slip numbers if you want to track deposits and withdrawals carefully.

Money should have entered the next available check number, but if it didn't, click the down arrow to open the Number drop-down menu and then choose Next Check Number. If the number that Money enters is incorrect, enter the correct number.

5. Enter the date in the Date text box, if necessary.

Money puts today's date in the Date text box, so you don't need to do anything if you are recording a transaction you completed today. See the sidebar "Tips for entering transactions quickly" to discover fast ways to enter future and past dates and to fill in other parts of a transaction tab. Pressing Ctrl+D enters today's date.

6. Enter whom you're paying the money to in the Pay To text box, or whom you received the money from in the From text box.

The Deposit form has a From text box rather than a Pay To text box. As the "Tips for entering transactions quickly" sidebar explains, you can simply type in the first few letters of a name (if you received or paid money to this person or party before) to scroll the list of names and go to the one you want.

For deposits, enter the name of the person or business who wrote you the check or checks you deposited. For withdrawals, enter **Cash** if you withdrew cash from the bank. For ATM withdrawals, Money enters the word *Cash* automatically.

If you've entered this name in the register before, the amount you last paid or received appears in the Amount text box. Not only that, but the category that you assigned to the last transaction with this person or company appears in the Category text box. You may not have to change the amount or category choices. If this transaction is identical to the one you recorded last time, your work is almost done and you can skip to Step 10.

7. Enter the amount of the transaction in the Amount text box.

To enter a round number, you don't have to enter the decimal point or trailing zeroes. In other words, to enter "$21.00," all you have to type is "21." Money adds the zeroes for you.

8. In the Category text box, enter a category (or category and subcategory).

Creating and choosing the right categories and subcategories is so important that I devote most of Chapter 4 to the subject. By assigning categories and subcategories to income and expense transactions, you can discover where you spend your hard-earned money and where it comes from — critical information, especially if you itemize on tax forms.

Expense categories are at the top of the drop-down list. Payments require an expense category. Deposits require an income category, which are found in the middle of the drop-down list.

9. **If you care to, write a few words in the Memo text box to describe the transaction.**

   Write a memo if for any reason you may come back to the account register in the future, see the transaction, and not know what it was for.

10. **Click the Enter button or press the Enter key.**

   Click the New button if you want to clear the entry form and record another transaction.

Don't be alarmed if the transaction you just entered doesn't appear on the register's last line. Transactions appear in date order. The "How's your view of the register?" section, later in this chapter, explains how to display transactions in different ways.

By the way, if you start recording a transaction but then decide to finish it later or start all over, click the Cancel button. The Edit button is for altering a transaction you entered already. The "Changing, or editing, transactions" section later in this chapter explains how to do that.

If you entered a deposit where you should have entered a withdrawal, or entered a withdrawal where you should have entered a deposit, click the Options button on the transaction form, choose Change Transaction Type To, and choose Withdrawal or Deposit on the submenu.

Speed techniques for entering transactions

As shown in Figure 3-5, the Editing tab of the Options dialog box offers a bunch of options for speed demons. These options are designed to take some of the tedium out of recording transactions, but they're not for everybody. Choose Tools➪Options, select the Editing tab in the Options dialog box, and try your hand with the following entry options after you get comfortable with Money.

Tips for entering transactions quickly

Money offers a bunch of techniques for entering transactions quickly on transaction forms:

✔ **Dates:** A fast way to enter the date is to click the down arrow to the right of the Date text box and make the minicalendar appear. If the calendar shows the right month, simply click a day. Otherwise, click the arrows on either side of the month name to go backward or forward month by month, and then click a day.

Press the + (plus sign) on the keyboard to advance the date by a day; press the – (minus sign) to go back a day.

✔ **Autocomplete:** Money "remembers" all the people and businesses you pay and from whom you receive payments. If you have entered a name in the Pay To or From text box before, all you have to do to make the entire name appear is to type the first few letters — Money fills in the rest. Or you can click the down arrow next to the text box, scroll through the list of people or businesses you entered on past occasions, and

click a name to enter it. This feature, which Money calls Autocomplete, ensures that you don't have to keep entering the same names repeatedly.

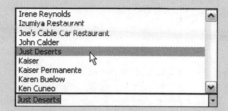

✔ **Doing the math:** Click the down arrow to the right of the Amount text box to see a minicalculator that you can use to do calculations — totaling the checks in a deposit, for example. Pressing the equals key (=) enters the total directly into the Amount text box. If you need a calculator that can handle advanced calculations, choose Tools⇨Calculator (or press Ctrl+K) to bring up the Windows calculator. You can cut and paste calculations that you make there into the Amount text box.

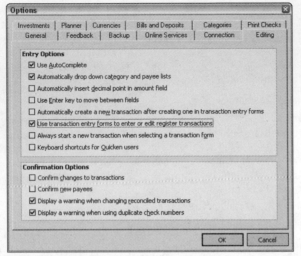

Figure 3-5:
These
options
take some
of the
tedium
out of
recording
trans-
actions.

Do you have to record past transactions?

I'm sorry to say it, but almost everyone has to record at least a few transactions from the past. When you set up an account, Money asks you to list or estimate a balance. If you follow Money's recommendation and enter the closing balance from your last bank statement, you have to enter all the transactions that don't appear on that statement because they haven't cleared the bank. In other words, if you wrote a check on June 30 and it didn't appear on the statement that you received on July 15, you have to enter that check in order to make your account balance.

To enter uncleared transactions, either use your own records or wait until next month's statement arrives and use it to record the absent transactions.

If you intend to use Money to help with tax returns, you'll need to record transactions back to beginning of your tax year, usually January 1. If today is September 30 or December 2, you have a great deal of work to do — or you can wait until next year to use Money in earnest. By way of encouragement, I can tell you that Money makes entering transactions an easy task, as this chapter and Chapter 4 show.

You can always change the opening balance of an account by changing the amount of the initial deposit. The opening balance of a brand new account is easy to figure out, but tracking an account you've had for a while requires a little detective work. You have to find out how much money was in the account as of the starting date that you entered when you set it up. That isn't easy. Rather than dig through old records, you may simply tinker with the initial deposit until the ending balance of the account matches the one on your last bank statement.

✔ **AutoComplete:** AutoComplete is great, of course. It keeps you from having to enter a payee name or category if you wrote a check or made a deposit from the same person or business before. All you have to do is enter the first few letters; AutoComplete does the rest. Still, if you like to exercise your fingers by typing, you can turn off AutoComplete by unchecking the Use AutoComplete check box.

✔ **Automatic drop-down categories and payee lists:** As soon as you move the cursor into the Pay To, From, or Category text box, a pop-up menu leaps on-screen so that you can choose a name and category. Some people find these menus annoying. They prefer to scroll the name and category lists by entering a letter or two. Uncheck the Automatically Drop Down Category and Payee Lists check box if you think the pop-up menus are a hindrance rather than a help.

✔ **Decimal points in the Amount text box:** This option makes entering the cents side of an amount a little easier. Entering a figure such as $23.27 requires pressing the period key to enter the decimal point, but if you choose Automatically Insert Decimal Point in Amount Field, all you have to do is type **2327** and Money enters the decimal point for you: 23.27. The downside of this option is having to enter two zeros when you enter a round number. With this option turned off, you can simply type **27** to enter $27.00, but if you select the option, you have to enter the zeros as well: **2700**.

✔ **Enter key for moving from box to box:** If you want to press the Enter key as well as the Tab key to move from box to box in transaction forms, select Use Enter Key to Move Between Fields.

✔ **Automatic new transactions:** This option makes for speedier entries. After you enter a transaction and click the Enter button, the particulars of the transaction — the payee, category, amount, and so on — remain on the entry form. To start another transaction, you have to clear the entry form by clicking the New button. Choosing Automatically Create a New Transaction After Creating One in Transaction Entry Forms clears the entry form right away. You don't have to click the New button.

✔ **Transaction entry forms for editing:** This option merely does what the Show Transaction Forms check box in account registers does — it makes an entry form appear on-screen. Don't bother unselecting the Use Transaction Entry Forms to Enter or Edit Register Transactions option. To remove an entry form, merely uncheck the Show Transactions Form check box in the account register.

✔ **Always start a new transaction:** Always Start a New Transaction When Selecting a Transaction Form. I'm having a contest to see which of you readers out there can be the first to figure out what this option does. This contest has no prize, but the winner is encouraged to submit his or her résumé to Microsoft.

   ✔ **Quicken keyboard shortcuts:** Quicken is a financial-tracking program
      similar to Money. Turncoats who have forsaken Quicken for Money can
      still use the Quicken keyboard shortcuts by selecting Keyboard
      Shortcuts for Quicken Users.

How's your view of the register?

Try using the View menu in the Account Register window like a TV remote-
control device to change channels when you get bored. As Figure 3-6 shows,
you can change views by clicking the triangle beside the word *View* and
making a choice from the drop-down list. No, the views are not especially
exciting, but I've seen worse on TV.

Click to open the View menu.

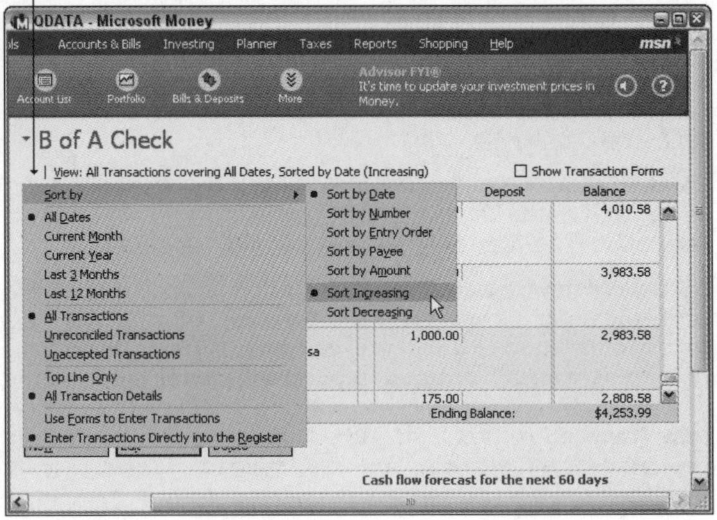

Figure 3-6:
The View
menu offers
many
different
ways to
arrange
transactions
on-screen.
Here, all
transaction
details are
shown.

Different kinds of registers offer different kinds of views. However, the
options fall into four categories:

   ✔ **Sort By options:** Options on the Sort By submenu determine the order
      by which transactions appear in the register. The default is Sort by Date,
      which arranges transactions in date order, as the way they are arranged
      on bank statements, but you can also arrange transactions by number,
      by the order in which *you* entered them, by alphabetical order of the
      payee's name, or by amount. The last two options on the submenu are
      for reversing the order of transactions.

- ✔ **Sort by date options:** Choose an option to show only transactions from the current month, current year, past three months, or past year.

- ✔ **Number of transaction options:** With the All Transactions option — you guessed it — all transactions appear in the register. However, to make only transactions that have not cleared the bank appear, select the Unreconciled Transactions option. This option is very handy when you are reconciling an account. Chapter 5 explains reconciling.

- ✔ **Amount of detail options:** To see more transactions on-screen, click the Top Line Only option. Only the first line of each transaction is shown. Select the All Transaction Details option or press Ctrl+T to see all parts of transactions, including categories and memo descriptions, as shown in Figure 3-6. Ctrl+T is a toggle key command. Press it to quickly change views.

- ✔ **Transaction forms options:** Choose the second option, Enter Transactions Directly into the Register, if you prefer doing that to entering transactions on forms. To enter a transaction directly into a register, click the last empty row and choose options from the drop-down menus that appear in the register columns. Personally, I find doing this very inconvenient, but you may like it.

Splitting deposits and withdrawals that don't fit in one category

Suppose that you try to record a transaction in a register but it doesn't fit in a single category. For example, suppose that you write a check to the Old Country Store to buy motor oil, a blouse, and a rocking chair. The transaction doesn't fall neatly in the Automotive, Clothing, or Household: Furnishings categories. And suppose that you deposit two checks at one time, one from your place of work and one from the New Jersey Lottery Commission. To record a transaction like that, you *split* it. Money offers the Split button on the transaction form for that very purpose, and you use it by following these steps:

1. **Record the transaction as you normally would.**

   If, like me, you don't have and never have had a good sense of what's normal, follow Steps 1 through 7 in the section "Recording checks, deposits, withdrawals, and debit card purchases in registers," earlier in this chapter.

   To total the checks in a deposit, click the down arrow beside the Amount box and total the checks on the minicalculator. After you click the equals button, the total is entered in the Amount box.

2. **Click the <u>S</u>plit button or press Ctrl+S.**

   You see the Transaction with Multiple Categories dialog box, shown in Figure 3-7. The Category list is already open so that you can select the first category.

   By the way, if you are depositing several checks, you can also click the Common Deposits button and choose Deposit Multiple Items from the menu to open the Transaction with Multiple Categories dialog box.

3. **For the first item that you purchased or deposited, select a category on the first line of the dialog box.**

4. **If you care to, enter a description in the Description text box on the first line.**

5. **In the Amount text box on the first line, enter the cost of the first item or the amount of the first check you deposited.**

6. **Repeat Steps 3 through 5 for each item you purchased or each check you deposited.**

   When you finish, the Sum of Splits figure should equal the Total Transaction figure, and the Unassigned figure should be 0.00. If the figures don't add up, tinker with the numbers in the Transaction with Multiple Categories dialog box until they do.

7. **Click the <u>D</u>one button to return to the transaction form.**

8. **Make sure that the transaction form is filled out properly; then click the Enter button.**

When a transaction has been split, the words "Split/Multiple Categories" appear in the Category text box of the register, as in Figure 3-8. To see how a transaction in a register was divided across categories, click the transaction, click the transaction form, and then click the Split button to open the Transaction with Multiple Categories dialog box.

Choose a category.   Enter an amount.

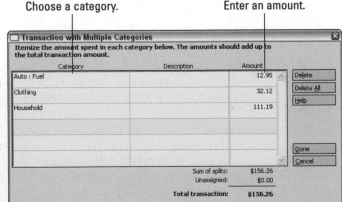

Figure 3-7: Splitting a transaction that doesn't fit into a single category.

This transaction was divided across categories.

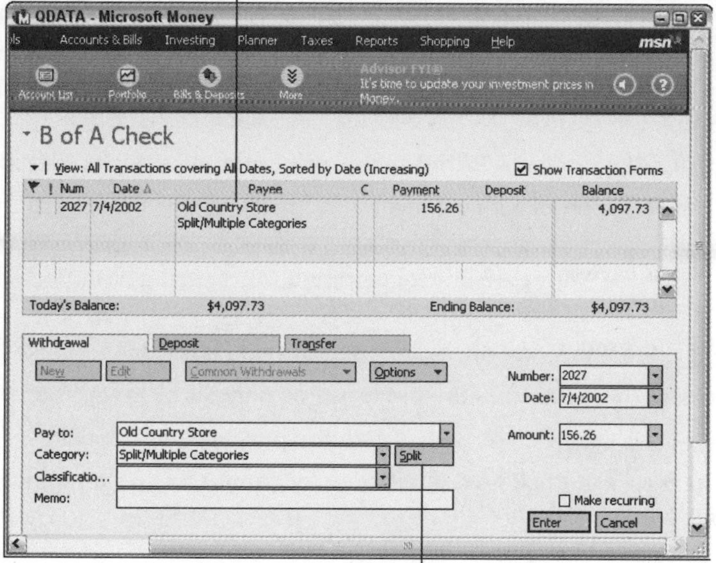

Figure 3-8:
When you
split a
transaction,
the words
"Split/
Multiple
Categories"
appear in
the register.

Click the Split button to see how
a transaction was split.

Suppose that you split a transaction but regret doing so. Click the transaction to select; then choose a single category in the Category box. That's all there is to it. Money removes the words "Split/Multiple Categories" and enters the name of the category you chose.

Recording a deposit or debit card purchase with cash back

Suppose that you deposit a check or make a debit card purchase and ask for a little cash back. Who doesn't need a little cash now and then? The problem with recording a cash-back deposit or debit card purchase with extra cash is that the transaction is really two transactions in one. In the case of the debit card purchase, part of the transaction is a debit card purchase and part is a cash withdrawal from a bank account. Likewise with cash-back deposits — part of the transaction is a deposit and part is a cash withdrawal.

Fortunately for you, Money offers special commands for recording these kinds of transactions. Follow these steps to record a cash-back deposit or debit card purchase:

1. **Open the register of the account in which you want to record the deposit or debit card purchase.**

   Earlier in this chapter, "Opening an account register" explains how to do that.

2. **Click the Withdrawal tab to record a cash-back debit card purchase; click the Deposit tab to record a cash-back deposit.**

3. **Click the Common Withdrawals or Common Deposits button.**

   A menu appears with commands for handling special kinds of transactions.

4. **To record a cash-back debit card purchase, click the Debit Card Purchase With Cash Back command; to record a cash-back deposit, click the Deposit With Cash Back command.**

   You see one of the dialog boxes shown in Figure 3-9.

5. **Enter the amount of the purchase or deposit in the Amount box.**

6. **In the Category box, categorize the purchase or deposit.**

7. **In the Cash Back box, enter how much money you took back with the purchase or deposit.**

8. **Click the OK button.**

   You see the Transaction with Multiple Categories dialog box (refer to Figure 3-7). From here, you can review the figures one last time or adjust them if need be.

9. **Click the Done button**

   You return to the account register. Notice, in the Category box, the words "Split/Multiple Categories." You have entered a split transaction — in this case, a withdrawal of cash as well as a payment or deposit. The amount box shows how much you actually spent or deposited.

10. **Complete the transaction as you normally would and click the Enter button.**

To examine a split transaction in a register, click the transaction, click the transaction form, and click the Split button. You see the Transaction with Multiple Categories dialog box (refer to Figure 3-7), which shows what took place in the transaction.

Transferring money between accounts

Sometimes, good luck comes your way; you earn a few extra dollars, so you transfer money from your checking account to a savings account or investment account. And sometimes, in a fit of panic, you have to transfer money from a savings account to a checking account to cover a couple of large checks. When you transfer money between real-life bank accounts, record the transfer in your Money account registers as well.

Transferring is more than meets the eye

It seems odd at first, but Money requires you to transfer funds not only when you transfer funds between bank accounts but also when you contribute to IRAs or other kinds of investments. Think of it this way: If you open an IRA and you write a $1,000 check for a contribution to your IRA, that $1,000 still belongs to you. You haven't really spent it. All you have done is transferred it from one account (checking) to another account (the retirement account with which you track the value of your IRA). Therefore, when you open a new account, you record the initial deposit as a transfer from your checking account to the new account.

You also transfer money between accounts when you pay a credit card bill. Here's how it

works: Each time you record a charge in a credit card account, the charge is added to the amount of money that you owe. Suppose that at the end of a month your account shows that you owe $200 because you charged $200 worth of items. To pay the $200 that you owe, you record a check for $200 to the credit card issuer, but in the register, the $200 is shown as a transfer from your checking account to your credit card account. After the transfer is complete, the $200 that you owed is brought to zero. The section "Recording a credit card payment" explains how to pay credit card bills.

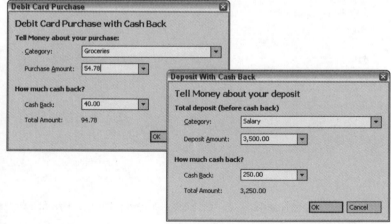

Figure 3-9: In the Cash Back box, enter how much you withdrew as part of your debit card purchase or deposit.

Follow these steps to record a transfer of money from one account to another:

1. **Open the register of the account from which you're transferring the money.**

   In other words, to transfer money from a checking to a savings account, open the checking account register.

2. **Click the Transfer tab.**

   You see the transaction form, shown at the bottom of Figure 3-10.

3. **Enter the date that the transfer was made in the Date text box.**

4. **In the Amount text box, enter the amount of the transfer.**

5. **Click the down arrow on the To drop-down list and select the account receiving the transferred money.**

   All the accounts you set up in Money appear on the To drop-down list. The name of the account from which you are transferring the money should already appear in the From text box. Leave the Pay To text box empty when transferring money between bank accounts.

   To speed the transaction, try clicking the Common Transfers button and selecting a bank or bank and transfer amount.

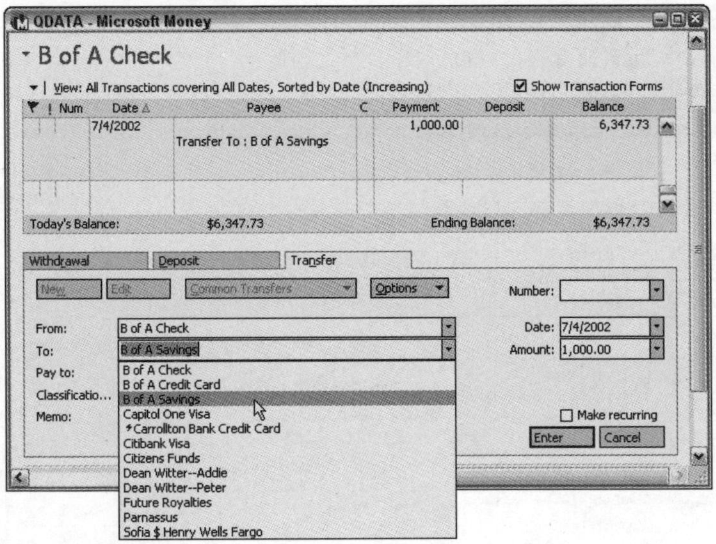

Figure 3-10:
Transferring
money
between
accounts
(bottom);
what a
transfer
looks like in
a register
(top).

6. **Enter a few words to describe the transaction in the Memo text box (optional).**

7. **Click the Enter button or press the Enter key.**

   The top of Figure 3-10 shows what a money transfer looks like in an account register. The transfer is counted as a debit — the amount you transferred is deducted from one account and added to the other.

Recording Transactions in Credit Card and Line of Credit Accounts

If you slogged through the previous few pages and discovered how to record checking and savings account transactions, you may experience *déjà vu* in the next few pages. Entering credit card and line of credit transactions is mighty similar to recording transactions made in savings and checking accounts.

Besides leaving credit cards at home, one way to keep credit card spending under control is to diligently record charges as you make them. As the amount that you owe in the credit card register gets larger and larger, you will be discouraged from spending so much with your credit card.

Recording credit card and line of credit charges

Credit card and line of credit account registers have a Charge form for recording charges. Figure 3-11 shows a Charge form. As does the Withdrawal form, the Charge form has places for entering a transaction date, amount, payee name, category, and memo. All the drop-down lists and keyboard tricks work the same way on a Charge form as on a Withdrawal form.

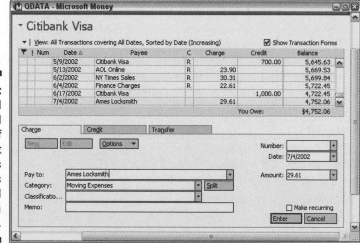

Figure 3-11: Record credit card and line of credit transactions exactly as you would record a check.

To fill in the Charge form, follow these steps:

1. **Open the account register.**

2. **Click the Charge tab.**

3. **Enter a reference number (optional).**

4. **Enter the charge date.**

5. **Enter the business you purchased the item from in the Pay To box.**

6. **Enter the amount of the charge.**

   Don't concern yourself with recording service charges and interest on your credit card. You can do that when you reconcile your account (a topic I explain in Chapter 5).

7. **Select a category.**

8. **Enter a description (optional).**

9. **Click the Enter button (or press Enter).**

Credit card and line of credit accounts track what you owe, not what you have. Don't forget this all-important detail. In the credit card register shown in Figure 3-11, you can clearly see the words *You Owe* where the words *Ending Balance* appear in a savings or checking account register. In effect, the You Owe number is a negative number. It represents an amount that you will have to pay out of your checking account one of these days.

Recording a credit

If you receive a credit from a bank or credit card issuer, perhaps because you overpaid, disputed a bill, or returned an item you bought, record the credit in the credit card account register. To do so, click the Credit tab and fill in the blanks in the Credit form. The Credit form works exactly like the Charge form (see the preceding section "Recording credit card and line of credit charges").

Be sure to record the credit in an expense category. Seems odd, doesn't it, to record credits as expenses? But when you recorded the purchase in the register, you assigned it to an expense category. Now that you're getting a refund, assign it to the same expense category so that the amount you spent in the category is accurate on your reports.

Recording a credit card payment

Before you make a credit card or line of credit payment, reconcile the credit card or line of credit account (Chapter 5 explains how). Then take note of how much of the debt you intend to pay, and follow these steps to make a payment to the bank or card issuer:

1. **Open the register (probably a checking register) of the account from which you intend to make the payment (see the section "Opening an account register," earlier in this chapter).**

2. **Click the Withdrawal tab at the bottom of the Account window.**

3. **Click the Common Withdrawals button, choose Credit Card Payment, and then choose the name of the credit card account where you track the credit card that you want to make a payment on.**

   The words "Credit Card Payment" and the name of the credit card account appear in the Category box on the transaction form, as shown in Figure 3-12.

Figure 3-12:
Paying all
or part of
a credit
card bill.

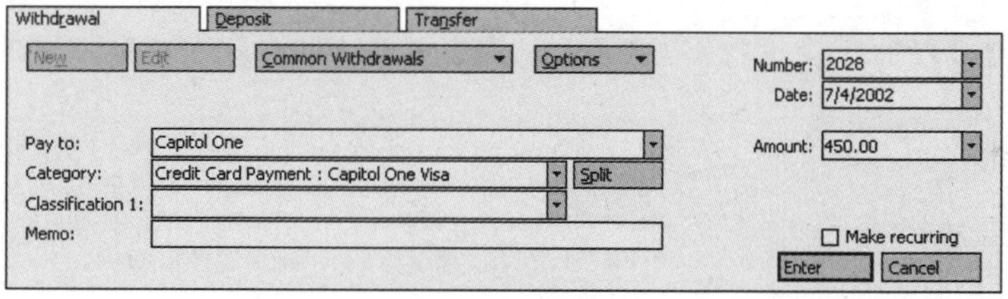

4. **Enter a check number in the Number text box if the number that appears there isn't correct.**

   Remember, you can click the down arrow and choose Next Check Number to enter the next available check number in the box.

5. **In the Date text box, enter the date that you wrote or will write on the check.**

6. **Enter the amount of the check in the Amount text box.**

   I hope that you can pay off the entire credit card or line of credit bill, but if you can't, Money doesn't care. Money continues to track what you owe from month to month.

7. **If you care to, write a few descriptive words in the Memo text box.**

8. **Click the Enter button or press Enter.**

   The amount you paid is deducted from the checking account. Meanwhile, the You Owe amount in the credit card or line of credit register decreases or is brought to zero. In effect, you have transferred money from your checking account to the account where you track credit card charges. Earlier in this chapter, the sidebar "Transferring is more than meets the eye" explains the mystery of why you transfer money between accounts to satisfy a credit card debt.

Right-click a credit card payment in a register and choose Go To Account: *Credit Card Name* (or press Ctrl+X) to go to the account register where you track credit card charges.

Fixing Mistakes in Account Registers

Everybody makes mistakes, and absolutely everybody makes mistakes when entering transactions in account registers. Most people do not have an expert typist's nimble fingers or sureness of touch. Therefore, the following sections explain how to find and fix mistakes, how to get from place to place in large registers, how to move transactions from one account to another, and how to delete and void transactions.

Finding a transaction so that you can fix it

Suppose that you made a terrific blunder somewhere in a register but aren't sure where. You categorized a transaction incorrectly, entered a transaction in the wrong account, or misspelled a name. Suppose that you made the error many times over. How can you fix the mistakes quickly without wasting an entire morning?

Fortunately, editing your transactions is easy in Money. But before you can fix errors, you have to find them. Read on to find out how to get around quickly in a register and how to find transactions with the Tools⇨Find and Replace command.

It helps to see more transactions on-screen when you are looking for a specific transaction. To see more transactions, uncheck the Show Transaction Forms check box, open the View menu in the upper-left corner of the register, and choose Top Line Only.

Moving around in an account register

One way to find a transaction is to eyeball the account register. With this technique, you put the register on-screen, move around in it like mad, and hope you find the transaction you are looking for. Table 3-1 presents keyboard and scroll bar techniques for getting around quickly in an account register.

Table 3-1	Keyboard and Scroll Bar Techniques for Moving around in Registers
Press/Click/Drag	***To Go...***
Ctrl+Home	To the first transaction in the register.
Ctrl+End	To the last transaction in the register.
↑ or ↓	To the previous or next transaction in the register.
PgUp or PgDn	Up or down an entire screen of transactions.
Scroll bar arrows	To the preceding or next transaction. Click the arrow at the top of the scroll bar to go up, the one at the bottom to go down.
Scroll bar	Up or down an entire screen of transactions. With this technique, you click the scroll bar but not the arrows or the scroll box. Click above the scroll box to go up; click below to go down.
Scroll box	Willy-nilly through the register. Drag the scroll box, the elevator-like object in the middle of the scroll bar, to go up or down very quickly.

Searching with the Find and Replace command

The surest way to pinpoint a transaction or a bunch of similar transactions is to choose Tools⇨Find and Replace (or press Ctrl+H). This command looks for transactions in all the registers, not just the one that is open, so you don't have to be in a specific register to start looking for transactions.

Follow these steps to look for transactions in your account registers:

1. **Choose Tools⇨Find and Replace.**

   You see the Find and Replace dialog box, shown in Figure 3-11. You can also press Ctrl+F to see this dialog box.

   From here, you can conduct a simple search of all your accounts, or an advanced search in which you tell Money in great detail where to search and what to search for.

2. **If you want to search only in investment or loan accounts, open the Search Across drop-down menu and make a choice.**

   You may as well start with a simple search and hope for the best. If you don't find what you are looking for, you can try an advanced search.

3. **Type what you are looking for in the Find This Text box, and if you know in which column of the register the thing is located, make a choice from the In This Field drop-down menu; then click the Next button.**

TIP

Figure 3-13 shows the fields you can choose from — Category, Payee, and so on — when you search regular accounts. If you are searching in a particular field, choose it in the In This Field drop-down menu *before* you type anything in the Find This Text box. That way, you can simply choose a field in the Find This Text drop-down menu instead of typing one in. For example, if you choose Payee, a list of payees appears on the Find This Text drop-down menu.

With a little luck, Money finds what you are looking for and you see search results like those in Figure 3-14. Examine the transactions and click the scroll bar, if necessary, to find the one you are looking for. A couple of pages hence, the section "Changing, or editing, transactions" explains how to fix transactions in the search results.

Figure 3-13: To start with, tell Money which accounts to search in and then conduct a simple or an advanced search.

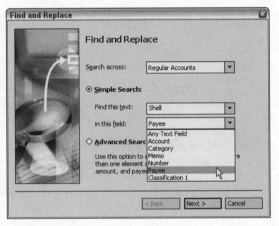

Figure 3-14: The results of a search. Click the Back button if you need to start all over.

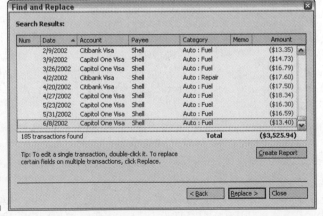

Try clicking the Num, Date, Account, Payee, Category, or Amount button at the top of the columns to arrange the transactions in a new way. For example, clicking the Date button arranges the transactions in date order. Clicking Payee arranges them in alphabetical order by payee. Click a button a second time to reverse the order (a little arrow on the button shows whether the column is arranged in ascending or descending order).

What if Money can't find what you are looking for — or, as often happens, the Search Results list is too long and you need to pinpoint one or two transactions? I'm afraid you have to click the Back button and start all over.

  4. **Click the Back button to return to the Find and Replace dialog box (refer to Figure 3-11).**

     Time to conduct an advanced search.

Conducting an advanced search

Sometimes you really have to beat the bushes to find the transaction you are looking for. To begin searching, click the Advanced Search radio button in the Find and Replace dialog box (refer to Figure 3-13) and then click Next. The dialog box offers eight tabs for entering search criteria. Table 3-2 explains what the eight tabs are. Fill out one tab or a combination of tabs. You needn't fill out all the tabs. Do your best to tell Money precisely where the thing you are looking for is located and what you know about it.

Click the Next button when you are done. You see a list of transactions that met your criteria (refer to Figure 3-14). Double-click a transaction to change it in any way. The next section explains how to edit transactions.

Table 3-2	Searching for Transactions in the Find and Replace Dialog Box
Tab	*What It Does*
Text	Searches for specific words. For example, if you are searching for a check on which you wrote "Damn the torpedoes" on the Memo line, type **Damn the torpedoes** in the Find Transactions with This text box.
Account	Selects which accounts to search in. To search in specific accounts, click the Clear All button and then click the names of the accounts you want to search.
Date	Searches in specific date ranges. Either click the down arrow next to the Range text box and select a time period, or enter a From and To date in the text boxes.

(continued)

Table 3-2 *(continued)*

Tab	What It Does
Amount	Searches for transactions of a certain amount. Enter a specific amount or number range in the From and To box.
Category	Searches in specific categories. Click the Clear All button and then click a Select button to narrow the search to income, expense, or tax-related categories. You can also click next to individual categories to search for them. Check the Show Subcategories check box to narrow the search to subcategories. (Chapter 4 explains more about fixing categorization errors.)
Payee	Searches for specific payees. Click the Clear All button and then click the name of the payee or names of the payees for which you recorded transactions.
Details	Searches by transaction type (payments, deposits, unprinted checks, unsent online bill payments, transfers) reconciliation status (unreconciled and reconciled), and check number.
Classification	Searches for transactions that you classified a certain way, if you use classifications. (Chapter 4 explains classifications.)

Changing, or editing, transactions

All right, so you found the transaction that you entered incorrectly. What do you do now? If you are staring at the transaction in an account register, either double-click it or click it and then click the Edit button on the transaction form. Then go right into the transaction form, fix the mistake in whatever text box or drop-down list it is located in, and click the Enter button.

If you found the error by way of the Tools➪Find and Replace command (see the previous section in this chapter), double-click the transaction in the Search Results list (refer to Figure 3-14). When the Edit Transaction dialog box appears, repair the transaction and click OK.

Suppose, however, that an error was made in numerous places. You misspelled a payee's name. You categorized several transactions incorrectly. In that case, follow the directions in the previous section of this chapter to display the errant transactions in the Find and Replace dialog box (refer to Figure 3-14). Then follow these steps to fix the transactions *en masse:*

1. **Click the <u>R</u>eplace button in the Find and Replace dialog box.**

   You see the Replace screen, shown in Figure 3-15.

2. **On the <u>R</u>eplace drop-down menu, choose which part of the transactions needs repairing.**

   You can change payee names, category assignments, memo text, or transaction numbers.

3. **In the <u>W</u>ith box, either type a new entry or choose one from the drop-down menu.**

   If you chose Payee or Category on the Replace drop-down menu, a list of payees or categories is made available on the With menu.

4. **Click the check boxes next to transactions you want to edit, or click the Replace <u>A</u>ll the Transactions Found radio button to edit all the transactions in the list.**

5. **Click the Next button.**

   A "last chance" dialog box appears and lists all the transactions that will be altered. If you are prudent, look through the list one last time. If you are daring and reckless, click the Finish button right away. You can click the Back button if you get cold feet.

6. **Click the Finish button.**

Figure 3-15: Use the Replace screen in the Find and Replace dialog box to change several transactions simultaneously.

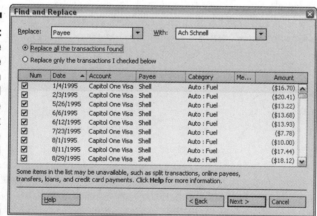

Voiding and deleting transactions

To strike a transaction from an account register, either delete or void it. What's the difference? A deleted transaction is erased permanently from your financial records. It may as well have never happened. But a voided transaction stays in the account register, where **VOID** clearly shows that you entered the transaction but voided it later on. What's more, a voided transaction can be "unvoided."

Void a transaction when you want to keep a record of having made it. For example, if you start writing check number 511 but accidentally enter the wrong payee name, void the check instead of deleting it. That way, the account register records what happened to check number 511 and you know that the check wasn't lost or stolen. Likewise, if you stop payment on a check, void it (and explain on the Memo line why you stopped payment).

History records what happened to voided transactions, but deleted transactions are lost forever in the prehistoric murk.

Voiding a transaction

Follow these steps to void a transaction:

1. **Click the transaction in the register.**

2. **Choose Edit⇨Mark As⇨Void.**

You can also right-click a transaction and choose Mark As⇨Void or press Ctrl+V to void it.

After a transaction has been voided, **VOID** appears in the balance column of the register, and R (for Reconciled) appears in the C (for Cleared) column to show that the transaction has cleared. Figure 3-16 shows a voided transaction in a register. (Chapter 5 explains what reconciling is.)

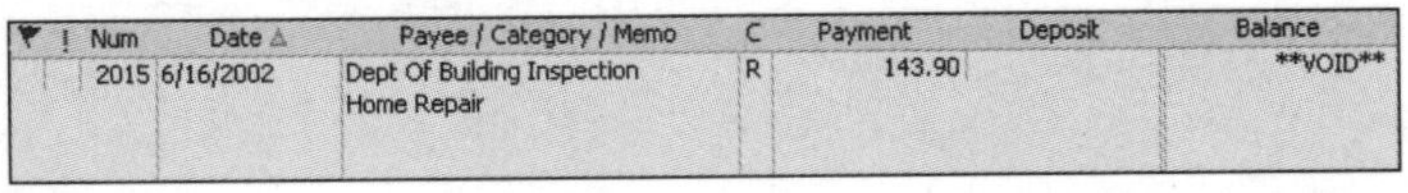

Figure 3-16:
A voided
transaction.

▼	!	Num	Date △	Payee / Category / Memo	C	Payment	Deposit	Balance
		2015	6/16/2002	Dept Of Building Inspection Home Repair	R	143.90		**VOID**

To unvoid a transaction, click it in the register and choose Edit⇨Mark As⇨Void all over again (or right-click and choose Mark As⇨Void). The Void command is what is known in computer jargon as a *toggle* — something you can turn on and off like a toggle switch. The term comes from the ancient Romans, who used to toggle their togas when going in or out of the baths.

Deleting a transaction

Follow these steps to delete a transaction:

1. **Click the transaction in the register.**

2. **Choose Edit⇨Delete, or right-click and choose Delete from the shortcut menu, or press Ctrl+D.**

   Sorry, you can't delete a transaction by pressing the Del key.

3. **Click Yes when Money asks whether you really want to go through with it.**

If you try to delete a transaction that is marked as cleared in the register (R appears in the C column), Money warns you that deleting the transaction could upset your account balance and put the account out of sync with bank records. I strongly suggest clicking No in the dialog box to keep the transaction from being deleted. Very likely, the transaction was cleared because it appeared on bank records, so it should appear on your records as well. Investigate the matter before deleting the transaction.

You cannot delete an online payment that has been sent to Online Services. You can, however, send instructions to cancel the payment, as long as you do so within a couple of days of sending it. (See Chapter 8 for more information.)

Flagging Transactions So That You Can Review Them

It so happens now and then that a check you've written or charge you've made needs looking after. A charge on your credit card is under dispute. A check you wrote hasn't been cashed and you're not sure why. In cases like these, you can flag the transaction. Flagging makes it easier to follow up checks and credit card charges. A flag appears in account registers beside transactions that have been flagged, as shown in Figure 3-17. Move the pointer over the flag icon and a pop-up box tells you why the flag is there.

Figure 3-17:
A flag icon appears beside transactions that have been flagged.

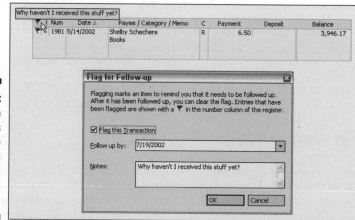

To flag a transaction, click in the register and choose Edit➪Flag for Follow-Up or right-click and choose Flag for Follow-Up. You see the Flag for Follow-Up dialog box, shown in Figure 3-17. In the Follow Up By box, enter a date to tell Money how long to leave the flag icon in the register. In the Notes box, enter the note that will appear when you move the pointer over the flag icon.

To find a transaction that you flagged, scroll through the account register or go to the Home Page. On that page is a list of flagged transactions. Click a transaction to see it in the Edit Transaction dialog box.

Moving a Transaction from One Account to Another

Suppose that you discover an error that has nothing to do with incorrect categories, amounts, or payee names. Suppose that you committed the grievous error of entering a transaction in the wrong account register. Before you are put in leg-irons, move the transaction to the correct account.

Money gives you two ways to move transactions between accounts:

- **From an account register:** If you find the errant transaction in a register, either click it and then choose Edit➪Move to Account or right-click it and choose Move to Account on the shortcut menu. You see the Account dialog box. In the Select New Account for Transaction list, select the name of the account to which you want to move the transaction; then click OK.

- **From the Find and Replace dialog box:** If you find the errant transaction by way of the Tools➪Find and Replace command (the "Searching with the Find and Replace command" section a few pages back explains how), double-click it to open the Edit Transaction dialog box. Then click the down arrow on the Account drop-down list box and select the name of the account in which the transaction rightfully belongs.

After you move a transaction to a different account, go to the other account and make sure that the transaction landed correctly. Very likely, the transaction needs to be renumbered or given a new date.

Printing a Register

Besides fretting over income taxes in April, you also have to print all your account registers from the previous year. Your accountant, if you have one, wants to see them. Even if you don't have an accountant, you should still print the account registers and tuck them away with copies of your income tax forms. Leaving behind a paper trail is important in case a posse from the IRS comes to track you down.

Follow these steps to print all or part of an account register:

1. **Open the account register that you want to print (see the section "Opening an account register," earlier in this chapter).**

2. **Choose File➪Print or press Ctrl+P.**

   You see the Print Report dialog box, shown in Figure 3-18. Theoretically, you can print part of a register from this dialog box by entering page numbers in the From and To text boxes. However, it is impossible to tell by looking at a register what page you are on or how many pages are in the register altogether. Oh well, so much for printing a handful of pages, although you can blindly try your luck with the From and To text boxes if you want.

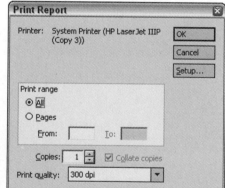

Figure 3-18:
Printing an account register.

3. **If you want to try your luck with printing less than the entire register, click the Pages radio button and enter page numbers in the From and To text boxes.**

4. **Click OK.**

If the register doesn't print correctly, the problem could be that Money and your printer aren't on speaking terms. See the "Printing Reports and Charts" section, near the end of Chapter 14, for more information.

To solve the problem of printing part of a register, create an Account Transactions report and customize it so that only transactions from a certain year or other time period appear. (See Chapter 14 for more information.)

Chapter 4

Categorizing Your Spending and Income

In This Chapter

▶ Identifying categories, subcategories, and classifications

▶ Creating your own categories and subcategories

▶ Creating tax-related categories for tax-reporting purposes

▶ Setting up a classification

▶ Recording transactions by category, subcategory, and classification

▶ Reassigning transactions to different categories

▶ Changing and deleting category and subcategory names

You've probably withdrawn money from an ATM machine, noticed the dwindling account balance, and asked yourself, "Where did the money go?" Or perhaps you balanced a checking account and scratched your head, asking, "Why did I write so many checks?"

Money can help you find out. By assigning each transaction to a category, you can discover a great deal about your spending habits and sources of income. You can generate a report or graph and find out how much you spent on clothing and dining and office supplies. You can find out how much you earned in interest income and how much you earned from different clients. You can even find out how much you are allowed to deduct for income tax purposes.

This chapter explains how to categorize and classify transactions in account registers. You figure out how to choose categories and how to create meaningful categories that work for you. You also explore how to rename categories, delete categories, and recategorize transactions. You may still have to write the same number of checks, but at least you'll have a better idea why.

Looking at the Ways to Categorize Income and Spending

Money offers four ways to categorize a financial transaction. What are the four ways? You can categorize a transaction by category, subcategory, classification, and tax-related status.

By category

By assigning transactions to categories, you can create neat-looking charts that give you the big picture on your spending, as shown in Figure 4-1. (See Chapter 14 for more about charts.) You'll see where all your money is spent and where the money comes from.

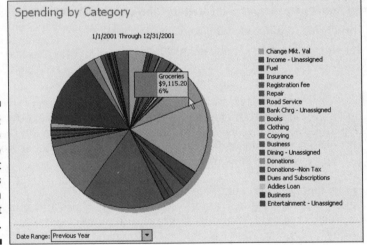

Figure 4-1: Each slice in this pie chart represents spending in a different category.

By subcategory

Divide a category into subcategories when you want to closely examine spending or income. The report in Figure 4-2 shows yearly expenses in four Automobile subcategories: Fees-License, Fuel, Insurance, and Repair. After you have used Money for a while, try running a report like this one to how much it costs to drive your car for one year.

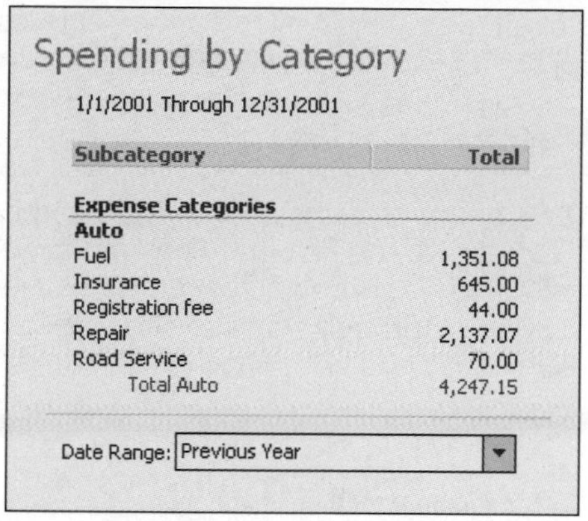

Spending by Category

1/1/2001 Through 12/31/2001

Subcategory	Total
Expense Categories	
Auto	
Fuel	1,351.08
Insurance	645.00
Registration fee	44.00
Repair	2,137.07
Road Service	70.00
Total Auto	4,247.15

Date Range: Previous Year

Figure 4-2: A subcategory report.

By classification

Most people don't need to bother with classifications, but they can be useful for tracking things such as rental properties. As the owner or manager of an apartment building or office building, you need to know precisely how much income the property generates and how much it costs to maintain. The only way to track income and costs, which fall in lots of different expense and income categories and subcategories, is to create a classification.

By tax-related status

By giving a category tax-related status, you can tell Money to include categories and subcategories in tax reports. An accountant may need two or three hours to examine account registers, find all the tax-related transactions, and total them — time that you will be charged for. Money can do it in about six seconds. (Chapter 13 looks at tax preparation with Money.)

Setting Up Your Own Categories and Subcategories

Money gives you a set of generic categories and subcategories so that you can start entering transactions right away. To see the complete list, click the Categories button on the Navigation bar (you may have to click More first) and then choose Categories (or choose Accounts & Bills⇨Categories & Payees or press Ctrl+Shift+C). The list is fine and dandy, but sooner or later you have to give serious thought to which categories and subcategories suit you, especially if you use Money to manage a business or track tax-deductible expenses. If you don't see what you need in the generic lists, then create your own!

Sit down and compose a list of all the categories and subcategories you need for your business or personal finances *before* you begin creating categories and subcategories. That way, you get it right from the start and you lower the odds of having to recategorize transactions later on.

Money offers two different ways to create categories and subcategories. You can make them up as you go along with the fast but dicey method, or you can thoughtfully create them all at one time with the slow but thorough method. The following sections describe the thorough way and the fast way to create categories and subcategories.

Creating a new category

Follow these steps to set up a new category:

1. **Click the Categories button on the Navigation bar, choose Accounts & Bills⇨Categories & Payees, or press Ctrl+Shift+C.**

   Doing so takes you to the Categories window.

2. **If necessary, click the <u>C</u>ategories button on the left side of the window to see the Categories list.**

   Figure 4-3 shows the Categories list. While you're viewing the window, you may want to scroll down the list of categories and subcategories and examine the ones already there. Expense categories appear at the top of the list and Income categories appear at the bottom.

   In Figure 4-3, I chose Categories, Subcategories and Category Groups from the View menu, but the View menu offers other ways of displaying categories and subcategories. Try experimenting with the other views when you have a minute or two to spare.

3. **Click the Ne<u>w</u> button along the bottom of the screen.**

   The New Category dialog box asks whether you want to create a new category or add a subcategory, as shown in Figure 4-4.

4. **The Create a <u>N</u>ew Category? radio button is already selected, so click the Next button.**

5. **Type a name for the category in the <u>N</u>ame box.**

   The name you enter will appear on the Category drop-down list when you record transactions, so be sure to choose a meaningful name.

6. **Click the <u>I</u>ncome or <u>E</u>xpense radio button and click the Next button.**

   All categories fall under the Income or Expense heading. Income categories describe sources of income; expense categories describe how you spend money.

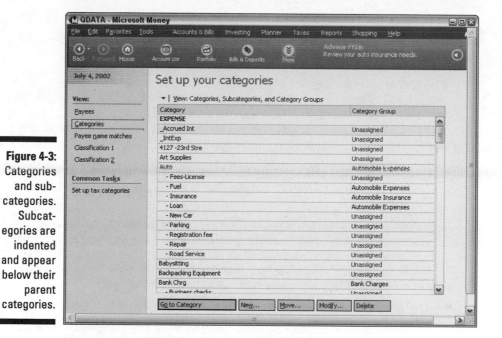

Figure 4-3:
Categories
and sub-
categories.
Subcat-
egories are
indented
and appear
below their
parent
categories.

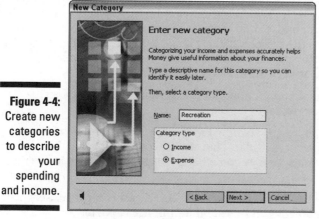

Figure 4-4:
Create new
categories
to describe
your
spending
and income.

7. Select a category group from the list.

A *category group* is a broad means of defining the category. Money uses category groups to make calculations in the Tax Estimator, Home Worksheet, and other features (see Chapter 12). When you select a category group, a description appears on the right side of the dialog box.

8. **Click the Finish button.**

   There it is — your new category, alive and kicking on the Categories &
   Payees window.

The following steps are not absolutely necessary for creating a category,
but try following them to acquaint yourself with the Categories window. You
can always go to this window when you want to learn more about a category.
By taking the following steps, you will always know what your new category
is for.

1. **Make sure that you highlight the new category on-screen and then
   click the Go to Category button that is along the bottom of the
   window.**

   You see a Categories window like the one shown in Figure 4-5. You can
   also get here by double-clicking a category on the Categories window.
   The window presents a bunch of different amenities. For example, you
   can see a graph showing how much you spent or took in, as well as a
   miniregister that shows account activity in the category.

2. **If you want, enter an abbreviation in the Abbreviation box.**

   The Abbreviation box represents an alternate way to assign a category
   to a transaction. Besides selecting a category from the drop-down list on
   the transaction form or typing the first few letters of the category name,
   you can type a two- or three-letter abbreviation. After you type the two
   or three letters and press Tab to move to the next part of the transaction
   form, Money enters the entire category name for you. (Big deal, I say. It's
   not as if selecting from the drop-down list or typing the first few letters
   of a category name is very difficult.)

3. **Enter a few words of commentary in the Comment box to describe
   why you created this category.**

   The Comment box is worth visiting. Enter a few words to describe the
   category and why you created it. That way, if you forget what the new
   category is for, you can always come back to the Categories window and
   find out.

4. **Select the Include on Tax Reports check box if you want transactions
   made under this category to be calculated in tax reports.**

5. **Click the Back button to return to the Categories window.**

   While you are in the Categories & Payees window, you may want to
   create a few more categories. To create subcategories for your new
   category, see the next section, "Creating a new subcategory," and begin
   at Step 3.

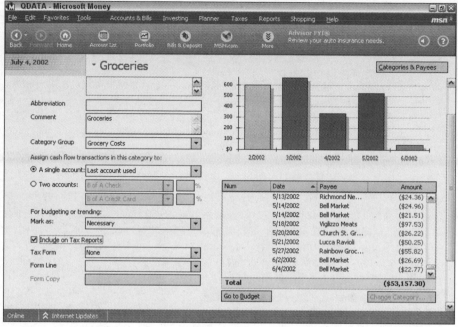

Figure 4-5:
The left side
of the
Categories
window
offers
options for
entering an
abbreviation
and giving
the category
tax-related
status.

The other options in the Category window — Category Group, Assign Cash Flow Transactions, Budgeting — are not for everybody. These options pertain to subjects covered in Chapter 12, where you discover how to get Money's help in planning ahead:

- ✔ **Category Group:** When you draw up a budget, you are given the choice of declaring how much you will spend or earn in each category or in each category group. Budgeting by category is hard work because there are so many categories. Many people opt to budget by category group to save time. You may choose a new category group from this drop-down menu.

- ✔ **Assign Cash Flow Transactions:** Money can project how much money you will have at future dates. The program does its soothsaying by examining the amount of money in different accounts over time. If earning or spending in the category you just created is done mostly by way of a certain bank account, choose it to help with cash-flow projections.

- ✔ **For Budgeting or Trending:** When you draw up a budget, you are also asked to declare by category which spending is necessary and which discretionary. Choose one or the other if you intend to get Money's help with budgeting.

The fast but dicey way to set up categories

Two of this chapter's sections, "Creating a new category" and "Creating a new subcategory," explain the thorough way to handle categories, but you can also create categories on the fly without visiting the Categories window. Follow these steps:

1. **Enter the entire transaction on the transaction form except for the category and subcategory.**

   In other words, enter numbers or letters in the Number, Date, Amount, Pay To, From, and Memo text boxes. Chapter 3 explains how to enter a transaction in a register.

2. **Click in the Category text box and type the name of the new category.**

Or, to create a new subcategory, choose a category, type a colon (:), and then type a subcategory name.

3. **Press the Tab key.**

   You see the New Category dialog box. I hope it looks familiar.

4. **Make sure that the name you entered appears correctly in the dialog box; then click the Next button.**

5. **Select a category group.**

6. **Click the Finish button.**

   The name of the category you created takes its place on the Category drop-down list so that you can select it in the future.

Creating a new subcategory

The best way to create a new subcategory is to go straight to the Categories window and start from there. Follow these steps:

1. **Click the Categories button on the Navigation bar, or choose Accounts & Bills⇨Categories & Payees to go to the Categories window.**

2. **If necessary, click the Categories button to view categories.**

   You will find this button on the left side of the window under View.

3. **Select the parent category of the subcategory you want to create.**

   In other words, to create a subcategory of the Education category, scroll to and select Education in the Categories window.

4. **Click the New button.**

   You see the New Category dialog box.

5. **Click the Add a Subcategory to an Existing Category radio button; then click Next.**

6. **Enter a name for the subcategory in the Name box; then click Next.**

7. **Select a category group.**

   Category groups are another one of those bold attempts by Microsoft to do your thinking for you. The Tax Estimator and other features you select can use the group you select in budget projections and tax estimations

8. **Click the Finish button.**

   Check it out — your new subcategory appears in the Categories window underneath its parent category. Either start all over to create another subcategory, or leave the Categories window by clicking the Back button.

Getting Ready for Tax Time with Tax-Related Categories

Giving a category tax-related status when you create it is one thing. But how do you give an existing category tax-related status? Simply, that's how.

Money offers a special window for handling tax-related categories. In the window, you can click a check box to make sure a category is figured into the tax reports you can generate with Money. And you can assign a category or subcategory to a line item on a tax form. As shown in Figure 4-6, Money offers the Tax Software Report that connects category and subcategory totals to specific income tax forms (W-2, Schedule A, Schedule C, and so on). The Tax Software Report makes filling out income tax forms easier. All you have to do is get the figures from the report and plug them into the right places on the tax forms. However, to make the process work, you have to know more about the tax forms than most people know or care to know.

Figure 4-6:
The Tax
Software
Report
presents
figures for
use in
preparing
federal
income tax
returns.

Tax Form Line	Amount
SCHEDULE C	
Gross receipts	66,646.99
Subtract line 2 from line 1	66,646.99
Gross Profit	66,646.99
Gross Income	66,646.99
Car and truck expenses	4,133.15
Insurance (not including health)	1,053.00
Other business expense	
Bank Chrg	146.55
Copying	146.38
Other business expense	292.93
Total Expenses (Add lines 8 through 27)	5,479.08
Tentative profit or loss (Subtract line 28 from line 7)	61,167.91

Let others do the work

Don't bother to keep tax records when others do it for you. Employers, for example, keep careful track of their employees' federal income, state income, Social Security, and Medicare tax-deduction information. Why keep those numbers yourself when your employer pays someone to do it? Besides, you have to use your employer's numbers when you file your income tax return.

Similarly, you can track tax-deductible mortgage interest payments, but why bother? At the start of the year, the bank sends you a statement that indicates how much you paid in interest during the previous year. Use Money to keep track of only the tax-related income and expenses that no one tracks for you.

Follow these steps to give an existing category or subcategory tax-related status so that it is figured into tax reports, and, if possible, assign tax forms and line items to a category or subcategory:

1. **Click the Categories button on the Navigation bar, or choose Accounts & Bills⇨Categories & Payees to get to the Categories window.**

2. **Click the Set Up Tax Categories button.**

   You can find this button on the left side of the window under Common Tasks. After you click the button, you see the Categories window, only this time, drop-down menus appear in the lower-right corner so that you can mark categories for tax reports and assign categories to line items on tax forms, as shown in Figure 4-7.

   Where possible, the generic categories and subcategories that Money creates automatically are assigned tax forms and form lines. You can see them by scrolling down the list. Tax-related categories show an X in the Tax column. In the Tax Form and Form Line columns, you can see where tax forms and lines have been assigned to categories and subcategories.

3. **Scroll down the list until you find a category or subcategory whose tax status needs changing; then click the category or subcategory to select it.**

4. **Select the Include on Tax Reports check box.**

5. **Click the down-arrow on the Tax Form drop-down list and select a tax form.**

   Being able to tag categories and subcategories to tax forms (such as a W-2, Schedule B, or Form 1040) is a neat idea, but you have to know the tax forms well to pull it off. You have to know, for example, that tax-exempt interest is reported on the Interest Income line of the Schedule B form. Who besides a tax accountant knows that?

If you want to be able to run Tax Software Reports, study your income tax returns from past years to see which forms and form lines to assign to the categories and subcategories that you use. You can also speak to an accountant. Be aware that tax forms change yearly, so what goes on one line one year may go somewhere else the next.

6. **Click the down arrow on the Form Line drop-down list and select the form line on which the income or expense is reported.**

7. **If you use multiple forms (more than one W-2, for example) to report your income, enter the number of forms you use in the Form Copy text box.**

8. **Click the Back button to return to the Categories window.**

Choose a category.

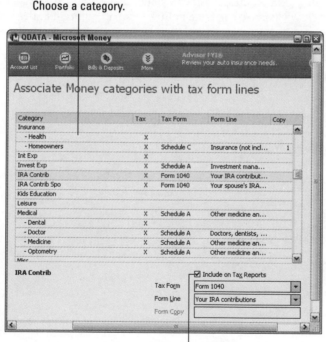

Figure 4-7: Assigning a tax form and line to a category.

Click to include it on tax reports.

Setting Up and Defining a Classification

At the beginning of this chapter, I explain that a classification is an umbrella grouping under which you track income and expenses in many different categories and subcategories. You can create two classifications in each

Money file. When you generate some types of reports, you can ask Money to tell you everything it knows about transactions assigned a certain classification.

Classifications permit you to track income or expenses in several different categories and subcategories simultaneously. A property manager, for example, can create a class named after each building he or she manages. As well as categorizing expenses for building repairs and income from rent, the manager may classify them by property. Then, for time to time, the manager may run classification reports to see precisely how much each property generates in income and costs in upkeep.

The following sections explain how to set up a new classification. You also find out how to define the *classes* and *subclasses* that go into the classification. When you enter a transaction, you can select a class and subclass from special drop-down lists on the transaction form. In Figure 4-8, the user has named the classification Properties, the class in question is the building at 1020 Lakeshore Drive, and Apt. 2 is a subclass. The transaction records a check that was written to cover plumbing repairs done to Apartment 2 at 1020 Lakeshore Drive.

Classification name

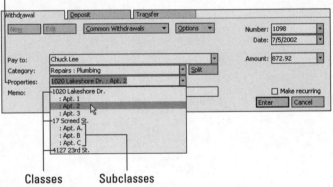

Figure 4-8:
Choosing a
subclass
from the
Classification
drop-down
list.

Classes   Subclasses

Setting up a classification

As with categories and subcategories, the starting point for setting up a classification is the all-purpose Categories window. Follow these steps to set up a classification:

1. **Click the Categories button on the Navigation bar, or choose Accounts & Bills⇨Categories & Payees.**

   You see the Categories window.

2. **Click the Classification 1 button.**

   You see the Add Classification dialog box, as shown in Figure 4-9.

3. **At the bottom of the dialog box, select one of Money's names either by clicking a radio button or by clicking the last radio button and entering an original name for the classification.**

   Money's six suggestions for naming the new classification appear next to the six radio buttons. If you click the Properties radio button, for example, the new classification is called Properties, and the word *Properties* appears on your transaction forms (refer to Figure 4-8).

   If you don't like Money's suggestions for a name, you can always click the last radio button and enter a name of your own in the text box.

4. **After you select or enter a name, click OK.**

   You return to the Categories window, where the name you chose or entered appears on the left side of the window on a button below the Categories button.

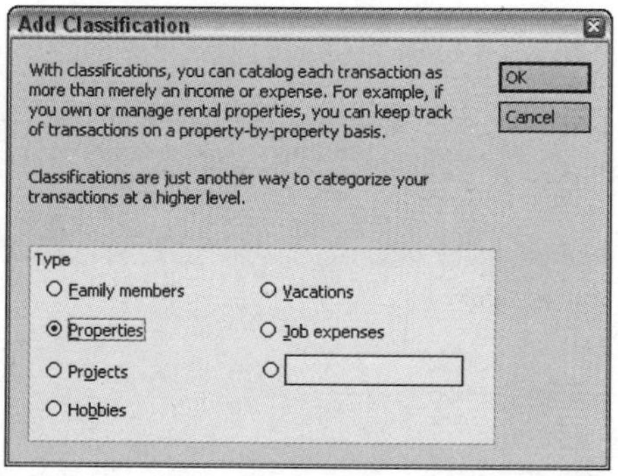

Figure 4-9:
To name the classifi-cation, either select a name or click the last radio button and enter your own choice for the name.

The next step is to define classes and perhaps subclasses for the new classification. By the way, if you set up two classifications in a Money file, you get two sets of classification drop-down lists on the transaction forms that appear in account registers.

Defining the classes and subclasses

Follow these steps to define the classes that appear on the first classification drop-down list on transaction forms:

1. **If necessary, click the Categories button on the Navigation bar, or choose Accounts & Bills⊏>Categories & Payees to open the Categories & Payees window.**

2. **Click the classification button that is named after the classification to which you want to add the classes.**

   In other words, to create classes for the Properties classification, click the Properties button. The Categories window lists classes and subclasses in the classification, if you have already created any, as shown in Figure 4-10.

3. **Click the New button.**

   You see the New Class or Subclass dialog box, as shown previously in Figure 4-10. Under Add, make sure that the first radio button is selected.

4. **Enter a name for the item in the Name text box and click OK.**

   The name you enter appears in the Categories & Payees window.

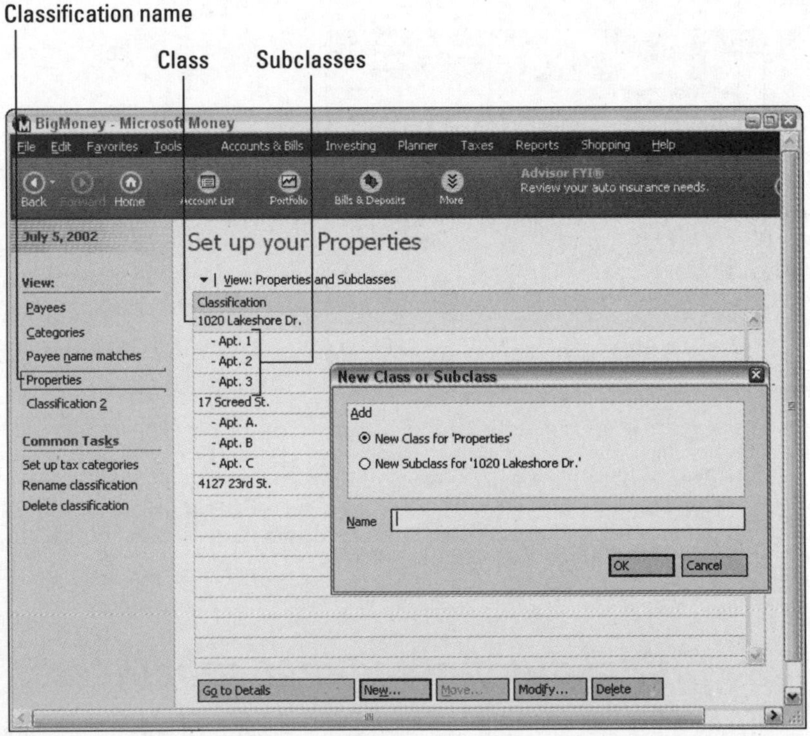

Figure 4-10:
Classes and subclasses for a classification called Properties, as well as the New Class or Subclass dialog box for creating classes and subclasses.

The steps for defining the subclasses that appear on the second classification drop-down list are going to be very familiar:

1. **If necessary, click the More button on the Navigation bar and choose Categories, or choose Accounts and Bills⇨Categories & Payees to go to the Categories window.**

2. **Click a classification button on the left side of the window to see the list of classes in the classification.**

3. **Select the class under which you want to define a subclass.**

   For example, to define a subclass called Apt. 1 that is to be subordinate to the 1020 Lakeshore Drive class, select 1020 Lakeshore Drive.

4. **Click the New button.**

   The New Class or Subclass dialog box appears (refer to Figure 4-10).

5. **Under Add, click the New Subclass for radio button.**

6. **Enter a name for the sub-class in the Name text box and click OK.**

Correcting Transactions Recorded in the Wrong Category

Don't feel foolish if you recorded transactions in the wrong category or subcategory. It happens all the time. Luckily for you, Money offers a special button called Move for reassigning all the transactions in one category to another category. And if you need to reassign only a handful of transactions, you can use the Find and Replace command to reassign transactions one at a time.

The Move button is very powerful indeed. When you use the Move button to reassign all the transactions in one category to another category, you delete the first category as well. For example, suppose that you assigned the Vacation category to a bunch of transactions when you should have assigned the Leisure category. If you use the Move button to move all Vacation transactions to the Leisure category, you delete the Vacation category from the Categories list as well. Use the Move button only when you want to drop one category altogether and move all its transactions elsewhere.

Another point about the Move button: If you attempt to move transactions in one category to another category and the category you want to move includes subcategories, you lose the subcategory assignments when you make the move. However, you can move subcategory assignments from one subcategory to another subcategory with the Move button.

Moving all transactions from one category to another category

To change category or subcategory assignments throughout your account registers, follow these steps:

1. **Click the Categories button on the Navigation bar, or press Ctrl+Shift+C to go to the Categories window.**

2. **If necessary, click the <u>C</u>ategories button on the window to make the categories and subcategories appear.**

   To see the categories and subcategories, you may need to open the View menu and choose Categories and their Subcategories.

3. **Scroll down the list and select the name of the category or subcategory whose transactions you want to reassign.**

   For example, if you erroneously assigned transactions to the Education: Kids subcategory when you should have assigned them to the Childcare category, select the Education: Kids subcategory on the list.

   Remember, the category or subcategory you select is deleted from the Categories window after you finish reassigning the transactions. Be sure to examine transactions carefully before you delete anything.

4. **Click the <u>M</u>ove button.**

   As shown in Figure 4-11, you see the Move Transactions dialog box. This is where you tell Money where to reassign the transactions in the category or subcategory you chose in Step 3.

5. **In the <u>C</u>ategory text box, select the category or subcategory to which you want to reassign the transactions.**

6. **Click OK.**

Figure 4-11:
Use the
Move
Transactions
dialog box
to assign
transactions
to a
different
category.

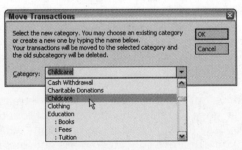

In the Categories list, the category or subcategory you chose in Step 3 has been deleted. Meanwhile, all transactions in your registers that were assigned the old category or subcategory are assigned the one you chose in Step 5.

Reassigning transactions to new categories

Instead of making a wholesale reassignment of one category or subcategory to another, you may decide to examine transactions one at a time and choose which ones need reassigning. To do that, you have to search for transactions in the account registers, examine each transaction, and then either choose a new category or subcategory or move on without moving the transaction.

The "Finding a transaction so that you can fix it" section in Chapter 3 explains everything you need to know about finding transactions. However, here are shorthand instructions for finding and fixing transactions that were assigned the wrong category or subcategory:

1. **Choose Tools⇨Find and Replace, or press Ctrl+H.**

   You see the Find Transactions dialog box.

2. **Select Category from the In This Field drop-down list; then, on the Find This Text drop-down list, select the category or subcategory whose transactions need reassigning; finally, click the Next button.**

   As shown at the top of Figure 4-12, the Search Results list shows transactions assigned to the category you chose. At this point, you can reassign the transactions one at a time or click the Replace button to reassign several transactions simultaneously.

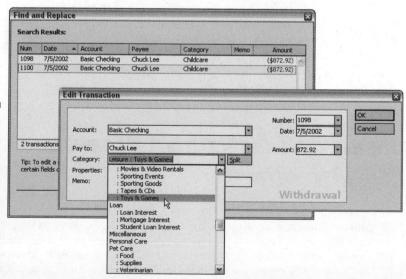

Figure 4-12: Searching for and repairing transactions that were assigned a specific category or subcategory.

3. **Assign the transactions to new categories:**

   - **One at a time**. Double-click a transaction that needs a new category. You see the Edit Transaction dialog box, as shown at the bottom of Figure 4-12. Choose a new category or subcategory from the drop-down list and click OK.

   - **Several at one time**. Click the Replace button. You see the Replace screen, shown in Figure 4-13. Select the check box next to each transaction that needs a new category assignment, choose Category on the Replace drop-down menu, choose a new category on the With list, and click the Next button. Then click the Finish button on the next screen, which asks, `Are you sure?`

By the way, when you reassign a transaction that has been reconciled, Money beeps and warns you not to change the amount of the transaction you are about to edit. Don't worry about the warning. You are concerned with the category assignment, not the amount of the transaction.

Check transactions that need reassigning.

Choose Category.   Choose a new category.

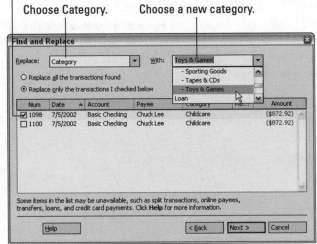

Figure 4-13:
Assign new categories *en masse* from the Replace screen.

Renaming and Deleting Categories and Classifications

After you have worked with Money for a while and you have refined the list of categories and classifications you want to work with, you can delete unnecessary categories and classifications. And if a category or classification name isn't descriptive enough, you can rename it. The following sections explain how to delete and rename categories, subcategories, and classifications.

After you rename a category or classification, transactions throughout the account registers that were assigned the old category or classification name are automatically given the new name. So when you rename, you also change the names of category, subcategory, or classification assignments throughout your registers.

Renaming a category or subcategory

Follow these steps to rename a category or subcategory:

1. **Click the Categories button on the Navigation bar, or choose Accounts & Bills⇨Categories & Payees to go to the Categories window.**

2. **If necessary, click the Categories button on the window to see the list of categories and subcategories.**

   If you don't see subcategory names but need to see them, choose Categories and their Subcategories from the View menu.

3. **Scroll down the list and select the category or subcategory whose name you want to change.**

4. **Click the Modify button, or right-click and choose Modify (choose Rename if you are dealing with a subcategory).**

   You see either the Modify Category dialog box or the Modify Sub-Category dialog box.

5. **Enter a name in the New Name text box and click OK.**

Renaming a classification

Follow these dance steps to change the name of a classification:

1. **Click the Categories button on the Navigation bar, or choose Accounts & Bills⇨Categories & Payees to open the Categories window.**

2. **On the left side of the window, click the button named after the classification whose name you want to change.**

3. **Click the Rename Classification button.**

   Look for the button under Common Tasks on the left side of the window. The Rename Classification dialog box appears.

4. **Enter a name in the New Name text box and click OK.**

   Back in the Categories window, the button you clicked in Step 2 has a new name. Classification assignments throughout your account registers have new names, as well.

Deleting a category or subcategory

When you no longer need a category or subcategory, you can delete it. However, be careful, because if you delete a category or subcategory to which transactions are assigned, the transactions lose their category assignments. In other words, you end up with transactions to which no category is assigned — and that defeats one of the primary reasons people use Money, which is to categorize their spending and income to find out where the money came from and where it went.

Try to delete a category or subcategory to which categories are assigned and you see the Delete Category dialog box. From this dialog box, you can assign transactions to a different category before you delete the category in question, but do you really want to do that? Suppose that some transactions belong in one category and others belong in another category. No, reviewing the transactions one at a time before you delete the category to which they are assigned is wiser. This chapter's "Reassigning transactions to new categories" section explains how to review transactions as you change their category or subcategory assignments.

After you reassign the transactions whose category you want to delete, follow these steps to delete a category or subcategory:

1. **Click the Categories button on the Navigation bar, or choose Accounts & Bills⇨Categories & Payees to open the Categories & Payees window.**

2. **Click the <u>C</u>ategories button on the window, if necessary, to see the list of categories and subcategories.**

    If you intend to delete a subcategory, you may need to choose Categories and their Subcategories from the View menu to see subcategories.

3. **Scroll through the list and select the category or subcategory you want to delete.**

4. **Click the De<u>l</u>ete button, or right-click and choose <u>D</u>elete from the shortcut menu.**

That's all she wrote — the category is gone from the Categories window. However, if you try to delete a category with subcategories underneath it, a dialog box warns you that deleting a category also deletes its subcategories. If you try to delete a category to which transactions are assigned, you see the Delete Category dialog box.

Whatever you do, don't delete a category with subcategories. Investigate the matter first and find out whether you need the subcategories for tracking your finances.

A fast way to remove deadwood categories

When you install Money on your computer, the program gives you a bunch of generic categories that you may or may not need. Very likely, you don't need many of them. To quickly remove them, you can use a special button called Remove Unused Categories. After you click the button, Money removes all categories and subcategories on the Categories list to which no transaction has been assigned.

Follow these steps to remove deadwood categories that take up space on the Categories list:

1. Choose Tools⇨Options to open the Options dialog box.

2. Click the Categories tab.

3. Make sure that a checkmark appears in the Ask Me Before Removing Each Category

check box, and if a checkmark doesn't appear, select the check box.

4. Click the Remove Unused Categories button. A dialog box asks whether you want to remove a certain category.

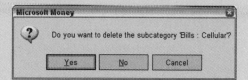

5. Click Yes or No.

6. Keep clicking Yes or No until you ax all deadwood categories and subcategories.

Deleting a classification

After you delete a classification, all transactions throughout the registers that were assigned the classification are no longer assigned to it. Therefore, I suggest that you think twice before deleting a classification. Think twice and think hard. Going back through the registers and reassigning transactions to a classification that you deleted is hard work that you'll want to avoid.

Follow these steps to delete a classification that you no longer need:

1. **Click the Categories button on the Navigation bar, or choose Accounts & Bills⇨Categories & Payees to open the Categories window.**

2. **On the left side of the window, click the button named after the classification that you want to delete.**

3. **Click the Delete button.**

   You can find this button under Common Tasks on the right side of the window. A dialog box warns you of the drastic nature of what you are about to do.

4. Ignore the dialog box and click <u>Y</u>es to delete the classification.

Back in the Categories window, the classification button now has the generic name Classification 1 or Classification 2, and all class and subclass names have disappeared from the screen.

You can delete a class or subclass by right-clicking it and choosing Delete.

Chapter 5

Balancing an Account

*U*ntil I started using Money, I never *reconciled,* or balanced, my checking or savings accounts. But Money makes balancing an account very easy indeed. No kidding, you can do it in four or five minutes.

This chapter explains what reconciling is, how to reconcile the transactions in your records with the bank's records, and what to do if you can't get an account to reconcile. Because reconciling a credit card account can be slightly tricky, you can find instructions in this chapter for reconciling credit card accounts as well as checking and savings accounts. *Bon voyage!*

How Reconciling Works

Reconciling is your opportunity to examine your records closely and make sure that they are accurate. When you reconcile an account, you compare your records to the bank's, fix any discrepancies you find, enter transactions that appear on the statement that you forgot to enter in the register, and click in the C (for Cleared) column next to each transaction that appears both in the register and on the bank statement.

In an account register, transactions that have cleared the bank — transactions that have been reconciled — show an R (for Reconciled) in the C (for Cleared) column, as shown in this Figure 5-1. Here, you can see that some transactions have cleared the bank and some are still waiting to clear.

What does *reconcile* mean, anyway?

In financial terms, *reconcile* means to compare one set of records to another for the sake of accuracy. When you reconcile an account in Money, you compare the transactions on the statement that the bank or brokerage house sent you to the transactions you entered in the Money register.

If you find a discrepancy between your records and the bank's, you can be pretty sure that the error was made on your side. Not that it doesn't happen, but banks don't err very often when recording financial transactions. Yes, bank lines move too slowly and banks have been known to nickel-and-dime their customers with all kinds of petty charges, but banks are sticklers for accuracy.

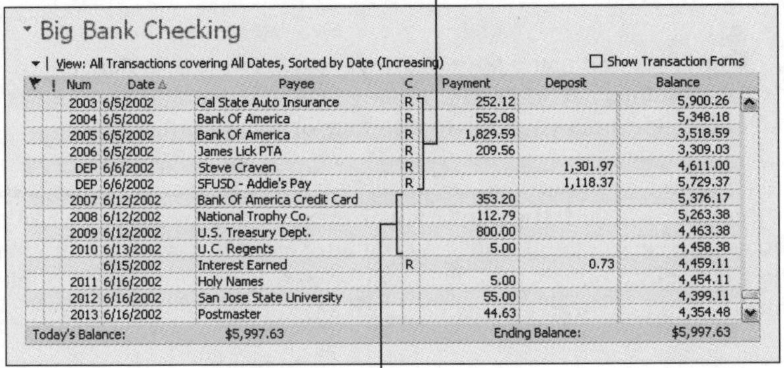

These transactions have cleared the bank.

Figure 5-1:
An R appears in the C (for Cleared) column when a transaction has cleared the bank.

▾ **Big Bank Checking**

▾ | View: All Transactions covering All Dates, Sorted by Date (Increasing) ☐ Show Transaction Forms

▼	Num	Date △	Payee	C	Payment	Deposit	Balance
	2003	6/5/2002	Cal State Auto Insurance	R	252.12		5,900.26
	2004	6/5/2002	Bank Of America	R	552.08		5,348.18
	2005	6/5/2002	Bank Of America	R	1,829.59		3,518.59
	2006	6/5/2002	James Lick PTA	R	209.56		3,309.03
	DEP	6/6/2002	Steve Craven	R		1,301.97	4,611.00
	DEP	6/6/2002	SFUSD - Addie's Pay	R		1,118.37	5,729.37
	2007	6/12/2002	Bank Of America Credit Card		353.20		5,376.17
	2008	6/12/2002	National Trophy Co.		112.79		5,263.38
	2009	6/12/2002	U.S. Treasury Dept.		800.00		4,463.38
	2010	6/13/2002	U.C. Regents		5.00		4,458.38
		6/15/2002	Interest Earned	R		0.73	4,459.11
	2011	6/16/2002	Holy Names		5.00		4,454.11
	2012	6/16/2002	San Jose State University		55.00		4,399.11
	2013	6/16/2002	Postmaster		44.63		4,354.48

Today's Balance: $5,997.63   Ending Balance: $5,997.63

These have not been reconciled yet.

Balancing an Account

Balancing an account is a two-step business. First, you tell the program how much money in interest the account earned (if it earned any) and how much you had to pay the bank for checks, ATM withdrawals, and other services (if you had to pay anything). Then you move ahead to the Balance dialog box, where you make your records jibe with the bank's and click off each transaction that appears both on your bank statement and in the register. Before you begin comparing the register to the bank statement, lay the bank statement flat on your desk. And you may want to put checks in numerical order (if you intend to reconcile a checking account), and your ATM slips in date order (you *have* been saving your ATM slips, haven't you?). With a little luck, you can reconcile without having to glance at checks and ATM slips. But if something goes amiss, you may have to examine the paperwork closely.

Telling Money which transactions cleared the bank

Follow these steps to tell Money which transactions cleared the bank and reconcile an account:

1. **Click the Account List button on the Navigation bar to go to the Accounts window.**

2. **Click the Balance an Account button.**

   You can find the button under Common Tasks on the left side of the window. A button called Balance This Account is also available on account register windows. After you click the button, you see a list of your accounts that includes the day they were last reconciled.

3. **Click the name of the account you want to balance.**

   You see a Balance dialog box like the one in Figure 5-2. This dialog box is where you enter information from the bank statement. The Starting Balance text box shows the amount of money in the account as of the last time you reconciled it (or the account's opening balance, if you recently opened the account).

4. **If necessary, enter the date listed on the bank statement in the Statement Date text box.**

5. **In the Ending Balance text box, enter the closing balance from the bank statement.**

Figure 5-2:
The
Balance
dialog box,
where you
tell Money
what the
bank told
you.

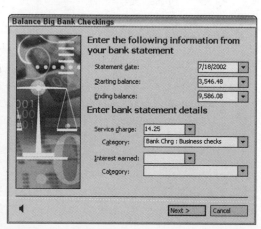

6. If you have to pay a service charge, enter it in the Service Charge text box, and categorize the service charge as well.

Banks are like mosquitoes: They like to bite. Banks do it by charging customers all sorts of miscellaneous fees. The fees appear on bank statements. You may get charged for ordering checks, or calling for information, or using an ATM, or sneezing too loudly. Scour the statement for evidence of service charges and enter the sum of those charges in the Service Charge box. For a category, choose Bank Charges: Service Charge, or something similar. (And for more on categorizing, turn to Chapter 4.)

7. In the Interest Earned text box, enter an amount if the account earned any interest, and categorize the interest payment as well.

You may use the Investment Income: Interest category and subcategory, for example.

Before you click the Next button to move ahead, compare what you entered in this dialog box to what is on your bank statement one last time. Entering numbers incorrectly in this dialog box is one of the primary reasons that people have trouble reconciling their bank accounts.

8. Click the Next button to move ahead to the Balance Account window, shown in Figure 5-3.

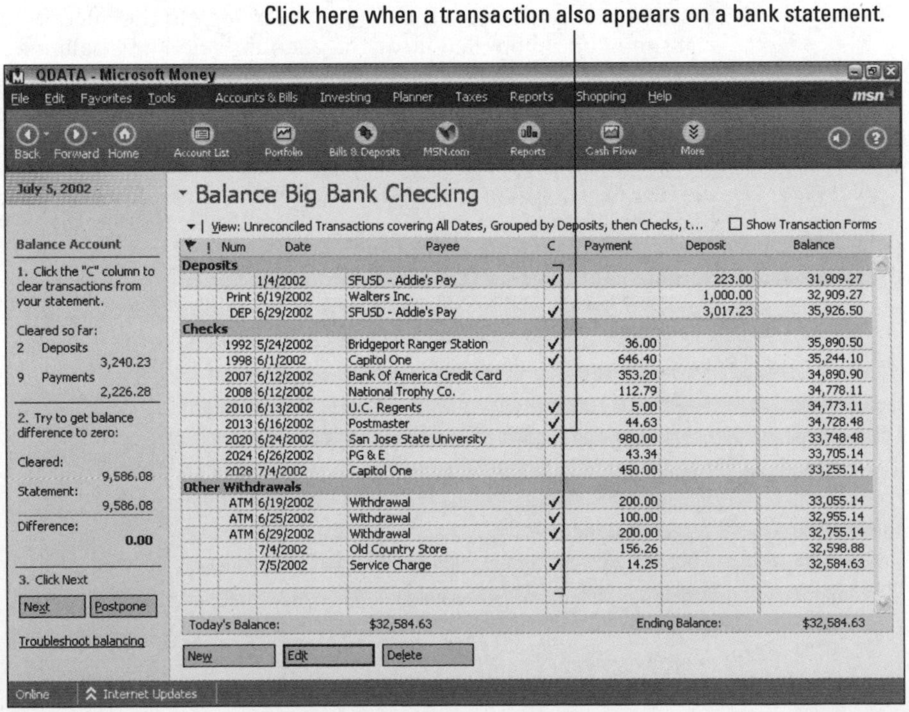

Click here when a transaction also appears on a bank statement.

Figure 5-3: Compare transactions in the register to the transactions on the bank statement; click in the C column next to each transaction that appears in both places.

Only transactions in the register that have not been reconciled appear in the window. Deposits and other transactions that brought money into the account appear at the top of the window; following that are withdrawals and other transactions that record when money was taken out of the account.

If you entered a service charge and/or interest payment in the Balance dialog box (in Steps 6 and 7), the amounts already appear on the window along with a checkmark to show that they have been cleared.

In Figure 5-3, the account has been reconciled successfully. You can tell by looking at number 2 ("Try to get balance difference to zero") on the left side of the window. There, the sum of the cleared transactions ($9,586.08) and the sum of the transactions on the statement ($9,586.08) are equal. When you click the C column in the register to clear transactions, the Cleared amount changes. The Statement amount does not change. It comes from the Balance dialog box (refer to Figure 5-2), where you entered it in the Ending Balance text box.

Many people think that reconciling accounts is easier when transactions are shown on one line rather than two. To show transactions on one line, open the View menu and choose Top Line Only.

9. **Examine your bank statement and click the C column next to each transaction on the statement that also appears in the register.**

   As you click transactions, the Cleared figure and Statement figure gradually fall in line with each other. If all goes well, they show the same amount and the Difference figure shows 0.00, as in Figure 5-3.

   To remove a checkmark in the C column, click it again. The next section in this chapter explains how you can fix mistakes in the register while you reconcile. The section after that offers strategies for recognizing and fixing reconciliation problems.

   If you have trouble finding a transaction in the register, open the View menu and select Sort⇨Sort by Date or Sort⇨Sort by Number. The Sort by Date command lists transactions in date order, and Sort by Number command lists them in numerical order on the Num column.

10. **Click the Next button when the account is reconciled.**

    You will find the Next button in the lower-left corner of the window. A Balanced! screen appears and tells you that your account is balanced.

11. **Click the Finish button.**

    Back in the register, all those checkmarks in the Balance Account window turn to R's in the register. The transactions you clicked off in the Balance Account window have cleared the bank and are reconciled with your records.

If the reconciling business makes you tired or if you find something better to do, click the Postpone button. Later, you can pick up where you left off by clicking the Balance This Account button on the Account window.

Fixing mistakes as you reconcile

Glancing at the bank statement, you discover that you made a mistake when you entered a transaction in a register — you entered the wrong amount or check number. Or perhaps you forgot to enter a transaction altogether. It happens. Cash withdrawals from ATM machines, which usually are made on the spur of the moment, often fail to get recorded in account registers.

Here is how to fix a mistake in a transaction:

1. **Click the transaction that needs correcting.**

   If you need to enter a brand-new transaction, go straight to Step 2.

2. **Click the Show Transaction Forms check box.**

   As shown in Figure 5-4, a transaction form appears in the window. The form looks and works like the transaction forms you know and love in account registers.

Click to see a transaction form.

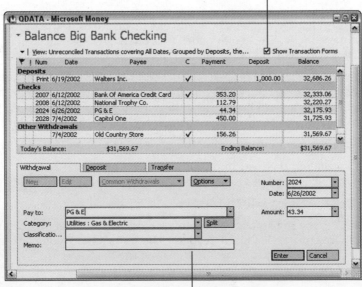

Figure 5-4:
Fixing an entry error in the Balance Account window.

Fix the error or enter a new transaction.

3. **Fix the error or enter a new transaction**

- **New transaction:** Click the Ne<u>w</u> button and enter the transaction.

- **Repair an error:** Enter the correct amount, check number, date, or whatever needs correcting.

4. **Click the Enter button.**

Help! The Darn Thing Won't Reconcile!

Not being able to reconcile a bank account is frustrating. You pore over the bank statement. You examine checks and ATM slips. You gnash your teeth and pull your hair, but still the thing won't reconcile. No matter how hard you try, the Difference figure that lists the difference between the cleared amount and the statement amount cannot be brought to 0.00.

To help you get out of the jam you are in, Money offers techniques for recognizing and fixing reconciliation problems. And Money also has a gizmo called AutoReconcile (which gets its own section later on in this chapter) that may or may not be able to help you reconcile your bank account.

A checklist of things to do if you can't reconcile

If an account won't balance, a number of different things can be wrong. The following sections explain how to recognize and fix reconciliation problems.

A transaction was not entered

The primary reason that accounts don't reconcile is because a transaction that is listed on the bank statement has not been entered in the register. ATM withdrawals, for example, are easy to forget and often do not get entered in account registers.

Remedy: Look for a transaction on the bank statement that is equal to the Difference amount on the Balance Account window. If the Difference amount is $35.20, chances are you forgot to record a $35.20 transaction in the register. Look for a $35.20 transaction on the bank statement and, if necessary, click the Show Transaction Forms check box to display a form and enter the transaction. Be sure to enter the date correctly. If the difference is $20.00, $40.00, or another round number, chances are you forgot to enter an ATM withdrawal.

An amount in the register is incorrect

Another reason accounts don't reconcile is that amounts were entered incorrectly in the register. This problem is a sticky one and is hard to track down. Look for transposed numbers and numbers entered backward. For example, $32.41 and $34.21 look alike at a glance, but there is a difference of $1.80 between the numbers.

An old accountant's trick: If the difference between what you have and what you should have is evenly divisible by 9, you probably transposed a number.

Remedy: Click the transaction, click the Show Transaction Forms check box, and change the amount on a transaction form.

A transaction was entered twice

Look for duplicate transactions in the register to make sure that no transaction was entered twice.

Remedy: Delete one of the transactions by pressing Ctrl+D or right-clicking it and choosing Delete from the shortcut menu.

A check was entered as a deposit or vice versa

Making an error like this is easy. Fortunately, detecting it is easy, too.

Remedy: Clear your checks and withdrawals first; then clear your deposits. You'll notice during this process whether a deposit, check, or withdrawal is missing. Click the transaction and then click the Show Transaction Forms check box. On the transaction form, edit the transaction to make it a deposit or a withdrawal. If you feel comfortable doing so, you can also right-click the transaction and choose or Change Transaction Type To — Withdrawal or Change Transaction Type To — Deposit.

The Ending (Statement) balance is incorrect

If you enter the Ending balance incorrectly in the Balance dialog box (refer to Figure 5-2), you cannot reconcile an account no matter how hard you try. Compare the Statement figure on the Balance Account window to the ending balance on your statement to see whether the figures match.

Remedy: Return to the Balance dialog box (refer to Figure 5-2) and enter a correct Ending Balance figure. To do so, click the Postpone button to return to the Accounts window, click the Balance This Account button, and then click the Next button. You see the Balance dialog box again, where you can enter a correct Ending balance this time. Click Next again to return to the Balance Account window.

A service charge or interest earned is incorrect

Besides entering the ending balance incorrectly, you may have entered an incorrect amount in the Service Charge or Interest Earned text box in the Balance dialog box (refer to Figure 5-2). Compare the interest and service charges on your statement to the ones on the Balance Account window to see whether an amount is incorrect.

Remedy: Click the service charge or interest entry in the Balance Account window, click the Show Transaction Forms check box, and enter a correct figure on the transaction form.

The bank statement was not flipped over

I'm embarrassed to admit it, but one or two times I wasn't able to reconcile an account because I forgot to turn over the bank statement and examine the transactions listed on the other side of the page — very stupid of me.

Remedy: Turn the page, note the transactions, and click to put a checkmark next to them.

Many bank statements include a total of all debits (payments) and a total of all credits (deposits). By comparing these numbers to the Deposits and Payments numbers on the Balance Account window (refer to Figure 5-3), you can quickly see where you are out of agreement.

If all else fails, you can try Money's AutoReconcile gizmo to find out why the account won't balance. This contraption scours the register for transactions that it thinks were entered incorrectly and gives you the chance to enter them correctly so that the account can be reconciled. Follow these steps to try it:

1. **Click the Next button.**

   Although the account isn't balanced, click the Next button as though it is in balance. You see the Balance dialog box shown in Figure 5-5.

2. **Choose the second option button, Use AutoReconcile to Help Find the Error.**

   If you are in luck and Money can find the error, the Possible Error dialog box on the right side of Figure 5-5 appears.

3. **Read the description of the error and click Yes or No to change the transaction in question or to let it stand.**

Forcing an account to balance

If, despite your detective work, you can't find the problem that keeps your account from balancing, you can force the account to balance. Forcing an account to balance means to enter what accountants call an "adjustment transaction" — a fictitious transaction, a little white lie that makes the numbers add up. Don't tell anybody I said so, but if the difference between what your statement says and what the Balance Account window says is just a few pennies, enter the adjustment transaction and spare yourself the headache of looking for the error. A few pennies here and there never hurt anybody.

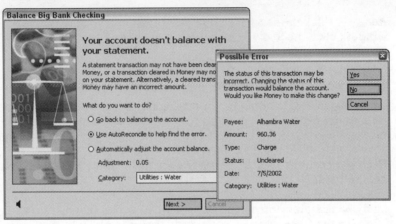

Figure 5-5:
Forcing an account to balance (left); the AutoReconcile gizmo (right).

The words "Account Adjustment" appear in the register on the Payee line when you force an adjustment transaction. Money gives you the chance to categorize the transaction on your own. After you have torn out your hair trying to discover why an account won't balance, follow these steps to force an adjustment transaction:

1. **Click the Next button on the Balance Account window.**

   Click the Next button even though the account has not been reconciled. The Balance dialog box appears (refer to Figure 5-5). It tells you that the account isn't in balance and asks what you want to do about it.

2. **Choose the Automatically Adjust the Account Balance option button.**

3. **Choose a category from the Category drop-down menu.**

4. **Click OK.**

Reconciling a Credit Card Account

Reconciling a credit card account is done in much the same way as reconciling a checking or savings account. The only difference is in the Balance dialog box (refer to Figure 5-2), where you tell Money how much the statement says that you owe.

When you reconcile an account, you clear credits as well as charges made to your credit card. Before you start reconciling, make sure that the credits the card issuer owes you have been entered in the credit card register (see Chapter 3 for more on recording credits).

Lay the credit card bill flat on your desk and follow these steps to reconcile a credit card account:

1. **Click the Account List button on the Navigation bar or choose Accounts & Bills⇨Account List to go to the Accounts window.**

2. **Click the Balance an Account button.**

   The button is located under Common Tasks on the left side of the window. You see the list of accounts and the date they were last reconciled.

3. **Click the name of the credit card account you want to balance.**

   You see the Balance dialog box, shown in Figure 5-6. The amount you owed as of the last time you reconciled the account appears in the Total Amount You Owed Last Month text box.

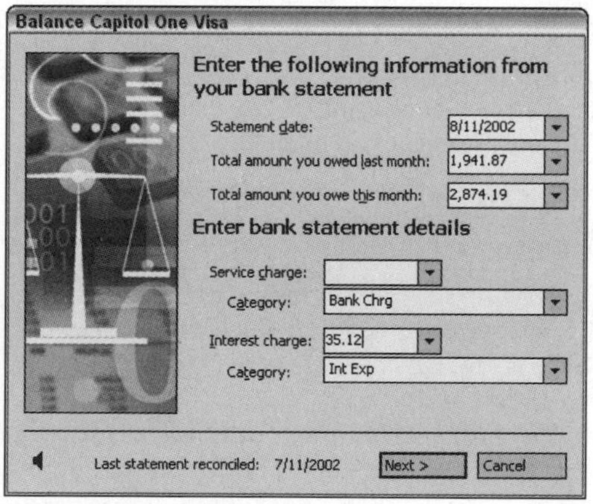

Figure 5-6:
When you reconcile a credit card account, start by telling Money how much you owe this month.

Balance Capitol One Visa	
Enter the following information from your bank statement	
Statement date:	8/11/2002
Total amount you owed last month:	1,941.87
Total amount you owe this month:	2,874.19
Enter bank statement details	
Service charge:	
Category:	Bank Chrg
Interest charge:	35.12
Category:	Int Exp
Last statement reconciled: 7/11/2002	Next > Cancel

4. **In the Statement Date text box, enter the date on your credit card statement.**

5. **In the Total Amount You Owe This Month text box, enter the amount the statement says that you owe, including service and interest charges.**

   In other words, enter the amount you would have to pay if you were to pay off all debt you owe to the credit card issuer.

6. **In the Service Charge text box, enter the annual fee if you are being charged an annual fee, and categorize the expense in the Category text box.**

   Some credit card issuers charge an annual fee. Record an annual fee in the Service Charge box. For a category and subcategory, choose Bank Charges: Service Charge or a similar category.

7. **In the Interest Charge text box, enter the amount you must pay in interest to service the credit card debt.**

   Most people don't pay off their credit card debt each month, so they have to pay an interest charge. And if you take out cash advances, you have to pay interest for those, too. For a category and subcategory, choose Bank Charges, Bank Charges: Interest Paid, or a similar category.

8. **Click the Next button.**

   You see the Balance Account window, which lists all transactions in the register that have not been reconciled. If the Balance Account window looks familiar, that is because it looks and works exactly like the Balance Account window for reconciling savings and checking accounts (refer to Figure 5-3).

9. **Examine your credit card statement and click the C column next to each transaction on the statement that also appears in the register.**

   To change the amount of a charge or credit, click it in the register and then click the Show Transaction Forms check box. That step brings up the transaction forms so that you can alter the transaction.

10. **Click the Next button after the account is reconciled.**

    A Balanced! screen appears.

11. **Click the Pay Bill Later button to pay the credit card bill later on, or click the Pay Bill Now button to open the Edit Transaction dialog box and record a bill payment.**

Guess what? You can use the same techniques for fixing reconciliation problems in credit card accounts as you can in checking and savings accounts. See the "Help! The Darn Thing Won't Reconcile!" section, earlier in this chapter, to find out how to fix reconciliation problems, or use the AutoReconcile gizmo to find and fix errors.

Chapter 6

Writing and Printing Checks

. . . .

. . . .

*N*ot every Money user needs to print checks. Checks are expensive, for one thing. If you order checks from Microsoft Money Checks, the official vendor, an order of 500 checks can cost between $70 and $89.50, depending on the kind of check you order, whereas most banks charge about $15 for that many checks. So, printing checks with Money costs five to six times as much as writing checks by hand.

But printing checks with Money can save time, especially if you run a small business and print lots of checks. When you write a check by hand, you have to write it twice (once when you record it in a register and once when you scribble on the paper check). When you print a check with Money, you enter it only once when you record it in a register. The printer handles the rest. What's more, you can *batch-print* checks (print a dozen or so at one time). Small-business owners who print lots of payroll checks or monthly expense checks ought to seriously consider printing checks with Money.

Another advantage of printing checks is being able to itemize the payment on the check stub. As long as you print checks on wallet-size or voucher checks (I explain those shortly), you can itemize the payment by splitting it (as I discuss in Chapter 3). The split-transaction information appears on the check stub.

But the best reason for printing checks has nothing to do with saving time or itemizing — it has to do with appearances. Printed checks are more professional looking. They make a good impression on creditors and clients. A printed check says "I mean business," whereas a handwritten check with spidery lettering says "Thank you, kind sir or madam, for honoring my little check." Everyone who works in a profession where appearances count — supermodels, for example — ought to print checks.

This chapter explains everything you need to know about printing checks — from choosing the right type of checks to ordering checks, telling your printer how to print checks, and adjusting checks that don't print correctly. You also discover how to record checks in a register, print a full sheet or a partial sheet of checks, and print addresses on checks.

By the way, if you came to this chapter to find out how to record a check in a register, you came to the wrong place. You should be in Chapter 3.

Deciding What Kind of Check to Order

Your first decision is what kind of check to order. Checks are printed on sheets and loaded into the printer like sheets of paper. As shown in Figure 6-1, the choices are wallet-size, standard business, or voucher checks. Checks and check envelopes are available in standard as well as European sizes. Most companies that make checks, Microsoft included, offer the opportunity to print company logos on checks and customize the checks in other ways. Table 6-1 compares and contrasts the three types of checks that you can print with Money. These prices come from Microsoft Money Checks, the Microsoft affiliate that offers checks for use with Money.

Figure 6-1:
The three types of checks: wallet-size (left), standard business (middle), and voucher (right).

Table 6-1				Checks for Use with Money
Name	*Size*	*Checks per Sheet*	*Cost per 500/Cost per Check**	*Description*
Wallet size	2.83" x 8.5"	3 checks	$70/14¢	The smallest check. It includes a 2.5" stub for tracking expenses. This check is for individuals, not businesses.
Standard	3.5" x 8.5"	3 checks	$75/15¢	The largest check. It does not include a stub, although you can list tax-deductible expenses on the Memo line. For small businesses.
Voucher	3.5" x 8.5"	1 check	$89.50/18¢	Includes ample room — two-thirds of a page — for listing expenses. For small businesses that need to itemize checks in detail.

*Prices listed here are from Microsoft Money Checks, are for standard-color checks, and are current as of July 2002. Premier-color checks, which come in a variety of colors, cost more. You can buy checks in sets of 250, 500, 1,000, or 2,000. Third-party vendors offer different prices for checks.

Ordering the Checks

Besides ordering from Microsoft Money Checks, you can order checks from third-party vendors. Table 6-2 lists vendors whose checks are compatible with Money. Checks are available in many different colors and designs, so shop around. Perhaps you can find checks in soft lilac, paprika, icy periwinkle, and the other chichi colors whose names grace clothing catalogues.

Table 6-2	Vendors Offering Checks for Use with Money	
Company	*Phone*	*Internet Address*
Best Checks	800–521–9619	www.bestchecks.com
Compuchecks	800–356–5581	www.compuchecks.com
FormSystems	800–325–5568	www.checksforless.com

(continued)

Table 6-2 *(continued)*		
Company	*Phone*	*Internet Address*
Microsoft Money Checks	800–432–1285	www.microsoft.com/money/checks.htm
PC Checks & Supplies	800–322–5317	www.pcchecks.com
Sensible Solutions	888–852–4325	www.sensible-solutions.com

After you know how many checks you want and in what size you want them, your next step is to contact a company that sells checks. Do that by calling the company or visiting its Web site (refer to Table 6-2). I recommend calling the company because the friendly human on the other side of the phone connection can likely answer all your questions.

When you order checks, you will be asked for the following information, most of which appears on the face of a check:

✔ Your name, address, and phone number.

✔ Your bank's name and the city, state, and zip code in which it is located.

✔ Your bank's *fractional number*. When you deposit a check, you usually list the first four numbers of the fractional number on the deposit slip. Here's an example of a fractional number: 66–55/4321.

✔ Your checking account number.

✔ The starting check number. See the sidebar "Choosing a starting number for the checks" to find out the ins and outs of choosing a number.

✔ The size of the checks — wallet, standard business, or voucher.

✔ Whether you have a laser printer, ink-jet printer, or an antique continuous-feed printer.

Choosing a starting number for the checks

When you choose a starting number for the checks, be sure to choose one that won't conflict with the numbers on checks you write by hand. Bankers frown and even call you on the telephone when you write two checks with the same check number. And if you try to record two checks with the same number in a checking register, a dialog box asks whether you really want to do that.

Writing checks with duplicate numbers is a *faux pas,* but it is easy to do when you write checks and print checks from the same account. Your spouse, checkbook in hand, could be on a shopping spree while you are at home printing checks. Or you could write a few checks from the checkbook, forget to record them in Money, and then print checks with the same numbers without thinking about it.

To keep from writing checks with duplicate numbers, choose a starting number for the printed checks that is far, far removed from the check numbers in your checkbook. For example, if the checks in your checkbook are numbered 600 to 650, choose 1501 as the starting check number for printed checks. That way, you can't write and print checks with duplicate numbers.

Printing the checks you order isn't absolutely necessary. You can always tear one off and write it by hand when you buy a pillbox hat at the thrift store or pay for a pizza.

Getting Your Printer Ready to Print Checks

To print checks, Money and your computer have to be on speaking terms. They have to understand each other and be able to work together. And your printer has to know which kind of check to print — a wallet-size check, standard business check, or voucher check.

Very likely, Money and your printer have already been introduced. When you install Money, the program gets information about your printer from the Windows operating system. You probably don't have to tinker with the printer settings, but you do need to tell the printer what kind of check to print.

Follow these steps to open the Check Setup dialog box and tell your printer everything it needs to know to print checks, including which font to use:

1. **Choose File⇨Print Setup⇨Check Setup.**

   You see the Check Setup dialog box, shown in Figure 6-2.

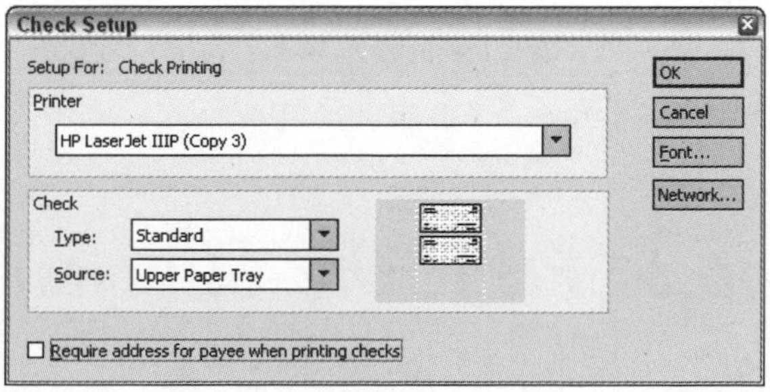

Figure 6-2:
Use the Check Setup dialog box to tell Money about your printer and the style of check that you intend to print.

2. **In the Printer drop-down list, select which printer to print the checks with, if necessary.**

   More than one printer appears on the drop-down list if you or someone else has set up a second or third printer to work with your computer. Select the printer from which you will print the checks.

3. **Click the down-arrow on the Type drop-down list and select which style of check you will print.**

   Select an option from the top of the list if you have a laser printer. Choices for continuous-feed printers, also known as pinwheel printers, appear on the bottom of the list. (If you migrated to Money from Quicken, additional choices appear on the Type drop-down list for printing on Quicken check forms. See Chapter 21.)

4. **If necessary, click the down-arrow on the Source drop-down list and select the tray through which you will feed checks to the printer.**

   Don't bother with the Source drop-down list if your printer has only one tray.

5. **Click the Font button and choose a font for printing your checks, if you want.**

   A *font* is a typeface design. Unless you choose otherwise, checks are printed in Courier New font in 12-point type. But you can choose a more stylish font or different type size in the Check Printing Font dialog box. Click OK when you're done.

6. **Click the check box called Require Address for Payee When Printing Checks if you want payee addresses to appear on your checks.**

   As long as an address is on file for a person or business to which you write a check, the address appears on the check — that is, it appears if you select this check box. As Chapter 10 explains, Money gets addresses from the Payees Details window. If you ordered window envelopes along with checks, you can print addresses on the checks, insert them in window envelopes, and save yourself the trouble of having to address envelopes.

7. **If your computer is connected to a network and you intend to print checks on a network printer, click the Network button and select the printer in the Connect to Printer dialog box.**

8. **Click OK to close the Check Setup dialog box.**

At Last — Time to Print the Checks

The moment of truth has now arrived. You're ready to actually print the checks!

The following pages explain how to record a check before printing, print a practice check, make adjustments, print a full sheet or a partial sheet of checks, print one check or several checks at a time, and include an address on a check in case you want to mail it in a window envelope.

Recording checks that you intend to print

Recording a check that you intend to print is not very different from recording a handwritten check. The only difference is that you select Print This Transaction from the Number drop-down list on the Withdrawal form rather than enter a check number, as Figure 6-3 shows.

These checks have not been printed yet.

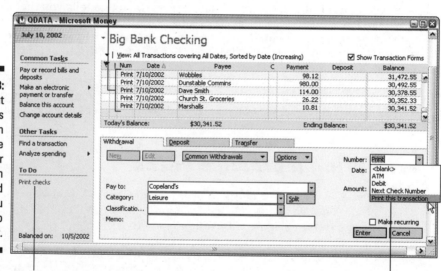

Figure 6-3: Select Print This Transaction from the Number drop-down list to record a check you want to print.

Reminder that checks need printing.

Choose Print This Transaction.

Chapter 3 explains everything you need or care to know about recording a check, but here are the raw details:

1. **Open the checking account register from which you want to write the check.**

2. **Click the New button.**

3. **From the Number drop-down list, choose Print This Transaction.**

4. **Enter the date that you want to appear on the check in the Date text box.**

5. **Enter the name of the person or business you are paying in the Pay To text box.**

   If you have paid this person or party before, you can enter the payee's name by typing the first couple of letters and pressing the Tab key.

6. **Enter the amount of the check in the Amount text box.**

7. **Describe the transaction by selecting a category and subcategory.**

8. **If you want, enter a word or two in the Memo box.**

   The words you type in the Memo box appear on the printed check.

9. **Click the Enter button (or press Enter).**

"When does the check get numbered?" you may ask. The check number is entered in the register automatically after the check is printed. Until the check number is entered, the word Print appears in the Num column of the register, as shown in Figure 6-3, and the To Do notice tells you that checks in the register need printing. On the Home Page, the words "Print Checks" also appear under the Reminders notice (turn to Chapter 1 to see how to make the Reminders notice appear on the Home Page if it doesn't appear there).

When you split a check payment, the split-transaction information appears on the voucher, or stub, of the check, provided that you're printing on wallet-size or voucher checks. (Wallet-size and voucher checks include a stub.)

Printing a practice check

After you've recorded a check to print, "Print Checks" appears in the Reminders notice on the Home Page and under "To Do" on the checking register page (refer to Figure 6-3). You're ready to go.

Before you print your first check, however, print a practice check. Insert one of the practice checks that came inside the Money 2003 box or a thin, transparent piece of paper into the printer. After you're done experimenting, you can lay the sheet of paper over a sheet of real checks and hold both sheets to the light to see whether the text landed in the right places.

Follow these steps to do a test run and see whether your printer handles checks correctly:

1. **Open the checking register if it is not already open.**

2. **Click the words "Print Checks" under the To Do notice or choose File⇨Print Checks.**

   You see the Print Checks dialog box, shown in Figure 6-4. For now, don't worry about the confusing options in this dialog box. You're interested only in the Print Test button.

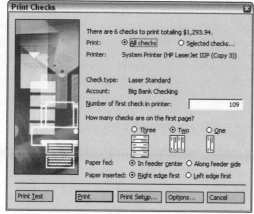

Figure 6-4:
Click the
Print Test
button to
make sure
that the
printer
handles
checks
correctly.

3. **Click the Print Test button.**

4. **Click Cancel to close the Print Checks dialog box.**

Money prints a check with a bunch of Xs on it and the words `This is a VOID check`. How does it look? If all is well, you don't need to read the next part of this chapter. It explains how to realign checks so that they print correctly.

As the "Printing partial sheets of checks" section that appears later in this chapter explains, to print a partial sheet of checks, you have to load the partial sheet into your printer as if you were loading an envelope. If you want to test how partial sheets print, follow the instructions here, but click the Two or One radio button in the Print Checks dialog box before running the test. Then tear off a practice check or two (or cut off part of the practice piece of paper you're using), load the partial sheet into your printer, and click the Print Test button.

Making adjustments to the text alignment

So, everything is slightly out of whack on your check? You can do something about that if you're using a laser printer. Visit the Print Checks tab in the Options dialog box and change the vertical and horizontal alignment settings. (If you're using a dot-matrix printer, you can fix the problem the old-fashioned way — by adjusting the sprockets on the printer.)

Take note of roughly how far out of position the text is, and then do the following to realign the text so that it falls correctly on your checks:

1. **Click the words "Print Checks" under the To Do notice to the left of the register or choose File⇨Print Checks to see the Print Checks dialog box.**

2. Click the Options button.

As shown in Figure 6-5, you see the Print Checks tab in the Options dialog box. You can also get here by choosing Tools⇨Options and then clicking the Print Checks tab.

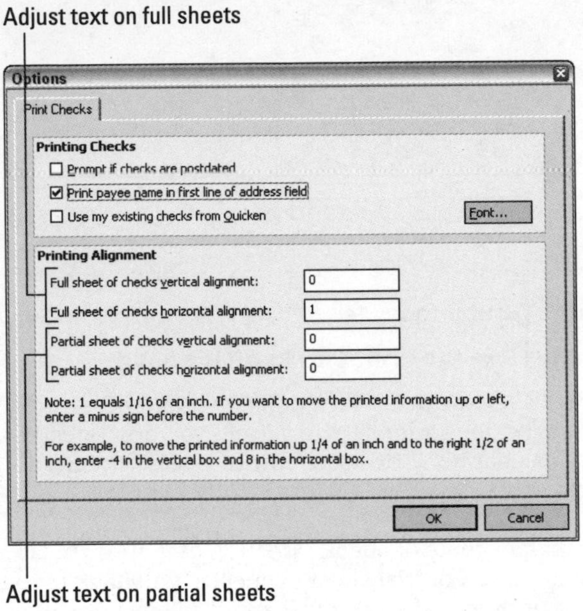

Adjust text on full sheets

Figure 6-5:
If you have a laser printer, you can go to the Print Checks tab to adjust where text falls on sheets of checks.

Adjust text on partial sheets

At the bottom of the tab are four text boxes for changing the horizontal (side to side) and vertical (up and down) alignment of text on sheets with all three checks and on partial sheets. The horizontal boxes move the text left or right on the check. The vertical boxes move it up or down.

3. Enter a number or numbers in the text boxes.

Enter a 1 to move text by a sixteenth of an inch, a **2** to move it by an eighth (two-sixteenths) of an inch — you get the idea.

To move text side to side, click in one of the horizontal text boxes and enter a positive number to move the text toward the right or a negative number to move it toward the left.

To move text up or down, click one of the vertical boxes and enter a positive number to move the text down or a negative number to move it up.

4. **Click OK after you're done.**

   You return to the Print Checks dialog box.

5. **Click the Print Test button.**

I hope the check prints correctly this time. If it doesn't, return to the Options dialog box and keep trying. As the prelate said to the layman, "Persistence and perseverance made a bishop of his reverence."

Printing a full sheet of checks

Take note of the number on the first check that you intend to print on, load a sheet or two of checks into the printer and then follow these steps to print on a full sheet of checks:

1. **Open the checking register and click the words "Print Checks" under the To Do notice or choose File➪Print Checks.**

   You see the Print Checks dialog box (refer to Figure 6-4).

   The top of the dialog box indicates how many checks need printing and how large of a bite the checks will take out of your checking account. If the bite is too large, you can always click the Selected Checks radio button and tell Money to print fewer checks, as Step 4 demonstrates.

2. **If necessary, enter a new check number in the Number of First Check in Printer text box.**

   The Number of First Check in Printer text box lists what Money thinks is the next available check number. This number may be wrong. Compare it to the first paper check you loaded in the printer and enter a new number, if necessary.

3. **Make sure that the Three radio button is selected.**

   The Three button tells Money to print a full sheet of checks. By the way, if you're printing voucher checks, which come one to a page, you don't see the Three, Two, or One radio button because you can print only one check on each page.

4. **Click the All Checks radio button to print all the unprinted checks in the register; click the Selected checks button to pick and choose which ones to print.**

   Clicking the Selected checks radio button opens the Select Checks dialog box, shown in Figure 6-6. To begin with, all the checks are selected, or highlighted, in the dialog box.

Figure 6-6:
Select
which
checks to
print in this
dialog box.
It opens
automati-
cally when
you click the
Selected
Checks
radio button.

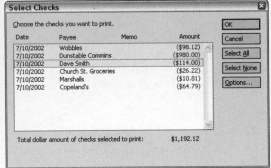

To print a handful of these checks, either click the Select None button to unselect all the checks and then click each one you want to print, or simply click each check you *don't* want to print to take its highlighting away and unselect it.

5. **Click OK.**

   You return to the Print Checks dialog box.

6. **Click the Print button.**

   The Print Checks dialog box shows you the numbers of the checks that "should have printed correctly." Examine the checks to see whether they printed correctly.

7. **Click the Finish button if the checks printed correctly; click Reprint if they didn't print correctly.**

   If, woe is me, you have to click the Reprint button, then turn a couple of pages ahead to the "Whoops! My Checks Didn't Print Correctly" section. That section explains what to do next.

Compare the numbers on the printed checks to the numbers in the Num column of the checking register to make sure that the numbers match. And be sure to sign the checks.

Printing partial sheets of checks

Wallet-size and standard business checks come three to a sheet, which makes printing them slightly problematic. After you print the first check on the sheet, for example, you are left with two blank checks. It would be a shame to waste them, so Money offers options in the Print Checks dialog box for print-ing on partial sheets.

To take advantage of the partial sheet options, you may have to get out the dreary manual that came with your printer. You have to find out how your printer accepts envelopes. Find out whether envelopes are fed to your printer in the center or along the side of the paper tray. Find out as well whether envelopes are fed right-edge first or left-edge first. The settings that apply to envelopes also apply to partial sheets of checks.

The previous section in this chapter, "Printing a full sheet of checks," explains how to print checks. The only difference between printing a full sheet and a partial sheet of checks is that you have to do three important things in the Print Checks dialog box (refer to Figure 6-4):

- ✔ **Click the Two or One radio button to tell Money how many checks remain on the sheet.**

- ✔ **Select the Paper Fed radio button that describes where on the paper tray the paper is fed to your printer (in the center or on the side).**

- ✔ **Select the Paper Inserted radio button that describes which edge of the paper is inserted in your printer (right or left edge first).**

As someone who writes and edits computer books, I shouldn't admit it, but I have a phobia of printers. I hate them. Rather than dicker with the options for printing on partial sheets of paper, I always try to print checks three at a time. That way, I never have to agonize over the partial sheet options. You can easily find a second or third bill that needs paying and use it to round out a check sheet. And if I can't find a second or third bill, I simply tear out the extra checks, carry them to a store, and use them like handwritten checks.

Including addresses on checks

As long as an address is on file for a person or business to which you write a check, the address appears on the check — that is, it appears on the check as long as you click the check box called Require Address for Payee When Printing Checks in the Check Setup dialog box. To get to that dialog box, choose File➪Print Setup➪Check Setup.

Money gets addresses from the Payees Details window, as Chapter 10 explains. To enter or view a payee's address, follow these steps:

1. **Click the More button on the Navigation bar and choose Categories or choose Accounts & Bills➪Categories & Payees to see the Categories window.**

2. **Click the Payees button.**

   You will find this button on the left side of the window. You see a list of payees after you click it.

3. **Either double-click the payee for whom you want to enter an address, or click the payee and then click the Go to Payee button.**

   You see the Payees window, with boxes for entering addresses and other kinds of juicy information.

4. **Enter an address.**

   The address you enter appears on printed checks if you instruct your printer to print addresses.

Whoops! My Checks Didn't Print Correctly

If you had to click the Reprint button in the Print Checks dialog box because your checks didn't print correctly, all is not lost; Money gives you a second chance to print the checks. When you click the Reprint button, the Select Checks to Reprint dialog box appears. From this dialog box, you tell Money which checks to reprint.

Before you reprint wallet-size or standard business checks that didn't print correctly, you may have to load the sheets sideways in your printer. Wallet-size and standard business checks come three to a sheet, so you have to load them sideways when only one or two checks remain on a sheet. The section "Printing partial sheets of checks," earlier in this chapter, explains all the issues that pertain to printing on partial sheets.

After you click the Reprint button in the Print Checks dialog box, follow these steps to reprint checks:

1. **Click the checks that need reprinting.**

   As you click each check in the Select Checks to Reprint dialog box, the check is highlighted.

2. **Make sure that the number in the Begin Reprinting Checks at Check Number text box is correct, and if it isn't, enter a new number.**

   This number should match the number on the first check that is loaded in your printer.

3. **Make sure that the number in the Checks Remaining on Sheet text box is correct, and enter a new number if necessary.**

4. **Click OK.**

   The Print Checks dialog box appears.

5. Examine your checks and click the Finish button if the checks printed correctly; click Reprint if they didn't print correctly.

As someone who has had to battle with printers, I hope that you don't have to click the Reprint button again.

Be sure to write VOID on checks that didn't print correctly and file them away with your canceled checks. That way, you have a record of what happened to them.

And on the subject of checks that didn't print correctly, what happens if you have to reprint three or four checks and you end up with a three- or four-check gap in the checking register? If you're a stickler for keeping good records, enter a transaction in the checking register for each check that needed reprinting and void it. In other words, if you botched check 1501 and reprinted it, enter a check transaction, give it number 1501, and then choose Edit⇨Mark As⇨Void (or press Ctrl+V) to void it.

Part II
Going Online with Money

The 5th Wave
By Rich Tennant

"Oh yeah, he's got a lot of money. When he tries to check his balance online, he gets a computer message saying there's 'Insufficient Memory' to complete the task."

In this part . . .

Part II is dedicated to Buck Rogers, that citizen of the future who banks online and pays all his bills in digital cash. You won't catch Buck Rogers standing in line at a bank or ATM machine. You won't see him reconciling his bank accounts from a measly paper statement. You won't see him thumbing through the newspaper in search of a stock quote, because Buck Rogers downloads stock quotes from the Internet.

If your computer is connected to the Internet, you're invited to go online and make like Buck Rogers. Here's your chance to take advantage of the Money program's many online features. This part of the book explains how.

Chapter 7

Getting Ready to Go Online

In This Chapter

▶ Exploring the online services that Money offers

▶ Getting the equipment and services you need to bank online

▶ Seeing whether your bank offers online services

▶ Setting up bank accounts to work online

▶ Canceling the online banking service

▶ Browsing the Internet without leaving Money

*T*he makers of Money 2003 are betting that people will soon rely on home computers to do their banking in the same way that people rely on ATM machines to do most of their banking today. Not so long ago, ATM machines were regarded with suspicion: "What if the machine shortchanges me?" However, most people don't think twice about using ATMs nowadays, and someday they probably won't think twice about banking online, either.

This chapter explains the steps you must take before you can start banking online. I describe the online services and equipment that you need, and show you how to find out whether your bank offers the services, how to sign up for them, and how to cancel them if it comes to that. Oh, and this chapter also explains how to cruise the Internet from inside Money.

Reviewing the Online Services That Money Offers

The Money program's online services enable you to do everything from pay your bills to investigate potential investments. Table 7-1 describes the Money online services.

Table 7-1	The Online Services That Money Offers
Service	*What You Can Do*
Online banking	Download records from your bank or credit card company to find out which transactions have cleared the bank (and then balance the account, if you so choose). Money automatically enters records that you download in the account register, which saves you some of the trouble of entering the records yourself. You can also download brokerage statements. *Cost:* Depends on whether you download transaction records directly into Money or go to the bank's Web site first. Varies from institution to institution. Some banks charge nothing and some charge $3 to $5 per month. See Chapter 8.
Online bill payment	Pay bills online. You can use this service to pay anyone, even Uncle Ernie. If your bank doesn't permit you to pay bills online, you can still do it through these third-party corporations: Microsoft Bill Pay, CheckFree, or Metavante. *Cost:* Varies from bank to bank and from service to service. My bank charges $5 per month for the first 25 payments (that's 20 cents per payment, which is cheaper than the 37-cent stamp it takes to mail a payment). After the first 25, payments cost 40 cents a piece. Microsoft Bill Pay charges $5.95 per month for the first 15 payments. After 15, payments cost 50 cents a piece. See Chapter 8.
Online stock and mutual funds	Download stock, bond, and mutual fund prices from the Internet. Money automatically enters the current prices of the stocks, bonds, and mutual funds in your portfolio in the Your Portfolio window. By using this service, your portfolio is always up-to-date. *Cost:* Free. See Chapter 9.
My Money Portfolio	Stay on top of your investments at the Money Central Web site. Your investments are updated automatically. *Cost:* Free.

Before you can start banking or paying bills online, you have to sign up with your bank. After you sign up, the bank assigns you a password or a PIN (personal identification number) similar to the PINs used in automatic teller machines. You have to supply the password or PIN number whenever you engage in an online activity.

Not all banks and financial institutions offer online banking, but the ones that offer the service do so in one of these ways:

- **Direct services:** You send instructions from inside Money to download a bank statement or transfer funds between accounts, and the instruction is sent directly from your computer over the Internet to the bank's computers. Usually, banks charge for this service.

- **Web services:** You go to the bank's Web site, enter your password, and download a statement to Money. You can't transfer funds with this type of online account. All you can do is view and download bank statements. Usually, this service is free.

When you pay a bill online through your bank, the payment order is sent to a third party such as CheckFree or the On-Line Services Corporation. Its computers contact your bank's computers and withdraw the money necessary for the payment. The third party sends a paper check or an electronic funds transfer to the payee. Which company handles these money transfers depends on your bank. Banks contract bill-pay services to other companies.

You can download up-to-date prices of stock quotes and mutual fund shares directly from the Your Portfolio window. As long as you enter the correct ticker symbol for the mutual fund or stock you want to update, the stock's price is updated. Anyone with an Internet connection can do this activity free of charge.

Laying the Groundwork

I'm afraid that getting online isn't as easy as counting one, two, three. Before you can start exploring cyberspace, you have to complete two or three irksome little chores. Sorry about that.

The following sections explain what equipment you need to go online, how to establish a connection between your computer and the Internet, how to investigate whether your bank offers online services, how to sign up for the services, and how to set up an account so that you can go online with it.

The good news is that you have to complete these irksome little chores only once.

The equipment you need

Before you even think about going online with Money, make sure that your computer is connected to or includes a modem. A *modem* — the word stands for "*m*odulator/*dem*odulator" — is a hardware device for sending and receiving files and messages over the telephone lines.

You need a .NET password!

Stop! Do not pass Go. Do not collect $200. Before you can use any of the online services, you need a .NET password from Microsoft. You can obtain the password at this Web address: `http://register.passport.com`. As Chapter 10 explains in excruciating detail, you have to enter your .NET password when you start Money. You need the password to bank online or record Money transactions online.

After you have your .NET password, you make it serve for all the PIN number and passwords that you have to enter to bank online. To tell Money which PINs and passwords to "remember" and enter for you, follow these steps:

1. **Choose File⇨Password Manager.**

2. **Select the Financial Institution Settings tab in the Password Manager dialog box.**

3. **Click the check boxes next to the PINs that you want Money to remember.**

   If you ever need to change a PIN, you can do it by selecting it and clicking the Advanced button.

4. **Click OK.**

You also need a browser, a computer program that connects to Web sites and displays Web pages (*browser* is not a contraction of the word *brown-noser,* by the way). When you installed Money, you also installed Internet Explorer, the browser made by the Microsoft Corporation, so a browser is already installed on your system. Click the Money Browser button in Money to make the program do double duty as a Web browser (you may have to click the More button before you can see the Money Browser button).

One more thing: You need an account with an Internet service provider (ISP). When you download stock quotes or bank online, Money runs piggyback on your ISP connection. Money can't establish or make the connection on its own.

Establishing an Internet connection

Before you can go online with Money, you need to establish a connection between your computer and the Internet. Chances are, Money already knows everything it needs to know about your connection because it gets the information from its cousin, Windows, when you install Money. If your computer can already connect with the Internet, you're home free, because Money rides piggyback on the connection that is already there.

Establishing the connection is really the job of Windows, not Money 2003. But if you're in a hurry and haven't established a connection yet, follow these basic steps:

1. **Choose Tools⇨Connection Settings.**

   You see the Connection tab of the Internet Properties dialog box. This is a Windows dialog box, not a Money dialog box. The settings you make here affect all your dealings with the Internet, not only the ones you have in the Money program.

2. **Click the Setup button.**

   You see the Internet Connection Wizard's first dialog box.

3. **Keep answering questions (and clicking the Next button) until you establish the connection.**

When you finish banking online, do you want to remain on the Internet or cut the connection right away? Money maintains the connection, but if you want to close down your connection to the Internet as soon as you finish banking online, choose Tools⇨Options and click the Connection tab in the Options dialog box. Then uncheck the Leave My Internet Connection Open After Downloading Internet Information check box.

Attention America Online subscribers: America Online doesn't make use of the Windows Internet connection settings. To run Money with America Online, do the following: Choose Tools⇨Options and click the Connection tab in the Options dialog box. Under Internet Connection, click the I Use America Online to Connect to the Internet check box, and click OK.

Disabling call waiting

Call waiting is wonderful unless you connect to the Internet by modem. The noise that call waiting makes to tell you someone is trying to call disrupts Internet connections. You can, however, enter a prefix before you call to disable call waiting for the duration of a telephone call. When you connect to the Internet by modem, make sure that your modem dials the prefix as well as the telephone number of your Internet provider. Find out what the prefix is and then follow these instructions to disable call waiting when you connect to the Internet:

✔ **In Windows 95 and 98:** Go to the Control Panel and double-click the Modems icon. Select a modem on the list, if necessary, and click the Dialing Properties button. Check the To Disable Call Waiting Dial, enter the prefix, and click OK.

✔ **In Windows 2000, Me, and XP:** Go to the Control Panel and double-click the Phone and Modem Options icon. On the Dialing Rules tab, click the Edit button, select the To Disable Call Waiting Dial check box, enter the prefix, and click OK.

Signing up with your bank

If the online banking services tickle your fancy, the next step is to get in touch with your bank and find out whether it offers online services and which services it offers. The fastest way to do this is to choose Accounts & Bills➪Online Services Manager and, in the Online Services Manager window, click the See the Financial Institutions Money Supports button. As shown in Figure 7-1, you go to a Web site that lists banks and whether they offer direct services or Web services.

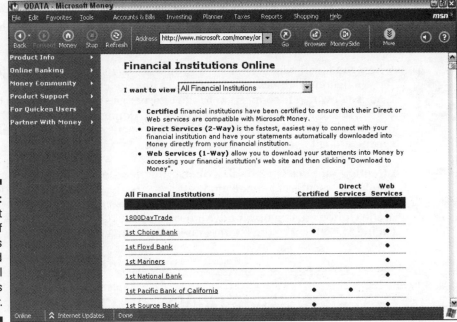

Figure 7-1: Seeing what kind of services banks and financial institutions offer.

Be sure to ask the bank or credit card company representative these important questions before you decide whether to bank online:

✔ Can I download transactions directly into Money without visiting the bank's Web site? Probably the person on the other end of the line will be confused by this question. Explain that you want to know whether it is necessary to go to the bank's Web site to download a bank statement. Explain that some banks permit Money users to download the data right into their Money file without visiting a bank's Web site.

✔ How much do the services cost? How much for bill payment and banking online? Do you charge a flat rate or do you charge per account? Is there a trial period for using the services?

> ✔ Can I transfer money between accounts?
>
> ✔ Which accounts can be online accounts? (For example, banks as a rule do not allow IRA accounts to be online accounts.)
>
> ✔ If I decide to cancel the service, what is the quickest way to do so?
>
> ✔ How will I be billed? Will the charges show up on my monthly bank statement, for example? If I bank online with more than one account, which statement will the bill appear on?

If you like the replies and decide to sign up for online banking, the bank or credit card company representative may ask for the following information, so be ready to provide it:

> ✔ Your address, home telephone number, and work telephone number
>
> ✔ Your account number(s) and perhaps your ATM card number
>
> ✔ Your birthday and birthplace
>
> ✔ Your mother's maiden name
>
> ✔ Your Social Security number
>
> ✔ Your e-mail address

What happens next depends on what kind of online services the bank offers. If the bank offers only Web services, you can get going very quickly. The bank will issue you a password. If you intend to bank online from inside Money, you usually have to wait a few days to receive a start-up kit in the mail. The kit includes the personal identification number (PIN) you need to access your accounts, as well as instructions for banking online.

Is online banking safe?

Occasionally, you read in the newspaper about an evil, twisted computer genius who crashes into others' computers and steals credit card numbers, account numbers, and the like. And stories like that make you wonder whether banking online is safe.

Banking online is safe. It's safe because banks and corporations such as Microsoft want it to be safe. Companies have poured millions of dollars into security measures to make banking on the Internet safe.

If you use an ATM card, you take a bigger risk than you do when you bank online. The odds that a thief will take your ATM card or demand your card's PIN number are higher than the odds that an evil hacker will steal your bank account's PIN number and use it to clean out your bank account.

Setting Up a Money Account So That It Works Online

After you learn your password or get your PIN number from the start-up kit that the bank sends, your next step is to give the account you want to work with online status. In other words, you need to set up the account so that you can use it to bank online and perhaps pay bills online. Connect to the Internet and follow these steps:

1. **Choose Accounts⇨Online Services Manager.**

   You go to the Online Services Manager window shown in Figure 7-2. The names of banks and financial institutions where you have open accounts are listed in this window. You gave Money the names of these banks when you set up your accounts.

   To begin with, all accounts are listed under "Banks and brokerages that are not set up for online." When you are finished declaring which accounts are online accounts, their names appear under "Banks and brokerages that are set up for online," as shown in Figure 7-2.

   If an account name isn't listed, it either isn't the kind of account that would offer online services (it's a loan account, for example) or it is held at an institution that doesn't offer the services.

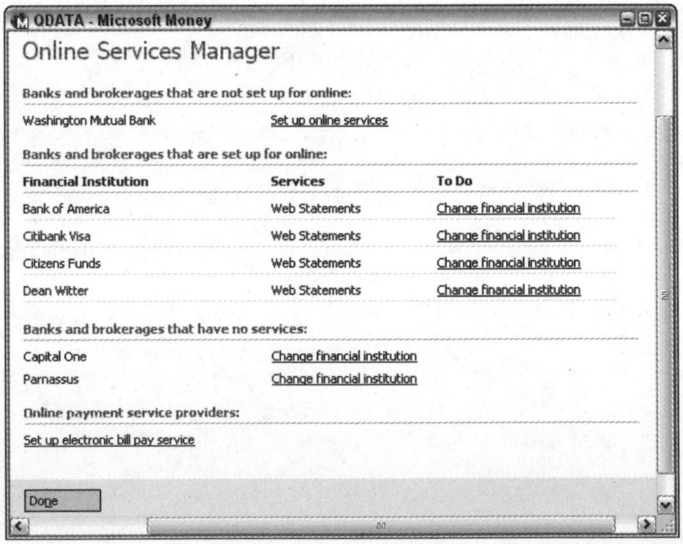

Figure 7-2:
The Online
Services
Manager
window.

2. **Click the Set Up Online Services button next to the name of the bank where you will bank online.**

   You see the Online Setup For window.

3. **Select the name of a bank or financial institution.**

   Probably the correct bank is already selected, but this is your chance to select the right name if you chose the wrong one when you set up the account.

4. **Click the Next button.**

   Money downloads information from the bank to your computer. What happens next depends on whether your bank offers Web services or direct services. Keep reading.

Setting up an account for Web services

If your bank offers Web services, you see a window that tells you how to go to your bank's Web site and enter an ID and password to download bank statements. The name of your bank has now been entered on the Favorites menu. Check it out. All you have to do to go to your bank's Web site is one of the following:

- ✔ Choose Favorites➪Favorite Web Sites➪Your Banks➪*Name of Your Bank*➪Web Statements Log On Page.

- ✔ Open the account register, click the Connect to Bank button, and choose Go To *Your Bank's Name* on the submenu.

Chapter 8 explains how to download a bank statement from your bank's Log On page.

Setting up an account for direct services

If your bank offers direct services, including the ability to pay bills online, you see the Log On window shown in Figure 7-3. Starting here and clicking the Next button as you go along, provide the information that Money needs to bank and pay bills online. In the course of filling in these windows, your computer will download information from your bank. Provide this information:

- ✔ **User ID (Social Security Number):** You know what that is, I hope.

- ✔ **PIN:** The personal identification number that the bank supplied you in the startup kit.

- ✔ **Account name:** The name of an account you want to bank online with.

✔ **Bill pay:** Declare whether you want to pay bills online as well as bank online.

✔ **Routing number:** The *routing number* (which you find in the start-up kit) consists of the first nine numbers in the lower-left corner of checks. On either side of the routing number is a colon (:).

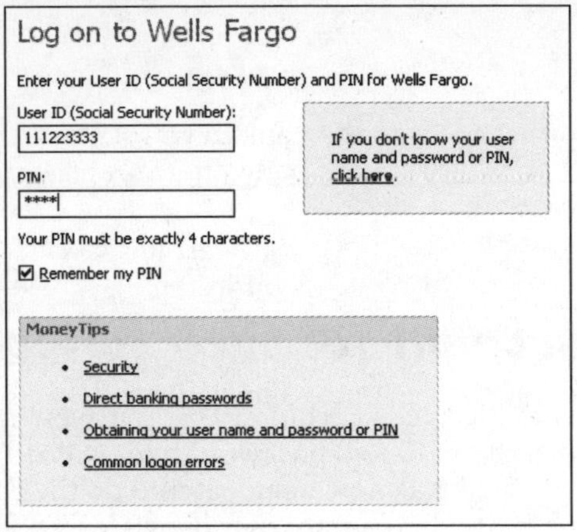

Figure 7-3:
Setting up a "direct services" online banking account.

Setting Up Bill Pay

If your bank doesn't offer online bill-paying services, you can still pay the bills online by getting the services of a third party. Money permits you to pay bills electronically with these third parties:

✔ **Microsoft Money Bill Pay:** To learn about this service, connect to the Internet and choose Shopping⇨Banking Center. You go to the Money Central Web site, where you can click links to learn about Microsoft Money Bill Pay and sign up for the service.

✔ **CheckFree:** Go to www.checkfree.com for more information.

✔ **Metavante:** Go to www.metavante.com for more information.

After you have signed up with a bill pay service, follow these steps to tell Money which one you want to use and provide the program with your Social Security and ID numbers:

1. **Choose Accounts & Bills⇨Online Services Manager.**

2. **Click the Set Up Electronic Bill Pay Service button.**

   You will find this button at the bottom of the Online Services Manager window.

3. **Choose which service you want from the Select an Online Payment Provider drop-down menu; then click the <u>N</u>ext button.**

4. **Enter your Social Security number and a password; then click the <u>N</u>ext button.**

   Money sends information to the third-party bill-paying service.

Changing Your Mind about the Online Banking Services

You tried. You tried your best and really put your heart into it, but banking online was not for you. It just didn't work out. You weren't ready for an online relationship.

To disable an online account and cancel the online banking services, do one of the following:

- **Direct services:** Choose Accounts & Bills➪Online Services Manager to go to the Online Services Manager window. Click the Modify Services button, and, in the window that appears, click No, I'd Like to Discontinue Using Direct Online Services.

- **Web services:** Since the service is free, simply stop using it.

- **Third-party bill-paying service:** Click the Bills & Deposits button to go to the Bills and Deposits window. Under "Common Tasks," click the Go to *Your Bill Pay Provider* button. You go to the Web site of the bill-paying company, where you can cancel the service.

One more task needs doing: Call the bank and deliver the bad news. Tell the bank representative, "Hey, it just wasn't working out, but it's not your fault. It's me. I need, like, more space, that's all."

Here's a way to find out a bank's telephone number very quickly: Click the Account List button, and in the Pick and Account to Use window, scroll to the bottom of the window and click the name of the bank that handles your online banking. You go to the What Would You Like to Do? window. Under "View Contact Information," click your bank's name. The Contact Information window tells you the number to call.

Browsing the Web in Money

Money has a split personality. Besides being a program for tracking your finances, Money is a Web browser. The makers of Money want you to be able to go straight from Money to the Internet and back again as you research investment opportunities, check the latest financial news, see how your stocks are doing, or, on a less serious but certainly more fun note, check the latest baseball scores.

As Figure 7-4 shows, Web pages show up inside the Money screen when you click a hyperlink and go on the Internet. That's very nice, of course, but how do you go back to Money? Where did your financial data go?

Click here to return to Money.

Figure 7-4: Money as a Web browser. Where did Money disappear to?

Here are thumbnail instructions for handling the Web browser side of Money's split personality:

✔ **Getting from Web page to Web page:** The Back and Forward buttons work just like buttons in a standard Web browser. Click Back or Forward to revisit Web pages or travel deeper into the Internet. By clicking the down arrow beside a button and choosing a Web page from the drop-down menu, you can leap forward or backward several Web pages simultaneously.

✔ **Returning to the Money screens:** There are three ways to get back to Money:

- Click the Money button to go to the Home Page.

- Click the Back button or open the Back button drop-down menu and select a Money window.

- Choose a menu command or click the More button and choose the name of a Money window from the drop-down list (refer to Figure 7-4).

✔ **Seeing a Web page in your browser:** Click the Browser button to dispense with Money and see a Web page in a real, live browser.

Cataloging your favorite Web sites

Suppose that you're tooling along in the Money browser and you come to a useful or fun Web site that you want to revisit later on. For occasions like that, Money offers you the opportunity to add the Web site to your Favorites list. Favorite Web sites are easy to revisit:

✔ To revisit the Web site in Money, choose Favorites⇨Favorite Web Sites and the name of the Web site on the submenu that appears.

✔ To revisit the Web site in Internet Explorer, choose Favorites⇨Financial Links and the name of the Web site. When you installed Money, the program put a new folder called Financial Links in the Internet Explorer Web browser.

With a Web site you want to revisit on-screen, choose Favorites⇨Add to Favorites. You see the Add Favorite dialog box. Enter a more descriptive name for the site, if necessary, and click OK.

If you intend to save more than a dozen Web sites, I suggest creating folders to keep track of them. Do that by clicking the New Folder button in the Add Favorite dialog box and entering a name in the Create New Folder dialog box that appears. Click the Create In button and choose a folder name to save a Web site in a particular folder.

Do the Web sites you added to the Favorites menu need reorganizing? Choose Favorites⇨Organize Favorites⇨Web Sites. You see the Organize Favorites dialog box. It offers buttons for deleting and renaming Web sites, as well as moving them to different folders.

Chapter 8

Banking and Bill Paying Online

• •

• •

*B*anking online and paying bills online represent a brave new world. If you've made the arrangements with your bank and have prepared Money for online banking (see Chapter 7), you're ready to blast off for that world. You're going to do for the first time what many people will consider routine by the year 2005. You're about to enter the future. You're about to take your digital cash into cyberspace.

In this chapter, you find out how to pay bills electronically over the Internet and how to keep tabs on a bank account by banking online. Throughout this chapter, I show you how to record online transactions and online payments in account registers. So strap yourself in. Liftoff is approaching.

Sending Bank Instructions over the Internet

After you record online transactions and online payments (I show you how shortly), they appear on the Connect window. As shown in Figure 8-1, this window also lists commands for downloading stock quotes and updating Money. The Connect window is where you tell Money which instructions to send to your bank, credit card company, or brokerage firm. After you give the instructions, you click the Connect button to go onto the Internet.

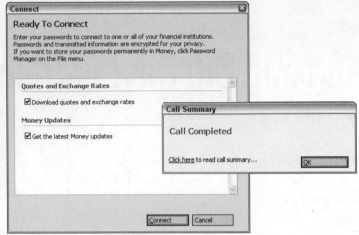

Figure 8-1:
Telling
Money
which
transactions
to send over
the Internet.

Connect to the Internet and follow these steps to send transaction instructions:

1. **Click the Internet Updates button and choose Update Now on the pop-up menu.**

   The Internet Updates button is located in the lower-left corner of the screen. You see the Connect dialog box after you click the button. The other way to bring up this dialog box is to choose Tools⇨Internet Updates⇨Update Now.

2. **Uncheck instructions that you *don't* want to send.**

   If you want to postpone sending an instruction, uncheck its name.

3. **Click the Connect button to send the instructions on the list.**

   If you are not using a .NET password, you will be asked to enter the PIN number of the account you are sending instructions to after you click the Connect button.

   You hear your phone dialing (if you have a modem rather than a DSL line) and then you see the Connecting dialog box. Then your modem initializes, you establish a secure connection, the Call Progress box appears, and the data transfers. If all goes well, the Call Summary dialog box appears with the Call Completed message (refer to Figure 8-1).

4. **Click OK in the Call Summary dialog box.**

   You see a Summary screen that lists the items that were downloaded or sent over the Internet.

You can always tell in Money when you're connected to the Internet. Glance at the lower-left corner of the screen. If you see the word "online," your computer is indeed connected to the Internet.

Getting transaction data automatically

People who bank online directly — that is, people whose PIN numbers are on file with Money — can retrieve information from their banks automatically whenever they connect to the Internet. Microsoft calls it "background banking." Without being asked, Money downloads your latest account balances. The program does this even when it isn't open. In order to engage in background banking, you need a .NET password (Chapter 10 explains what those are).

If automatic banking appeals to you, start by giving Money the PIN numbers it needs to access your account information. Choose File⇨ Password Manager, select the Financial Institution Settings tab in the Password Manager dialog box, and click check boxes next to the PINs of the bank accounts whose data you want. Then choose Tools⇨Internet Updates⇨ Customize Updates to go to the Customize Background Banking window. In the window, click the check boxes next to the names of accounts whose data you want, and choose how often you want to download the data automatically.

Banking Online

Remember the old movies and TV shows about Buck Rogers? Not one of them showed Buck banking online. Sure, you got to see Buck battle Ming the Merciless, but you never saw him battle his checkbook as he tried to balance it. Too bad Buck didn't have Money to download a bank statement and use it to update an account register, transfer money between online accounts, or send e-mail messages to a bank. (He could even have used e-mail to taunt Ming.)

Getting accurate, up-to-date account information

With the online banking service, you can find out how much money is in an account and which transactions have cleared the bank. After you get the information, you can compare it to the records in your account register and update the register with the downloaded information. You can even let Money do the work of recording transactions in registers. Instead of entering the transactions yourself, the bank "pours" them into the account register when you download.

Unless you specify otherwise, you get months and months of information the first time you download a bank statement. You don't want that. You want about a month's worth of transactions.

How you download statements from a bank depends on whether you use direct services or Web services to bank online. Better read on.

Downloading a bank statement with Web services

To download a bank statement with Web services, start by going to your bank's Log On page. You can get there with one of these techniques:

- ✔ Choose Favorites➪Favorite Web Sites➪Your Banks➪*Name of Your Bank*➪Web Statements Log On Page.

- ✔ On the Account List window, click Get Online Statements, and, in the next window, click the name of a bank.

- ✔ Open the account register, click the Connect to Bank button, and choose Go To *Your Bank's Name* on the submenu.

On your bank's Log On page, enter your online ID and password. Then follow the instructions on the page for downloading a bank statement. Each bank's instructions are a little different. Select the name of your account, look for a Download to Microsoft Money button, and click the button.

After the account information is downloaded to your computer, you see the Online File Received screen, shown in Figure 8-2. Follow these steps:

1. **On the Money Account name drop-down menu, choose the name of the account where the transactions belong.**

Figure 8-2: Downloading a bank statement with Web services.

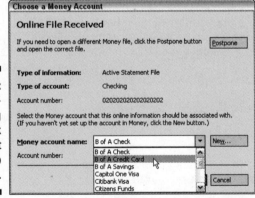

2. **Click the Next button.**

   The You Have Statements to Read window, shown in Figure 8-3, appears.

Click an account name to view the records you downloaded from the bank.

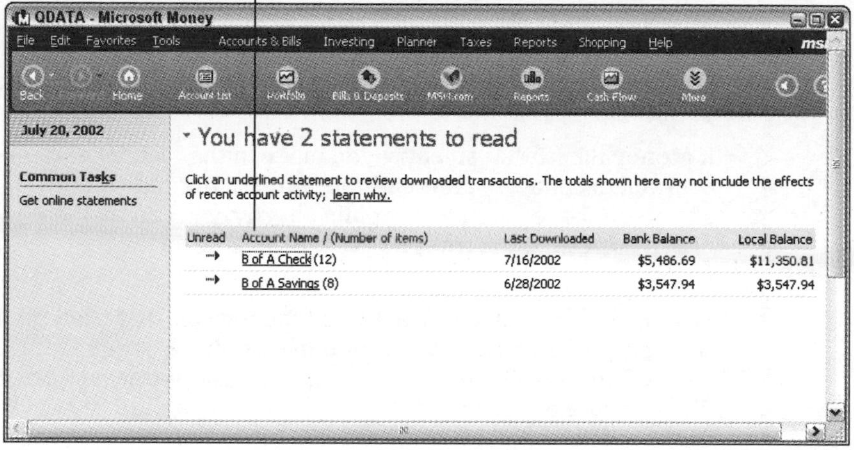

Figure 8-3:
The list of
downloaded
account
statements.

Downloading a bank statement with direct services

Options for getting bank statements appear automatically in the Connect dialog box — the dialog box you see when you click the Internet Updates button and choose Update Now. Money assumes that you want to download your bank statement whenever you connect to the Internet by way of Money. Enter your PIN, if necessary, and click the Connect button. The You Have Statements to Read window (refer to Figure 8-3) lists the bank statements you downloaded.

Viewing and updating a register whose transactions you downloaded

After you've downloaded transactions from the bank, you can compare the bank's records to yours for the sake of accuracy. By doing so, you make sure that the amounts in your register match the amounts in the bank's records. If you find a discrepancy, Money gives you the chance to fix it.

In the You Have Statements to Read window (refer to Figure 8-3), click the name of the bank account whose statement you want to examine. You see an account register like the one in Figure 8-4. Here's how to read confusing registers like this one:

✔ Under "Downloaded" on the left side of the screen, Money tells you how many transactions need reviewing.

✔ An exclamation point appears in the ! column where transactions need reviewing. An orange ! means that no match was found; a red ! means that a match may have been found; a green ! means a definite match was found.

✔ If Money thinks that an entry you made in the register and one you downloaded may be different, the words "Your Entry" and "Bank Entry" appear in the register. As I explain shortly, you can fix these discrepancies by selecting the transaction and clicking the Accept or Change button.

✔ Where you entered a transaction in the register that is identical to a transaction you downloaded from the bank, the words "Your Entry" and "Bank Entry" *don't* appear in the register. These transactions are very likely accurate. You can simply click the Accept button to acknowledge them.

✔ If you downloaded a transaction but it is nowhere to be found in your register, the transaction APPEARS IN CAPITAL LETTERS.

Click Change to edit it.

Click Accept to enter the boldface transaction.

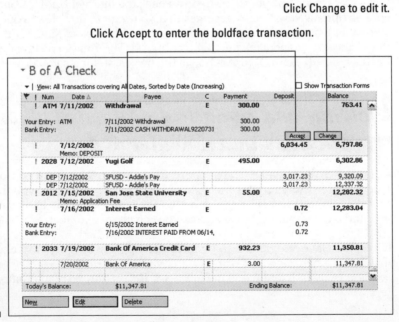

Figure 8-4: Reviewing transactions downloaded from the bank.

Your mission now, should you choose to accept it, is to examine the transactions, make sure they are accurate, and accept or edit them as necessary. You don't have to clear all the transactions. You can always uncheck the mysterious ones and clear them later, when the paper statement arrives.

Click each transaction that needs reviewing to select it; then do one of the following:

- ✔ **Accept it:** Click the Accept button. You hear a "beep," and that's the end of it. The transaction is officially entered in the register. Before you accept a transaction, make sure it is categorized correctly.

  Under Common Tasks, click the Reconcile Transactions button and choose Accept All Definite matches if you are certain that the matches are accurate and you want to save a little time.

- ✔ **Change it:** Click the Change button whenever the bank and your records differ. You see the Review Transaction Details window, shown in Figure 8-5. This window gives you the chance to repair the little problem.

Click here to edit a transaction.

Figure 8-5:
Changing transactions downloaded from the bank.

Review transaction details

The information below is based on data received from your financial institution.

Num	Date	Payee	Amount	Category
	7/11/2002	VISA INSTANT CASH TRA...	$300.00	
		Memo: VISA INSTANT CASH TRANSFERINSTANT CASH		

⦿ This transaction was entered into your register as a new transaction.

○ This transaction should be matched to a pre-existing transaction(s) in my register.

Select one or more transactions from your register:

	Num	Date	Payee	Category : Subcategory	Amount
☐	2023	6/26/2002	Sallie Mae	Education : Addies Loan	(168.76)
☐	2024	6/26/2002	PG & E	Utilities : Gas & Electric	(43.34)
☐	2022	6/26/2002	Pac Bell	Telephone : 282-3989	(82.85)
☐	2021	6/26/2(			
☐	2025	6/28/2(			
☐	DEP	6/29/2(			
☐	ATM	6/29/2(			
☐	2026	7/8/20(			

Edit Transaction

Account: B of A Check
From: Cash Withdrawl
Category: Misc
Classifica...
Memo:
Cleared

Number:
Date: 7/11/2002
Amount: 300.00

Split

OK
Cancel

Deposit

In the Review Transaction Details window, do one of the following:

- ✔ **Edit the transaction:** Click the transaction at the top of the window. The Edit Transaction dialog box appears (refer to Figure 8-5). Fix the transaction and click OK. Then click the Done button.

- ✔ **Assign the transaction to another entry in your register:** At the bottom of the screen is a list of unreconciled transactions in your account register. If the transaction is one you entered already, select its check box in the list and click the Done button.

Deciding how to download transactions

Be sure to visit the Online Services tab of the Options dialog box if you are serious about downloading transactions from banks. This tab gives you many opportunities to decide how you want to download stuff from the bank. Choose Tools⇨Options to open the Options dialog box. From top to bottom, here are the options on the Online Services tab:

✔ **Add a description to the Memo field:** Banks automatically enter descriptions in the Memo field for withdrawals, for example. Choose this option to enter those descriptions in your account registers.

✔ **Match transactions:** When looking for matches, this option tells Money to search a certain number of days in the past. Sixty days is usually adequate, because that represents about two statement periods.

✔ **Automatically accept all downloaded transactions:** I wouldn't touch this one with a ten-foot pole! I think you should review downloaded transactions before entering them in the register.

✔ **Overwrite transaction dates:** Instead of entering the date on which you made a transaction into the account register, Money enters the date on which the transaction cleared the bank.

✔ **Replace downloaded payee names with user-altered names:** Money offers a feature for filling in payee names for downloaded transactions. I don't cover it in this book because it doesn't work very well. You're welcome to try it, though, by choosing this option.

✔ **Automatically mark accepted transactions as Reconciled:** Choose this option if you don't want to balance your bank account against the monthly statements that the bank sends in the mail and you prefer to balance the account on the basis of transactions that you download from the bank.

✔ **Show standardized payee names:** The payee name feature again!

✔ **Enter electronic payments in the register:** Instead of entering the date on which you made an electronic payment, Money enters into the register the date the payment clears the bank.

✔ **After accepting a transaction:** What do you want to do after you click the Done button in the Review Transaction Details window (refer to Figure 8-5)? Choose an option from this drop-down menu.

Paying the Bills Online

Sure, paying bills online is disconcerting at first. That's your hard-earned money flying across cyberspace. Those coins that used to jangle in your pocket have been digitized and turned into bits and bytes — nothing you could feed a jukebox, for example.

On the other hand, you don't have to rummage through desk drawers to find stamps and envelopes when you pay bills online. As I note in Chapter 7, paying bills online is a little cheaper than paying bills by mail.

If you are paying bills through a Web service such as Microsoft Bill Pay or CheckFree, go to the Web site where you issue payments. People who use direct services can fire bills into cyberspace from inside Money. The following sections explain how to record an online payment, stop a payment, and inquire about a payment.

Money offers a shortcut to Microsoft Bill Pay. Click the Bills & Deposits button to go the Bills and Deposits window. Then click the Go to MSN Bill pay button. You'll find it under Common Tasks.

Recording the online payment

To record an online payment, follow these steps:

1. **Click the Account List button on the Navigation bar or choose Accounts & Bills⇨Accounts.**

   You land in the Account List window.

2. **Click the name of the bank from which you will pay the bill.**

   You go to an account register.

3. **Click the Make an Electronic Payment or Transfer button and choose Make an Electronic Payment on the pop-up menu.**

   The first time you record an online payment to a company or person and you click OK in the Edit Transaction dialog box, you see a dialog box for entering information about company or person. Here you tell Money everything you know about the payee. Be sure to enter the information correctly.

   You have to fill out the Online Payee Details dialog box only once for each payee. After you make the first online payment, Money doesn't ask you for the payee's address and phone number again. If a payee's address or phone number changes, go to the Categories & Payees window and record the changes there (see Chapter 10).

   If you don't have an account number, enter your name in the Account Number text box.

4. **Click the Submit Payment button.**

   When you click the button, you see the Edit Transaction dialog box. Except for the Due Date text box and the Number box, which says Epay (for Electronic Payment), this dialog box works exactly like the Withdrawal transaction form I describe in Chapter 3.

What about check numbers for online payments?

When you record an online payment and send it across the Internet, Money assigns it a check number that is far, far removed from the numbers on the checks you enter by hand. The check number isn't assigned until the payment has been sent. Money even puts the online icon — an envelope being struck by lightning — next to the check number in the register so that you know that the payment was made online.

Stopping a payment after it's sent

What? You sent a payment over the Internet and now you regret doing so? If you sent the payment in the past four days, you can try to stop it by following these steps:

1. **Click the Bills & Deposits button on the Navigation bar to go to the Bills and Deposits window.**

2. **Click View Electronic Transactions.**

   The View Electronic Payments and Transfers window appears. It lists all transactions you sent in the past 60 days.

3. **Select the electronic transaction you want to stop and click the Delete button.**

Transferring money between accounts

As long as both accounts are signed up for the online banking service and both accounts are at the same bank, you can transfer money between accounts. In fact, you can play digital Ping-Pong and send the money back and forth between accounts as many times as you wish. Sorry, you can't transfer money, for example, from a credit card account to a checking account. Also, you can't transfer money to someone else's bank account. Money laundering is not allowed.

Transfer funds between accounts the same way you record a normal money transfer in a register. However, choose Electronic Transfer (Xfer) in the Number box and click the Submit button to send the transfer across the Internet.

Chapter 9

The High-Tech Investor

*F*or investors who dabble in stocks, mutual funds, and bonds, being able to download share prices from the Internet with Money is too good to be true. Rather than update share prices yourself by entering numbers in text boxes, all you have to do is plug into the Internet, grab the numbers, and be done with it. No fooling — downloading share prices from the Internet with Money takes about two minutes. It's free, too.

Chapter 7 explains how to tell Money about your Internet connection so that the program knows how to get around in cyberspace. This chapter explains how to update a portfolio from the Internet. I also explain how to research investments over the Internet at Money Central, the official MS Money Web site, and how to research investments elsewhere on the Internet.

Downloading Stock and Mutual Fund Quotes

You can download stock, mutual fund, and bond prices as long as you have access to the Internet through an Internet service provider, a browser is installed on your computer, and you have entered ticker symbols for your investments. A *ticker symbol* is an abbreviated company name that is used for tracking the performance of stocks, mutual funds, and bonds. You can usually find these symbols on the statements you receive from brokers. Unless Money has a company's ticker symbol on file, you can't download the current price of a stock, bond, or mutual fund.

In Chapter 17, I explain how you can enter ticker symbols while you're describing the securities in an investment and retirement account, but here are shorthand instructions for entering ticker symbols in case you don't want to wear out your fingertips turning to Chapter 17:

1. **Click the Portfolio button on the Navigation bar or choose Investing⇨Portfolio.**

   You land in the Your Portfolio window.

2. **Double-click the name of the security that needs a ticker symbol.**

   The Price History window appears.

3. **Click the Details button.**

   You see a Details window like the one in Figure 9-1. If a Symbol text box doesn't appear in your window, the investment can't be updated by way of the Internet because it is not a stock, mutual fund, or bond.

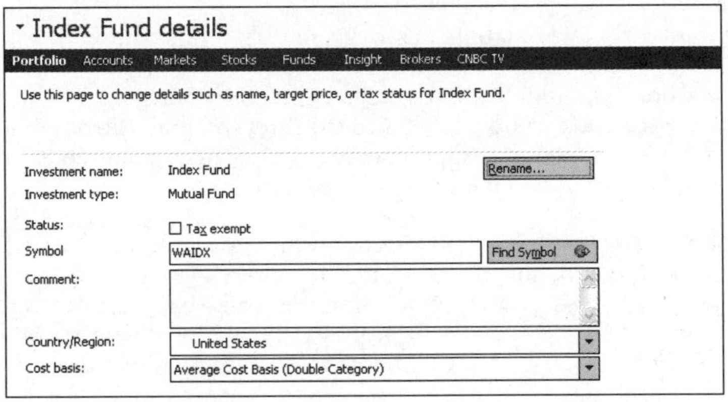

Figure 9-1:
Entering a
ticker
symbol.

4. **Enter the ticker symbol in the Symbol text box.**

   If you're running Money 2003 Deluxe, you can find out a company's ticker symbol by clicking the Find Symbol button in the Details window.

I am very happy to report that downloading stock, bond, money market, and mutual fund prices is one of the easiest tasks you can do in Money. As long as your connection to the Internet is running smoothly and you have provided an accurate ticker symbol for the securities whose price you want to download, all you have to do is click one or two buttons.

Follow these steps to update the prices of stocks, bonds, money market funds, and mutual funds in your portfolio:

1. **Click the Portfolio button on the Navigation bar or choose Investing➪ Portfolio to go to the Your Portfolio window.**

2. **As shown in Figure 9-2, click the Update Prices button and choose an option to update the price of the securities in your portfolio.**

Choose an Update option.   Choose which security prices to update.

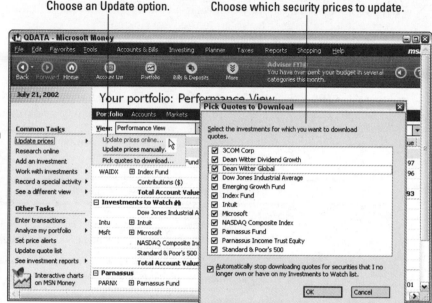

Figure 9-2: Click the Update Prices button and choose how you want to download security prices.

The window offers two ways to update the price of securities:

- **Update the price of all securities:** Click the Update Prices button and choose Update Prices Online from the submenu.

- **Update the price of a handful of securities:** Click the Update Prices button and choose Pick Quotes to Download from the submenu. You see the Pick Quotes to Download dialog box, shown in Figure 9-2. Uncheck the securities whose prices you *don't* want to update and click OK.

The Update Prices submenu also offers an option called Update Prices Manually. Choose this option to enter prices on your own, but why do that? This is the computer era. Make the computer do the work.

Money Central: Researching Investments Online

Money 2003 Deluxe users can take advantage of Money Central to research investments online. Money Central is a Web site with all sorts of tools for researching investments. To go to the Web site, choose Investing⇔Online Investing Research or click the Research Online button in the Your Portfolio window. Do the buttons in the Money Central Web site look familiar? Those are the same buttons you see along the top of the Your Portfolio window in Money. When you click a button in the Your Portfolio window — Markets, Stocks, Funds, Insight, Finder, Brokers or CNBC TV — you go on the Internet, straight to a page at Money Central. There, you can start examining investment opportunities. Table 9-1 describes the different pages of the Money Central Web site that you can go to by clicking a button in the Your Portfolio window.

Table 9-1	Pages in the Money Central Web Site
Page	*How It Can Help You*
Markets	Offers business articles, late-breaking news about the financial markets, and market statistics.
Stocks	Lets you gather detailed information about specific stocks.
Funds	Lets you get information about mutual funds.
Insight	More wisdom about the financial markets, including stock-picking strategies and *Jubak's Journal* (articles by a fellow named Jim Jubak, one of them financial gurus, I reckon).
Brokers	Offers links to well-known brokerage houses such as Ameritrade and TD Waterhouse.
CNBC TV	What's on CNBC TV, a cable TV channel, as well as links to articles about investing.

Money Central: Scrutinizing the Investments You Own

After you have downloaded stock and mutual fund quotes a few times, Money gets wind of the investments you own and starts giving you opportunities to look more closely at them, as shown in Figure 9-3. In the Your Portfolio window, you can right-click an investment, choose MSN Money Investor on the submenu, and choose an option from the submenu to go to the Money Central Web site and learn more about a company. This is a very convenient way to examine investments that you own.

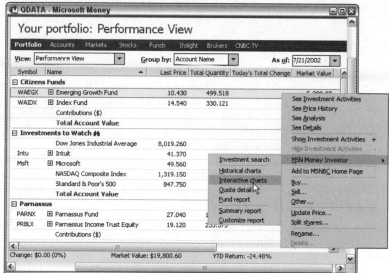

Figure 9-3:
You can research the investments you own starting from the Your Portfolio window.

Other Ways to Research Investments Online

It goes without saying, but Money Central isn't the only place on the Internet to research investments. You are hereby encouraged to get investment advice from as many places as you possibly can. In my opinion, there are no experts when it comes to handing out investment advice. They are just people with opinions. The following pages unscrew the inscrutable. They show you where to go on the Internet to research mutual funds and stocks.

Researching mutual funds on the Internet

Before you start dabbling in mutual funds, you need to know about how fees are levied, the different kinds of funds, and the risks. After you know that, you can start looking for a fund that meets your needs. Here are some Web sites where you can acquire the basics of mutual fund investing:

✔ **Brill's Mutual Funds Interactive:** An all-purpose Web site for mutual fund investing. Here, you can read about mutual fund investing or search for funds by name and read about them. Address: www.fundsinteractive.com

✔ **Mutual Fund Investor's Center:** An excellent Web site with articles about mutual fund investing. This site ranks mutual funds in various ways. You can also search for mutual funds using different criteria. Address: www.mfea.com

✔ **Mutual Funds Online:** Offers advice about choosing, buying, and selling mutual funds. Address: www.mfmag.com

At last count, investors could choose from among 10,000 mutual funds. After you know what you want in a mutual fund, check out Money Central to search for a mutual fund that fits your investment strategy. You can also search at these Web sites:

✔ **Morningstar.com:** The granddaddy of mutual fund analysis, this company offers reports on 7,000 mutual funds. You can get fund profiles, performance reports, financial statements, and news articles. Address: www.morningstar.com

✔ **SmartMoney.com:** Offers a sophisticated search engine for pinpointing mutual funds. Address: www.smartmoney.com

Researching stocks on the Internet

The stock market, it has been said, is 85 percent psychology and 15 percent economics. And that's only half the problem. The other half has to do with the market's hard-to-understand terminology and the numerous confusing ways to buy and sell stock.

To get general-purpose information about stocks and stock markets, read stock tips, and discover stock-picking strategies, try these sites, which are good starting places:

✔ **Briefing.com:** Get stock quotes, reports, and historical charts. Address: www.briefing.com

✔ **DailyStocks.com:** Provides links to market indexes, news sources, earnings figures, and newsletters. Address: www.dailystocks.com

✔ **Wall Street Research Net:** Offers links to many financial resources, including brokers sites and government data. Address: www.wsrn.com

Suppose that you want to target a stock but you don't know what it is yet. In other words, you believe that the future is bright for a certain industry and you want to buy shares in companies in that industry. Or you want to buy a certain kind of stock — stock in a foreign corporation, a small cap stock, or a blue-chip stock. Searching for stocks this way is called *screening*. From these Web sites, you can screen stocks and find the one you are looking for:

- **Market Guide's NetScreen:** Offers two stock-screening databases, one with which you can search using 20 variables and one using 75 variables. Address: www.marketguide.com

- **Quicken.com:** This stock screener is easy to use and its help instructions are genuinely helpful. (Click the <u>Investing</u> hyperlink and then the <u>Popular Stock Screens</u> hyperlink.) Address: www.quicken.com

- **Silicon Investor:** This screener is easy to understand and fill out. (Look under <u>Research</u> and click the <u>Stock Screener</u> hyperlink.) Address: www.siliconinvestor.com

Part III
Getting Your Money's Worth

The 5th Wave By Rich Tennant

"The first thing you should know about investing online is that when you see the exploding bomb icon appear, it's just your browser crashing — not your portfolio."

In this part . . .

The next four chapters show you how to get the most out of Money. They tell you how to draw up a budget, schedule bills so you can pay them on time, and get ready for tax season. Oh, and you also pick up a handful of housekeeping hints, such as backing up your data files, that make your trip to Moneyland more enjoyable.

Chapter 10

Some Important Housekeeping Chores

This chapter explains a handful of housekeeping chores that you must do from time to time. Sorry. Nobody likes housekeeping chores, but they have to get done.

In this chapter, you find out how to back up your data file so that you have a spare copy if your computer fails. You also discover how to restore a file — that is, load a backup copy of a file onto your computer. This chapter explains how to delete old bank accounts, create a second file for storing transactions, delete a file, and rename a file. You also find out how to archive a file to keep records of past transactions. For spies, secret agents, and people who often glance over their shoulder, this chapter also explains how to clamp a password on a Money file.

Backing Up and Restoring Money Files

Computers are wonderful machines — until they break down. If a computer breaks down entirely, it's worse than useless because the data on its hard disk drive can't be recovered. It can't be recovered, I should say, unless someone had the foresight to back up the data.

In computerese, *backing up* means to make a second copy of a file so that the data can be recovered if something evil happens to the hard drive where the original file is stored. As long as you have a backup copy of your Money file, it doesn't matter whether your computer is run over by a bulldozer or struck by lightning. It doesn't matter because you can always restore your data from the backup file. *Restoring* means to load the backup copy of a file onto a computer and use it instead of the original file from which the backup was made.

Telling Money how to back up your financial data

Backing up is so important that Money gives you the opportunity to do it when you close the program or close a data file. You may have already noticed the Back Up dialog box, shown in Figure 10-1. By clicking the Back Up button in this dialog box each time you close Money, you can make a backup copy of your data file.

Figure 10-1:
The Back
Up dialog
box appears
whenever
you close
Money.

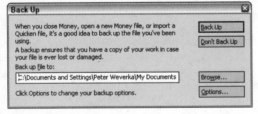

To be accurate, you make a backup copy to the C:\My Documents or the C:\Documents and Settings*Your Name*\My Documents folder on the hard drive. Instead of the data file being copied to a floppy disk that can be dropped in a drawer or filing cabinet, the backup copy is stored on the same computer that stores the original file. If something wicked happens to that computer — if it crashes or is stolen — you lose the Money data you so carefully assembled. You can't restore the file from a backup copy, because the backup copy is also on your computer.

To remedy this problem, you can tell Money that you want to make backup copies to a floppy disk, Zip disk, or other removable disk as well as the hard drive each time you close the program. Backing up this way takes all of five seconds. And by backing up this way, you always have a completely up-to-date copy of your data file on hand in case of an emergency.

Follow these steps to change the backup settings so that Money reminds you to back up to a floppy disk as well as the hard drive whenever you close the program:

1. **Choose Tools⇨Options.**

2. **Click the Backup tab in the Options dialog box.**

   You see the Backup tab, as shown in Figure 10-2. By the way, you can also reach the Backup tab by clicking the Options button in the Back Up dialog box (refer to Figure 10-1).

Figure 10-2: Enter a 1 in the Automatically Back Up to Floppy Every *X* Days text box to be reminded each time you use Money to back up your data file to a floppy disk.

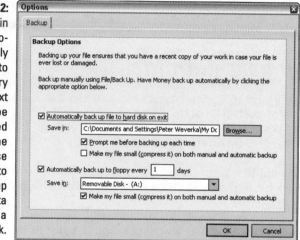

3. **Make sure that both Automatically Back Up File boxes are checked.**

   By doing so, you make sure that backup copies are made to the hard disk and to a floppy disk.

4. **Make sure that the check box called Prompt Me Before Backing Up Each Time is checked.**

   This way, you are reminded to make backup copies of your data.

5. **Enter 1 in the Automatically Back Up to a Floppy Every X Days text box.**

   Unless you change this setting, you are asked every 14 days whether you want to back up the data file to a floppy disk. But 14 days is not often enough. I think you should back up the data file to a floppy disk each day that you finish using the program.

6. **Click the Browse button and, in the Backup dialog box, choose a folder for storing backup copies of your Money file on the hard disk.**

   Backup copies are stored in the C:\My Documents folder by default, but most people reserve that folder for data files that they use on a daily basis. I suggest choosing or creating a more inconspicuous folder. The folder can be anywhere on your hard disk.

7. **Open the Save In drop-down menu and choose a removable disk apart from the floppy disk drive (A) if you want to make backup copies elsewhere.**

   If your computer is equipped with a Zip drive, for example, you can choose Removable Disk (D:) from the drop-down menu to make backup copies to a Zip disk.

8. **Click OK to close the Options dialog box.**

   You're all set. You will be reminded to back up your data file to a floppy disk or other disk whenever you close Money 2003.

Backing up your data file

Money gives you two ways to back up a data file. You can wait until you close the program and negotiate the Back Up dialog box as part of shutting down, or you can choose File➪Backup to back up the data file without closing the program (see the "Backing up on the fly" sidebar).

Assuming that you want to wait to back up your data, here are instructions for backing up a data file to the hard disk and a floppy disk when you close the program:

1. **Click the Close button (the X in the upper-right corner of the screen) or choose File➪Exit to close Money.**

   You see the familiar Back Up dialog box (refer to Figure 10-1).

2. **Click the Back Up button.**

   Your computer grinds away and then the deed is done — the file is backed up to the hard drive.

   As long as you followed the instructions earlier in this chapter in "Telling Money how to back up your financial data," you see the Back Up to Floppy dialog box. It tells you how many days have passed since the last time you backed up your data file to a floppy disk.

3. **Click the Back Up Now button.**

   That's all she wrote — the file is copied to the floppy disk.

Be sure to put the floppy or removable disk in a safe place. A *safe place* is one where nothing can be spilled on it and no one is tempted to use it for a drink coaster.

Backing up on the fly

You don't have to wait till you shut down Money to back up a data file. To back up in the middle of your work, choose File⇨Backup (or press Ctrl+B). In the Backup dialog box, click an option button to tell Money where to back up your data file; then click OK.

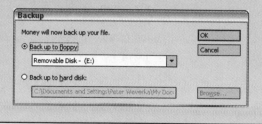

Restoring a file from its backup copy

Suppose that doomsday arrives and you have to restore a data file from its backup copy on a floppy disk, removable disk, or the hard disk. Perhaps you botched a find-and-replace operation or your computer went momentarily haywire. If that happens, follow these steps to start working with the backup copy of a file instead of the original copy:

1. **If you want to restore your data file from a floppy disk, put the floppy disk with the backup copy of your data file in the A drive.**

2. **Choose File⇨Restore Backup.**

   You see the Restore Backup dialog box.

3. **Click the Restore from a Backup File radio button (if it isn't already selected) and click the Next button.**

   The Restore Backup dialog box, shown in Figure 10-3, appears. Take a close look at the filename that is listed in this dialog box. What you do in Step 4 depends on whether that file is the one you want to restore.

Figure 10-3:
In this dialog box, tell Money where the backup file is located.

Restore Backup

Money recommends the default backup file. If you haven't backed up your Money file before or want to open a different file, click the second option.

⊙ Restore from default backup file:
Original file name: C:\Documents and Settings\Peter Weverka\My Docum...
Backed up to: E:\TEster Backup d1.mbf
on Wednesday, July 10, 2002 Backup file size: 2,367,792 bytes

○ Open a different backup file.

[< Back] [Restore] [Cancel]

4. **Click the Restore from Default Backup File radio button and then click the Restore button if the file listed in the dialog box is the one you want to restore; click the Open a Different Backup File radio button and click the Next button if you want to restore a different file from its backup copy.**

   If you clicked the first radio button, you see the Restore Target dialog box. Skip to Step 6.

   If you clicked the second radio button, you see another Restore Backup dialog box. This one lists all Money files — backup and otherwise — on the A drive, C drive, and other drives on your computer.

5. **In the Restore Backup dialog box, click the backup copy of the file that you want to restore; then click the Restore button.**

   Backup files have the word "Backup" in their name and have the extension .mbf. If the backup file you are looking for is not on the list, click the Select Other Backup File button and look for the file in the Restore dialog box.

   After you click the Restore button, you see the Restore Backup dialog box.

6. **Make sure that the Restore Backup dialog box lists the file that you want to restore from its backup copy; then click the Restore button.**

   In a moment or two, depending on how large the data file is, the backup takes the place of the original. Now, all you have to do is enter the financial transactions that you entered between the time you last backed up the file and the time you restored it. I hope there aren't many transactions to enter.

Transferring Your Money File to a New Computer

When you get a new computer, you may well ask yourself, "How do I get my Money data from my old computer to my new computer?" The answer is by backing up the data on your old computer, loading the Money software on your new computer (if necessary), and restoring the backed-up Money file on your new computer. In other words, pretend on your new computer that you just lost your Money data; then restore the data from a backup file.

The previous section in this chapter explains how to restore data from a backup file. Turn a couple of pages back and start reading. I'll wait for you here.

Pruning the Payee List

As you surely know, Money "remembers" the names of people and businesses that you enter in account registers. When you enter a payee name the second time, you have to type only the first two or three letters. Money enters the full name for you. And if you are the sort of person who would rather click than type, you can enter a payee name in an account register by selecting it from the Pay To drop-down list.

As wonderful as it is, the Payees list has a habit of getting very long. From time to time you need to prune the list to cut it down to size. That way, fewer names appear in the Payee To or From text box and you can find the name you need faster on transaction forms.

When you delete a payee on the list, nothing happens to his, her, or its name in the account registers. The payee's name remains intact for future generations to see and behold. Next time you try to enter the payee's name in a transaction form, however, the name doesn't appear automatically in the Pay To or From box after you type the first couple of letters.

Follow these steps to remove names from the Payees list:

1. **To get to the Payees list, click the More button on the Navigation bar and choose Payees, or choose Accounts & Bills⇨Categories & Payees and then Payees button.**

    The Payees window appears, as shown in Figure 10-4.

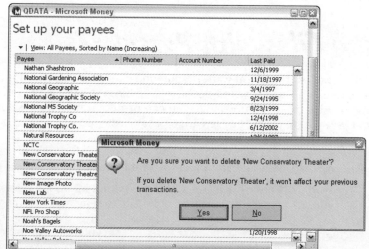

Figure 10-4: Prune the Payees list when it gets too long.

2. **Select a payee name on the list and click the Delete button.**

   A dialog box asks whether you really want to go through with it.

3. **Click the Yes button.**

You can edit information about a payee anytime. Simply go to the appropriate Payees window, double-click a payee's name, and change the information on the Payee screen.

Organizing Your Favorite Accounts, Reports, and Web Sites

If you have spent any time in Money, you know how to play favorites. By choosing Favorites⇨Add to Favorites, you can place an account, report, or Web site on the Favorites list. Then all you have to do to go to the account, report, or Web site is choose a command from the Favorites menu.

Also on the Favorites menu is a command called Organize Favorites. Choose Favorites⇨Organize Favorites when your Favorites lists get out of hand and need reorganizing. Money will take you to a window where you can prioritize your favorite accounts, reports, and Web sites, delete them, or rename them.

The Favorites lists are a very convenient device for getting around in Money. Use the Organize Favorites command to squeeze more pleasure and profit from the Favorites lists.

Protecting Files with Passwords

Probably the last thing you want is someone snooping in your Money file. To keep jealous colleagues, your spouse, future biographers, agents of Interpol, or anyone else from opening a file, you can protect it with a password. Money offers two ways to protect a file with a password:

- **Conventional password:** Enter the password each time you start Money. Fail to do so and you can't open the Money file.

- **Microsoft .NET password:** Use a .NET password. Microsoft offers the .NET password service for free. Instead of having to remember many passwords to many Web sites, you enter one password — your .NET password — at participating Web sites. The password is "encrypted," a computer term that means "buried so deep in the crypt no one can uncover it."

The following sections explain how to lock a file with a password, open a file that has been given a password, and change or remove passwords.

The Microsoft .NET password

You have no choice but to use a .NET password if you intend to record Money transactions online, download information from your bank, or see MoneySide information while you browse the Internet (these subjects are covered in Chapter 9). Here is some good news for people who use Hotmail or have an account with MSN (the Microsoft Network): You already have a .NET password. The same password that gets you into Hotmail or MSN can double as a password to Money.

Go to this Web site to get a .NET password: http://register.passport.com. One benefit of using a .NET password instead of a conventional one is that you can forget the .NET password and still recover it from Microsoft. If you forget a conventional password, you're plumb out of luck. You can't open your Money file.

Locking a file with a password

Connect to the Internet if you want a .NET password. Follow these steps to clamp a password — conventional or .NET — on a Money file:

1. **If necessary, open the file that needs a password.**

2. **Choose File⇨Password Manager.**

   You see the Password Manager dialog box shown on the left side of Figure 10-5. What you do now depends on whether you want a conventional password or you've signed up for a .NET password.

   - **Conventional password:** Type a password in the New Password text box; then type the same password in the Confirm new Password text box. It doesn't matter whether a password is upper-case, lowercase, or a combination of upper- and lowercase letters. If the password is Oaxaca, for example, it doesn't matter whether you enter oaxaca, OAXACA, or Oaxaca in the Password dialog box when you open the file.

   - **.NET password:** Click the Use Passport Sign-In button. You see the Sign In to Money dialog box shown on the right side of Figure 10-5. Enter your sign-in name, enter your password, and click the Sign In button. The password you entered is sent over the Internet to Passport.com, Microsoft's name for the Web site where .NET passwords are kept under lock and key.

   It's settled: Whoever tries to open the file next time, or whoever starts the Money program next time, will need the secret password.

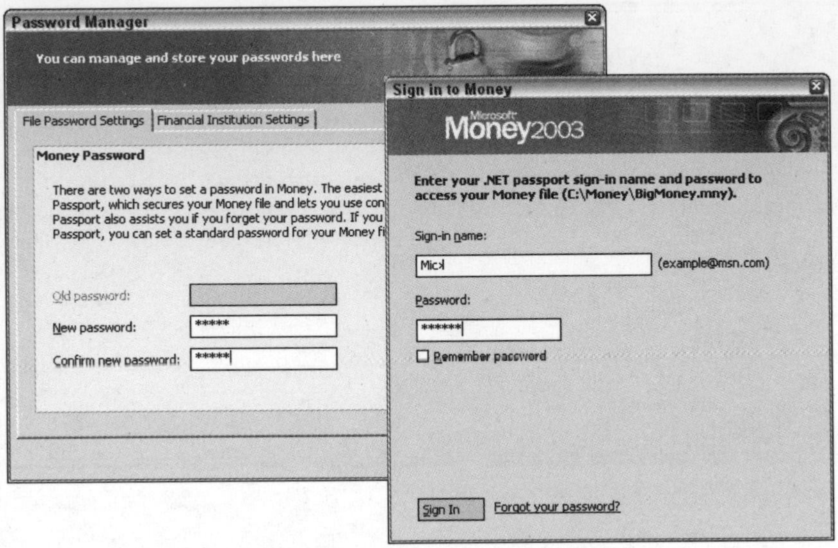

Password Manager

You can manage and store your passwords here

| File Password Settings | Financial Institution Settings |

Money Password

There are two ways to set a password in Money. The easiest
Passport, which secures your Money file and lets you use con
Passport also assists you if you forget your password. If you
Passport, you can set a standard password for your Money fi

Old password:

New password: `*****`

Confirm new password: `*****`

Sign in to Money

Money 2003

Enter your .NET passport sign-in name and password to
access your Money file (C:\Money\BigMoney.mny).

Sign-in name:

`Mic` (example@msn.com)

Password:

`******`

☐ Remember password

Sign In   Forgot your password?

Figure 10-5:
Designating
a conven-
tional
password
(left) and
a .NET
password
(right).

Opening a file that has been given a password

When you try to start Money or open a new Money file that has been given a
password, you see a Welcome screen like the one in Figure 10-6. I hope that
you know the password. If you do, enter it and click the Sign In button.

Some gratuitous advice about choosing passwords

Everybody has different advice for choosing a
password that isn't likely to be forgotten or discovered, and everybody agrees that you
shouldn't use your own name or the names of
family members or pets, because devious souls
try those names first when they try to crack

open a file. Here's a good tip for choosing passwords: Pick your favorite foreign city and spell
it backwards. My favorite foreign city is in
Mexico. If I used a password, it would be
`acaxa0`.

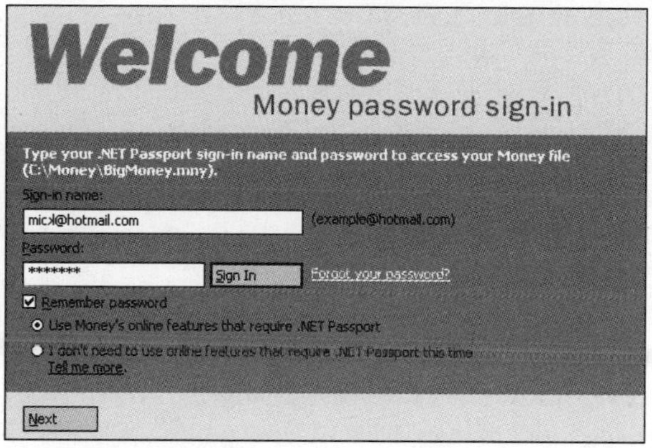

Figure 10-6:
Enter the
password
for a Money
file in this
dialog box.

Welcome
Money password sign-in

Type your .NET Passport sign-in name and password to access your Money file
(C:\Money\BigMoney.mny).

Sign-in name:

| mick@hotmail.com | (example@hotmail.com) |

Password:

| ******* | Sign In | Forgot your password? |

☑ Remember password
◉ Use Money's online features that require .NET Passport
○ I don't need to use online features that require .NET Passport this time
  Tell me more.

Next

People who enter .NET passwords have two extra choices to make on the
Welcome screen.

✔ **Remember Password:** Clicking this check box sort of defeats the purpose of having a password. Next time you open Money, your sign-in
name and password will already be entered on the Welcome screen. All
you or a cat burglar has to do is click the Sign In button to access the
Money file.

✔ **Online Features that Require .NET:** Make sure the first option button,
Use Money's Online Features that Require .NET Passport, is selected.
You got a .NET password to use those features, right?

If you don't remember the password and yours is a conventional password,
wag your head and proclaim, "Woe is me." All is not lost if yours is a .NET
password. You can go to this Web site on the Internet and recover your
stray password: `http://memberservices.passport.com`. Click the
I Forgot My Password link and take it from there.

Changing and removing passwords

How you change or remove a password from a file depends on what kind of
password you have. Start by choosing File➪Password Manager to open the
Password Manager dialog box. Then take the following steps:

✔ **Changing a conventional password:** Enter your current password in the Old Password text box, and enter the new password in the New Password and Confirm New Password text boxes. Then click OK.

✔ **Changing a .NET password:** Click the Change button. You see the Change Passports dialog box, shown in Figure 10-7. Make sure the first option button, Go to Passport.com to Change Details, is selected, and click the Finish button. Your browser opens to a screen at Passport.com, where you will find options for changing your password.

✔ **Removing a conventional password:** Enter your password in the Old Password text box and click OK.

✔ **Removing a .NET password:** Click the Change button to go to the Change Passports dialog box (refer to Figure 10-7); select the third option button, Disable Money's Passport Features, and click the Finish button. You see the Disable Passports dialog box. Select the Disable This Passport for Use in Money check box and click the Finish button.

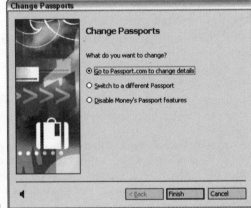

Figure 10-7:
Enter the password for a Money file in this dialog box.

Getting More Room in Account Registers

As you may have noticed by now, cash flow forecasts, a list of upcoming bills, and other extraneous items appear at the bottom of account register windows and the Portfolio window. Microsoft calls these items "personalized feedback." Figure 10-8 shows two account register windows, one with and one without personalized feedback. Some people think the window is too crowded already, and for those people, Money offers the opportunity to remove the so-called feedback (what an odd term!).

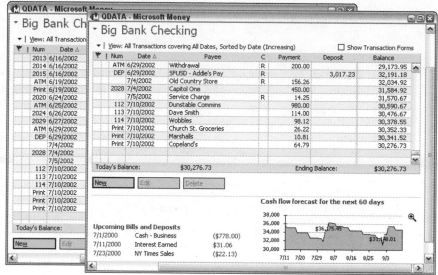

Figure 10-8:
Account register without (left) and with (right) "personalized feedback."

To remove the feedback, follow these steps:

1. **Choose Tools➪Options.**

2. **Click the Feedback tab in the Options dialog box.**

3. **Under Personalized Feedback in the Account Register and Portfolio window, click the Options button.**

4. **Choose an option button that describes how much feedback you want on-screen and click OK.**

Deleting and Closing Bank Accounts

When you close a bank account, you can either delete it or close it in the Accounts window. If the transactions in the account no longer matter for your financial history — and if the IRS wouldn't care whether a history of the account remains in your records — delete the account. More likely than not, however, you need the records in the account for reports, charts, and other financial analyses.

Rather than delete an account, simply close it. You can still view transactions in a closed account. To view them, go to the Accounts window, click the Sort Account List By button, and unselect Hide Closed Accounts on the submenu. Then double-click the name of the closed account to see its transactions.

Closing an account

Follow these steps to close an account:

1. Click the Account List button on the Navigation bar or choose Accounts & Bills⇨Account List to go to the Accounts window.

You see the Accounts window. The names of accounts that are closed are grayed out in the window.

2. Click the Set Up Accounts button.

You'll find this button under "Common Tasks." After you click it, you land in the Set Up Your Accounts In Money window.

3. Click the Close or Reopen Accounts button.

The Click to Check the Accounts You Want to Close window appears, as shown in Figure 10-9. In this window, closed accounts are checked off.

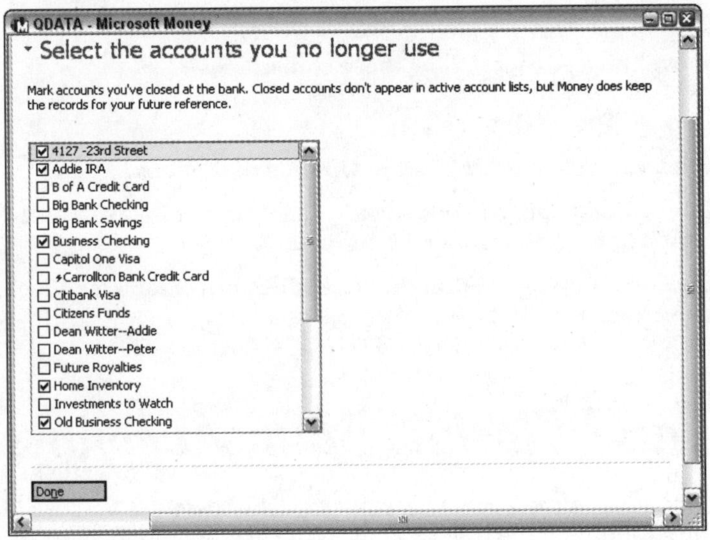

Figure 10-9: Click the check box next to an account name to close an account.

> **QDATA - Microsoft Money**
>
> **· Select the accounts you no longer use**
>
> Mark accounts you've closed at the bank. Closed accounts don't appear in active account lists, but Money does keep the records for your future reference.
>
> ☑ 4127 -23rd Street
> ☑ Addie IRA
> ☐ B of A Credit Card
> ☐ Big Bank Checking
> ☐ Big Bank Savings
> ☑ Business Checking
> ☐ Capitol One Visa
> ☐ +Carrollton Bank Credit Card
> ☐ Citibank Visa
> ☐ Citizens Funds
> ☐ Dean Witter--Addie
> ☐ Dean Witter--Peter
> ☐ Future Royalties
> ☑ Home Inventory
> ☐ Investments to Watch
> ☑ Old Business Checking
>
> Done

4. Click the check box next to the name of each account you want to close.

5. Click the Do_ne button.

The fastest way to close an account is to go to the Accounts window, right-click the name of the account you want to close, and choose Account Is Closed from the shortcut menu. For that matter, you can reopen an account that you closed by right-clicking its name and choosing Account is Open from the shortcut menu.

Deleting an account

Think twice before deleting an account. You might need the data later on. Follow these steps to delete an account:

1. **Click the Account List button on the Navigation bar or choose Accounts & Bills⇨Account List.**

   The Accounts window appears.

2. **Click the Set Up Accounts button.**

   The button is listed under "Common Tasks." Don't ask me why you click a button called Set Up Accounts to delete an account, but you do.

3. **Click the Delete an Account Permanently button.**

   The Select an Account dialog box appears.

4. **Click the name of the account you want to delete and then click OK.**

   A dialog box asks whether you want to delete the account or close it.

5. **Click the Delete Account radio button and click OK.**

Creating an Archive File for Past Transactions

An *archive file* stores all the previous transactions to a certain date for safekeeping. Archive your Money file at tax time, copy it to a floppy disk, and put it away with all your receipts and records from the previous year. That way, you have an electronic record of your financial transactions from the past.

Don't create an archive file on January 1. Wait until you have cleared all transactions from the previous year and filed your income tax returns.

Follow these steps to create an archive file:

1. **Make sure that the file you want to archive is open.**

2. **Choose File⇨Archive.**

   You see the Archive dialog box. Never mind all that verbiage; just glance at the text box in the lower-right corner to make sure that it shows January 1. All transactions in your registers prior to that day are copied to the archive file.

3. **If the date box doesn't show January 1, enter January 1 of this year.**

4. **Click OK.**

   You see the Archive dialog box. Money suggests a name for the archive file — it wants to name the file after last year.

5. **In the File Name text box, either enter your own name for the archive file or let Money's name stand.**

6. **Click OK.**

   You see the Archive dialog box.

7. **Click the check box next to the accounts whose transactions you want to include in the Archive file.**

8. **Click OK.**

Creating a Separate File for Financial Activity

You have to create a Money file for tracking a small business with Money. Self-employed people and people who operate very small businesses that require only one bank account can use their personal Money file, but all others need a separate file. As a rule, you need a separate file if you submit a separate income tax report for your business.

Read on to find out how to create a Money file and how to open a file. You also discover how to switch back and forth between the Money file where you track your personal finances and the one where you track your business's finances.

Creating the separate file

Follow these steps to create a new file:

1. **Choose File⇨New⇨New File or press Ctrl+N.**

   You see the New dialog box, shown in Figure 10-10.

2. **In the File Name text box, enter a descriptive name for the new file.**

   Be sure to choose a name that is easy to identify. Filenames can be 255 characters long (though it's hard to imagine anyone that longwinded). Filenames *cannot* include the following characters: / \ [ ] : (* | <> = + ; , ? (if you saw these characters in a comic book, you would think that I was swearing at you).

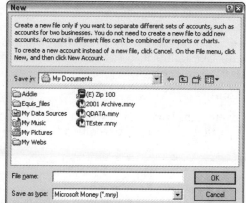

Figure 10-10:
Creating a
new file.

3. **Click OK.**

   The Back Up dialog box appears. Money wants to close the file that is on-screen and open the one you just created, but before it closes files or closes the Money program, it always asks whether you want to back up the file you have been working on.

4. **Click the Back Up button.**

5. **Click the Next button and fill out the Set Up Assistant dialog boxes, if you so choose.**

   If you already know your way around Money and you want to go straight to work, keep clicking next until you see the Skip Sign-In button, and click it.

   The new file appears on-screen. If you doubt me, look in the upper-left corner of the screen, where you see the name of the file you created.

Opening the Money file you want to work with

The fastest way to go from one file to another is to click File on the main menu and select a filename from the bottom of the menu. But if the name of the file you want to open is not on the File menu, follow these steps to switch from one file to another:

1. **Choose File⇨Open or press Ctrl+O.**

   You see the Open dialog box.

2. **Find and select the file you want to open.**

3. **Click the Open button.**

   Money insists on backing up a file when you close it to open another, so the Back Up dialog box appears. Earlier in this chapter, I explain all the details about backing up, but suffice it to say that you can click the Don't Back Up button if you're in a hurry.

4. **Click the Back Up button.**

   The new file appears on-screen. You can tell which file you've opened by reading its name on the title bar in the upper-left corner of the window.

Renaming and Deleting Files

Follow these steps to rename a Money file or delete one that you no longer need:

1. **Choose File⇨Open or press Ctrl+O.**

   You see the Open dialog box.

2. **Locate the file that needs renaming or deleting.**

3. **Right-click the file you want to rename or delete.**

   A shortcut menu appears.

4. **Either rename or delete the file:**

   • To rename: Click Rename and type the new name over the old one.

   • To delete: Click Delete and then click Yes when Money asks whether you are brave enough to really do it.

5. **Click Cancel or press the Esc key to close the Open dialog box.**

Chapter 11

Pinching Your Pennies

"**A** penny saved is a penny earned," according to Benjamin Franklin. Apart from finding a better-paying job (or a second job), the only way to make more money and stay out of debt is to save and spend wisely. This chapter explains how to get Money's help to do just that.

In this chapter, you find out how to set limits for your spending, plan for a big-ticket purchase such as a house or car, schedule bills so that you pay them on time, put yourself on a budget, and track the frequent flyer miles or points you earn with credit card purchases.

Being Alerted to Excessive Spending

One way to tighten your belt is to set monthly spending limits and have Money alert you when you spend too freely in a particular category. As soon as you overspend in the category, Money's FYI Advisor tells you as much. The clotheshorse in Figure 11-1, for example, has overspent in the Clothing category.

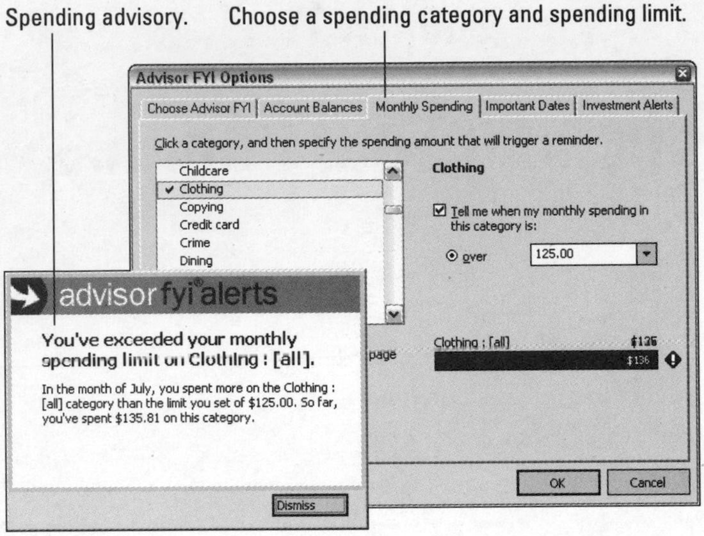

Spending advisory.   Choose a spending category and spending limit.

Figure 11-1:
The Advisor
FYI is one
way to keep
your
spending
under
control.

FYI advisories appear at the bottom of account registers, in pop-up boxes when you record a transaction that exceeds a spending limit (refer to Figure 11-1), on the Home Page, in the Money Express window, and in the Advisor FYI Options dialog box. They are hard to miss. Chapter 12 explains the FYI Advisor in detail. For now, follow these steps to see an FYI advisory when you overspend in a category:

1. **Choose Tools⇨Customize Advisor FYI.**

   You see the Advisor FYI Options dialog box.

2. **Click the Monthly Spending tab (refer to Figure 11-1).**

3. **Select the name of a spending category.**

   Choose the category in which your spending — how do I put this delicately? — is undisciplined. Usually that means the Clothing, Dining, or Entertainment category.

4. **Click the Tell Me When My Monthly Spending in This Category Is check box.**

5. **Enter a dollar figure in the Over text box.**

   Enter the amount you prefer to spend each month in the category. Exceed the amount and the FYI Advisor curls its lip and growls.

Purchase Wizard: Getting Advice for Gathering the Down Payment

Money offers a gizmo called the Purchase Wizard, a robotic financial counselor that you can use to get advice for gathering the down payment on a big-ticket item — a house or vacation house, car, or boat, for example. First the Purchase Wizard asks what you want to buy, how much it costs, and when you want to buy it. From there, the Purchase Wizard surveys your investment accounts, long- and short-term savings accounts, and cash accounts to see how you might acquire the item. At the end, you get written advice, some of it gratuitous and some of it useful, for obtaining your dream item.

Follow these steps to find out whether the Purchase Wizard can help you see your way to the thing you covet so much:

1. **Choose Planner⇨Purchase Wizard.**

   You land in a window that asks what you want to purchase, as shown in Figure 11-2.

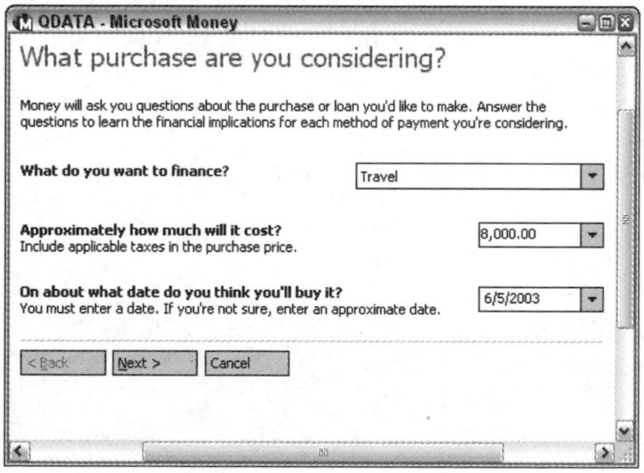

Figure 11-2:
Tell the Purchase Wizard what you want to buy, how much it costs, and when you want to buy it.

2. **From the What Do You Want to Finance? drop-down menu, choose an item, enter its cost in the next text box, enter the date you hope to purchase it in the next text box, and click the Next button.**

   If the item you want isn't on the drop-down menu, choose the closest thing to it.

   What happens next depends on what kind of item you want to purchase and how much it costs. You see a screen with strategies for purchasing the item — taking out a loan, selling securities, or refinancing, for example.

3. **Click the radio button next to a purchase strategy that whets your appetite and click the Next button for a detailed description of how you might buy the thing in question.**

Read the somewhat gratuitous advice. You can always click the Back button (or the Try Another button, in some cases) to backtrack and explore a purchasing strategy that you discounted before.

Scheduling Bills So That They Are Paid On Time

Everybody forgets to pay a bill now and then. Usually, an envelope with an ominous red warning appears in the mail, you pay the bill, and that's the end of it. But sometimes you have to pay a fee for being late. Credit card issuers, for example, are notorious for charging late fees. Mortgage lenders also do not tolerate tardiness. And if you forget to pay the IRS on time . . . well, I shudder to think what happens if you forget to pay the IRS.

To make sure that you pay bills on time, schedule them in the Bills and Deposits window. If you want, a list of due and overdue bills can appear on the Home Page (see Chapter 1 to find out how to make the list of bills appear). On the Home Page in Figure 11-3, for example, three bills or deposits are overdue and two are upcoming. Upcoming and overdue bills are listed in the Money Express window and the bottom of account register. They are made a part of the budgets you can create with Money and are used for cash-flow forecasting.

Looks like some bills need paying!

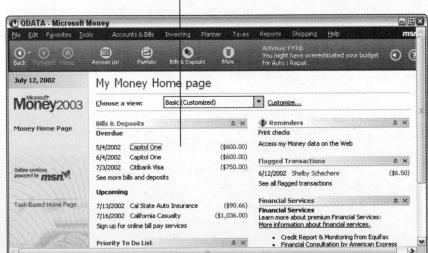

Figure 11-3:
You can put a list of overdue and upcoming bills in the Home Page, where it's difficult to miss them.

Which bills are candidates for scheduling? Any bill for which you have to pay a late fee. Go ahead and schedule the mortgage payment or rent, vehicle registration fees, credit card payments, alimony payments, and the like. But don't crowd the Bills and Deposits window with every bill you receive. The purpose of scheduling bills is to help pay them on time. A crowded Bills and Deposits window is very discouraging, for one thing. And facing all those bills is hard because it's difficult to identify in a long list of bills which ones are the most important and need to be paid first.

By the way, bills aren't the only things you can schedule. You can also schedule deposits and account transfers (I'll show you how later in this chapter). If your employer deposits your pay directly into a bank account, you can schedule the deposit. Or you can simply schedule the deposit to remind yourself to do so and to make your future income a part of the financial projections that Money does.

Scheduling a bill payment or deposit

Follow these steps to schedule a bill or deposit:

1. **Click the Bills & Deposits button on the Navigation bar or choose Accounts & Bills⇨Bills & Deposits List.**

   You go to the Bills and Deposits window, as shown in Figure 11-4. The window lists bills, deposits, transfers, and investment purchases that have been scheduled thus far, if you have scheduled any transactions. Days on the calendar appear in boldface when a bill is due or a deposit is expected (if you don't see the calendar, click the Show Calendar check box).

2. **Click the New button and, from the pop-up menu, choose Bill or Deposit.**

   You see the Create a Recurring Deposit or Create a Recurring Bill window like the one in Figure 11-5. In this window you describe the bill or deposit, how frequently it is made, and in which account register you will record it.

3. **Answer the questions in the Create a Recurring dialog box and click OK.**

   And no peeking over the shoulder of the next guy to see how he answered these questions.

Scheduled bills and deposits.

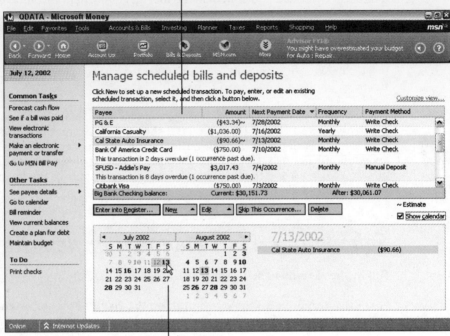

Click a date to scroll to a scheduled transaction.

Figure 11-4:
Scheduled
transactions
are listed in
the Bills and
Deposits
window.

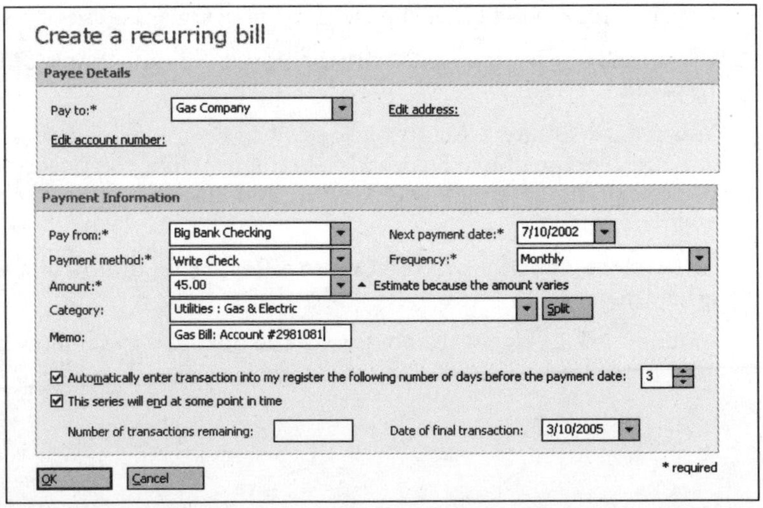

Figure 11-5:
In this
window,
describe bill
payments
and
scheduled
deposits you
intend to
make.

Questions with an asterisk (*) in the window must be answered. Here is the lowdown on scheduling a bill or deposit:

- **Pay To/Receive From:** Choose the person or business that you will pay or is paying you. These names come from the Payee list.

- **Pay From/Deposit To:** Choose the bank account that you will pay the bill from or enter the deposit in. The Bills and Deposits window (refer to Figure 11-4) has a button called Enter into Register. By clicking that button, you can enter the transaction without having to visit the account register.

- **Next Payment Date:** Enter the date when the next bill is due or the next deposit is to be made.

- **Payment Method:** In the case of a bill, tell how the payment will be made. Choose Print This Transaction if you print checks; choose Write Check if you will write the check by hand. In the case of a deposit, choose Manual Deposit if you make the deposit yourself; choose Direct Deposit if your employer deposits checks directly into your bank account.

- **Frequency:** Choose the option that describes how often the bill falls due or the deposit is made.

- **Amount:** Enter the amount and then click the arrow to open the pop-up menu and describe the amount:

  - **This Is a Fixed Amount:** The amount never changes and is the same from time period to time period. Choose this option to describe a bill or monthly salary that is the same each month.

  - **Estimate Because the Amount Varies:** You estimated the amount. Choose this option to describe an amount that changes from period to period. Money uses your estimates in cash-flow forecasts and budgets.

  - **Estimate Based on the Last Number of Instances:** If you have used Money for a while, choose this option as well as a number from the time period submenu and Money will find enter the average amount of the payment or deposit for you.

- **Category:** Choose a category or subcategory for the payment or deposit.

- **Automatically Enter Transaction:** Rather than click the Enter into Register button in the Bills & Deposits window (refer to Figure 11-4) to enter a transaction, you can have Money enter it for you if you choose this option.

- **This Series Will End:** Choose this option if you happen to know that the bill will stop falling due or the deposit will stop being made at a certain time in the future. Either enter the number of transactions that remain or enter an ending date in the text boxes.

The following are listed in the Bills and Deposits window: the payee; the account from which or to which the bill or deposit will be paid; the due date; the frequency of the payment or deposit; and the amount.

To get a very good look at when bills are due or deposits are supposed to be made, click the Go To Calendar button in the Bills and Deposits window. Instead of the baby bear calendar at the bottom of the window, you see a papa bear calendar in a new window called View Bills and Deposits on the Calendar.

How Money tells you to pay bills

After a bill or deposit is scheduled, Money gives you ten days' warning to pay it. In other words, you get ten days to get out of Dodge, and if you don't heed the warning but stick around and gamble at the saloon, Wyatt Earp and Doc Holiday ride you out of town on a rail (whatever that means).

Ten days before a bill is due, Money reminds you to pay it in these locations:

✔ **Money Express window:** The Money Express window, shown in Figure 11-6, lists upcoming bills and deposits. Chapter 1 explains how the Money Express window works. To pay a bill from the Money Express window, click it. In a moment, Money opens and you see the Bills and Deposits window, where you can record the payment.

✔ **Home Page:** If you so choose, you can make the "Upcoming Bills and Deposits" list appear on the Home Page (refer to Figure 11-3, and see Chapter 1 to learn how to make the list appear).

✔ **Account registers:** The "Upcoming Bills and Deposits" list appears on the bottom of account registers if the bills or deposits are to be recorded in the register.

Figure 11-6:
Upcoming bills and deposits appear in the Money Express window as well as the Bills and Deposits window.

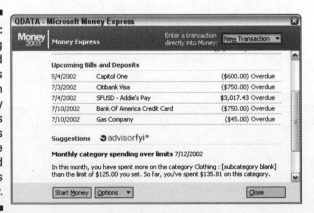

Recording a paycheck deposit automatically

The pop-up menu that appears when you click the New button in the Bills and Deposits window offers an option called Paycheck for recording paycheck deposits. Don't bother choosing this option button unless you want to keep track of how much of your gross income is devoted to taxes, Social Security, employee-sponsored IRA accounts, health plans, and what all. In other words, don't choose the Paycheck option unless you are a stickler for keeping records.

If your employer is worth anything, he or she keeps these records for you. You can consult your employer to get the numbers. If your employer contributes to an IRA account, record that contribution as a scheduled deposit in the IRA, not as a paycheck deposit in which part of your income is diverted to the IRA. The Paycheck option is really for people who want to track small business activity in Money.

If ten days isn't enough time, or if you don't want the Money Express icon to crowd your taskbar, follow these steps to tell Money precisely how to handle upcoming bills and deposits:

1. **Choose Tools➪Options and click the Bills and Deposits tab in the Options dialog box.**

2. **Unselect the Use Money Express check box if you don't want bills and deposits to appear in the Money Express window.**

3. **In the Remind Me text box, enter how many days ahead of their due dates you want to be reminded that bills are due.**

   While you're here, notice the Count Only Business Days check box. Click it to exclude weekends and holidays from the countdown. As for the Watch My Transaction for Recurring Payments check box, uncheck it if you don't want to be asked to schedule a transaction each time you pay or receive money twice from the same person or business.

4. **Click OK.**

Scheduling deposits, transfers, and investment purchases

Besides bill payments and deposits, you can schedule transfers and investment purchases in the Bills and Deposits window (refer to Figure 11-4). Schedule a transfer if, for example, you always transfer part of your paycheck to a savings account. You can also schedule an investment purchase if you regularly buy shares of a security.

In the case of transfers and investment purchases, the steps for scheduling the transaction are nearly identical to those for scheduling a bill payment: Starting from the Bills and Deposits window (click the Bills & Deposits button on the Navigation bar), click the New button, choose an option from the pop-up menu, and answer the questions in the dialog boxes (see "Scheduling a Bill Payment or Deposit," earlier in this chapter, if you need help).

Recording a scheduled transaction in a register

Terrible, isn't it, when a bunch of bills raise their ugly heads in the Bills and Deposits window or the Money Express window. How can you remove all those notices and start from a clean slate? I'm afraid you have to pay the bills (or else skip or cancel them, which is the subject of the next section in this chapter).

Many a Money user has recorded a bill that is due in the Bills and Deposits window but then forgotten to actually pay the bill. I don't know why that is. Having gone to the trouble of recording a bill payment, it seems that many people think that the bill is really paid. It's not paid. No, you still have to get out the old checkbook and mail the check.

Follow these steps to pay bills and make other transactions that you scheduled:

1. **In Money, click the Bills & Deposits button on the Navigation bar or choose Accounts & Bills⇨Bills & Deposits List; if you're starting from the Money Express window, click a bill or deposit that needs your attention to start Money.**

   You land in the Bills and Deposits window, as shown in Figure 11-7.

2. **Double-click the transaction that needs recording.**

   You can also select a transaction and then click the Enter into Register button or right-click the transaction and choose Enter into Register. As shown in Figure 11-7, you see the Record dialog box. Looks like a transaction form, doesn't it? And look — it's already filled out. Well, it's mostly filled out, anyway.

3. **If necessary, fill in the Number box.**

   You can either enter a check number or click the arrow for a drop-down list of options. Select Print This Transaction to print the check on your printer. The Electronic Payment and Electronic Transfer options are for banking online (see Chapter 8).

4. **If you are paying a bill or recording a transaction whose amount changes from month to month, enter the correct amount in the Amount text box.**

Double-click a transaction.

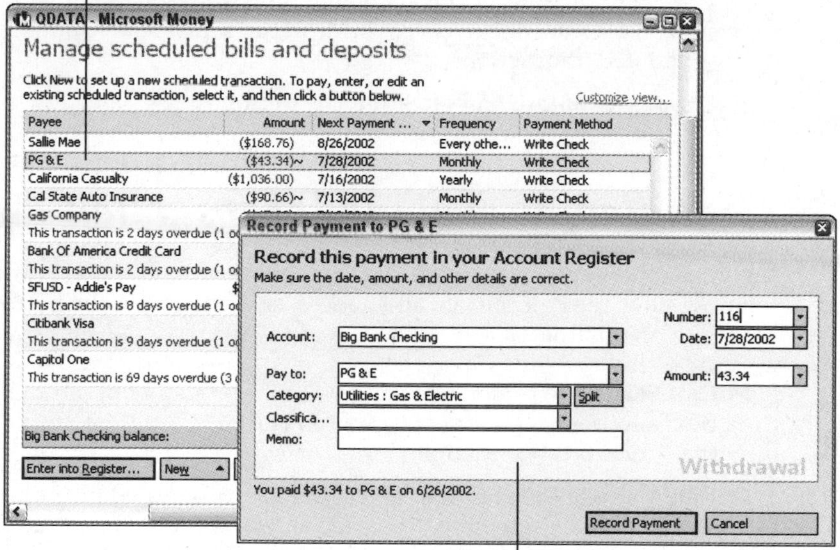

Figure 11-7:
Recording
scheduled
transactions
is pretty
simple —
most of the
boxes in the
Record
dialog box
are already
filled in.

QDATA - Microsoft Money

Manage scheduled bills and deposits

Click New to set up a new scheduled transaction. To pay, enter, or edit an existing scheduled transaction, select it, and then click a button below.   Customize view...

Payee	Amount	Next Payment ... ▼	Frequency	Payment Method
Sallie Mae	($168.76)	8/26/2002	Every othe...	Write Check
PG & E	($43.34)~	7/28/2002	Monthly	Write Check
California Casualty	($1,036.00)	7/16/2002	Yearly	Write Check
Cal State Auto Insurance	($90.66)~	7/13/2002	Monthly	Write Check
Gas Company				

This transaction is 2 days overdue (1 o
Bank Of America Credit Card
This transaction is 2 days overdue (1 o
SFUSD - Addie's Pay $
This transaction is 8 days overdue (1 o
Citibank Visa
This transaction is 9 days overdue (1 o
Capitol One
This transaction is 69 days overdue (3

Big Bank Checking balance:

[Enter into Register...] [New ▲]

Record Payment to PG & E

Record this payment in your Account Register
Make sure the date, amount, and other details are correct.

Account: Big Bank Checking   Number: 116

Pay to: PG & E   Date: 7/28/2002

Category: Utilities : Gas & Electric   [Split]   Amount: 43.34

Classifica...

Memo:

Withdrawal

You paid $43.34 to PG & E on 6/26/2002.

[Record Payment] [Cancel]

Fill in the blanks.

5. **Click the Record button or press the Enter key.**

In the Bills and Deposits window, a line is drawn through the transaction you just recorded (next time you start Money, the lines and recorded transactions disappear from the list). Meanwhile, in the Money Express window, the transaction you just recorded is removed from the list of upcoming bills and deposits. All's well that ends well.

TIP

To visit the account register where the scheduled transaction was recorded (and see what the new account balance is), right-click the transaction in the Bills and Deposits window and choose Go to Account from the shortcut menu.

Skipping a scheduled transaction

Suppose that you want to skip a scheduled transaction this month, perhaps because you already recorded it in a register. Better follow these steps:

1. **Click the Bills & Deposits button on the Navigation bar or choose Accounts & Bills⇨Bills & Deposits List to go to the Bills and Deposits window.**

2. **Find the transaction you want to skip and click it.**

3. **Click the Skip This Occurrence button.**

The Skip Scheduled Transaction dialog box asks skip it this time around, skip all overdue occurrences, or drop the transaction from the list of scheduled transactions.

4. **Choose an option and click the OK button.**

Changing a scheduled transaction

If you need to alter a scheduled transaction, select it in the Bills and Deposits window, click the Edit button, and choose an option from the button's pop-up menu:

✔ **Edit Series:** Takes you to a window that looks and operates just like the Bills and Deposits window (refer to Figure 11-5) so that you can change the scheduled transaction.

✔ **Edit a Single Occurrence:** Takes you to a window where you can choose the date of the scheduled transaction you want to change and then change the transaction.

Finding out when you last paid a scheduled bill

Click the See If a Bill Was Paid button in the Bills and Deposits window if you have second thoughts about whether a bill needs paying. After you click the button, you see a list of the scheduled transactions that you recorded in the last 60 days. The list tells you plain and simple which bills were paid and which might need paying again.

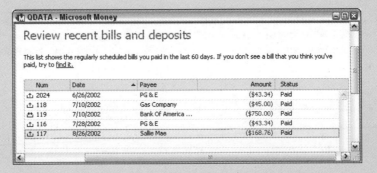

Canceling a scheduled transaction

You've been a loyal subscriber to the by-mail body-building course and you're as scrawny as ever, so you decide to quit making the monthly payments that you scheduled in the Bills and Deposits window. Follow these steps to cancel a scheduled transaction and remove it forever from the Bills and Deposits window:

1. **Click the Bills & Deposits button or choose Accounts & Bills⇨Bills & Deposits List to go to the Bills and Deposits window.**

2. **Select the scheduled transaction you want to abandon and click the Delete button.**

3. **Click Yes when Money asks whether you really want to delete the transaction.**

Budgeting with Money

Except for getting a higher-paying or second job, begging, borrowing, or stealing, the only way to save more money is to put yourself on a budget. A *budget* is a plan for keeping spending down in different areas, the idea being to make more money available for the things you want to do — go to college, go to Greece, pay off a credit card debt.

If you've ever tried to draft a budget on paper, you'll be delighted with the Money budgeting features. As long as you categorize expense transactions when you record them in registers (see Chapter 3), half the work of drafting your budget is already done. You already know how much you spend on groceries, clothing, and dining, for example. Now all you have to do is get Money's help to target the categories where you spend too much. In other words, all you have to do now is set budget goals for yourself.

This rest of this chapter explains how to draft a budget with Money, including how to set budget goals and, just as important, how to generate graphs and reports that tell you whether you've met your budget.

 I strongly recommend waiting at least three months before formulating a budget. The reason: Money gathers data about your spending habits from the transactions you enter in registers. You can save a good deal of time by using this data for budget projections. To use the data, however, you must have been recording transactions in Money for at least three months.

You formulate a budget in Money through the Budget Planner window, where you tell Money the following:

- ✔ What you expect your income to be
- ✔ How much you propose to set aside for saving and reducing debt
- ✔ How much you want to set aside for retirement
- ✔ How much you prefer to spend in different expense categories

After making these determinations, you can find out how much money will be left for spending or saving if you meet your budget. You also can generate reports and charts to see whether you've met your budget in each spending category.

Before you visit the Budget Planner window, however, I suggest taking these two steps:

- ✔ **Prepare your budget estimates.** The mechanics of drawing up a budget with Money 2003 are pretty simple, but a budget is not. Before you start formulating your budget, create and print a Monthly Cash Flow report, which can help you decide how much to spend each month in different categories. Chapter 14 explains how to create and print reports.
- ✔ **Gather the necessary documents.** Figures from paycheck stubs and bills come in handy when budgeting with Money.

Getting started

You can start formulating a budget by following these steps:

1. **Click the More button on the Navigation bar and choose Budget, or choose Planner⏎Budget Planner.**

   You see the Budget Planner window. The window offers links for creating budgets and examining a budget you already created.

   Before you start hammering away at your budget, try clicking the <u>Find Out What Experts Think about Budgeting</u> hyperlink. Doing so takes you to the Money Central Web site, where you can read about budgeting.

2. **Click the Create a Budget link.**

   The first Budget window appears. It outlines what budgeting entails.

   To formulate a budget, you give Money information about your income, your expenses, your savings goals, and how much you want to spend in each category. To get from window to window, click the Next button (or Previous button). These buttons are located on the bottom of windows.

3. **Click the Next button to go to the Enter Your Income window.**

   This window is shown in Figure 11-8. If you've scheduled any deposits in the Bills and Deposits window (see "Scheduling Bills So They Are Paid On Time," earlier in this chapter), the monthly amounts of those deposits already appear on the window and are marked by an icon. Your next task is to describe in this window what your monthly income is (and perhaps what your spouse's monthly income is as well). After you are finished, the Total Income Amount figure should describe your household's monthly income. Better keep reading.

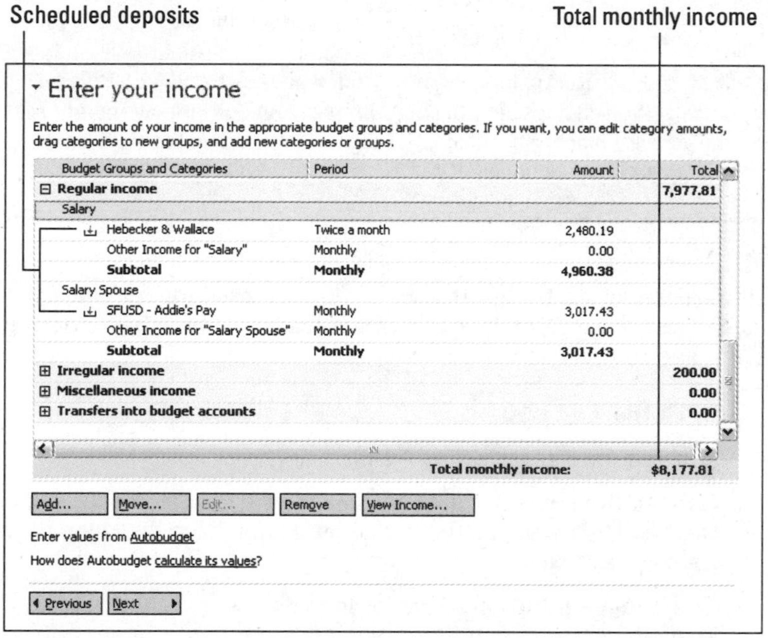

Scheduled deposits   Total monthly income

Figure 11-8: Telling Money your income. To stay within the budget, your spending cannot exceed your income.

Enter your income: Telling Money about your income

To stay within the budget you create, your spending cannot exceed your income. Unless your income varies wildly from month to month, you don't have to be a rocket scientist to complete this part of the budget. You can simply tell Money to get your average monthly income and enter it in the window. However, if you are self-employed or if you use Money to track a business, your income probably varies from month to month and estimating your monthly income is not as easy.

TIP

Some gratuitous budgeting advice

Budgeting is like dieting. It requires discipline. When you are on a diet, your stomach rumbles. You feel hungry all the time. At dinner parties, you have to say "Just a sliver, please" no matter how delicious the cake looks. The only pleasures in going on a diet are noticing how well your clothes fit and seeing the needle on the bathroom scale point to new, uncharted regions.

Similarly, the only pleasure in living with a budget is seeing the balances in your savings and checking accounts rise to new, uncharted heights. Having to compare prices in the supermarket and

go without fancy new duds is hard. Postponing a vacation is hard. Eating meat loaf at home when you could be enjoying *oie rotie aux pruneaux* (roast goose with prune stuffing) in a swanky restaurant is hard.

To make living with a budget easier, try to set realistic goals for yourself. Don't set yourself up for failure by making your budget too strict. Draft a budget that you can live with. Challenge yourself, but don't go overboard. That way, disciplining yourself is easier, more likely to be successful, and much more rewarding.

Follow these steps to report your income to the Budget Planner if you haven't scheduled any deposits or if you earn income beyond what you're scheduled to receive:

1. **Click the A̲dd button.**

   You see the Budget Group Name dialog box.

2. **Choose the second option button, A̲dd a Category to a Budget from the List Below, and choose budget group from the drop-down menu; then click Next.**

   The budget groups are Regular Income, Irregular Income, and Miscellaneous Income. After you add an income category from the Categories list in the next step, the category's name will appear under a budget group in the Enter Your Income window.

   The Choose Categories dialog box shown in Figure 11-9 appears after you click Next. Do these categories look familiar? They are the income categories in the Categories list.

3. **Choose income categories and subcategories by checking the boxes next to their names.**

4. **Click the Finish button to include each category's subcategories in the budget estimate.**

   You return to the Enter Your Income window.

Based on the transactions you have entered in your account registers, Money enters an average monthly income figure in the Amount column. But what if the figure doesn't truly represent your monthly income in the category? Either double-click the category or select it and click the Edit button. You see the Edit dialog box shown in Figure 11-10. Describe your monthly income as follows:

- **Recurring:** Choose the Recurring option. On the Period drop-down menu, choose the option that describes how often you receive income in the category. Enter the amount in the Amount text box.

- **Different each month:** Choose the Custom option. In the month text boxes, enter roughly how much you earn each month in the category.

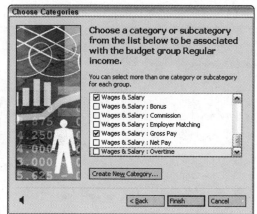

Figure 11-9:
Choosing budget categories and subcategories.

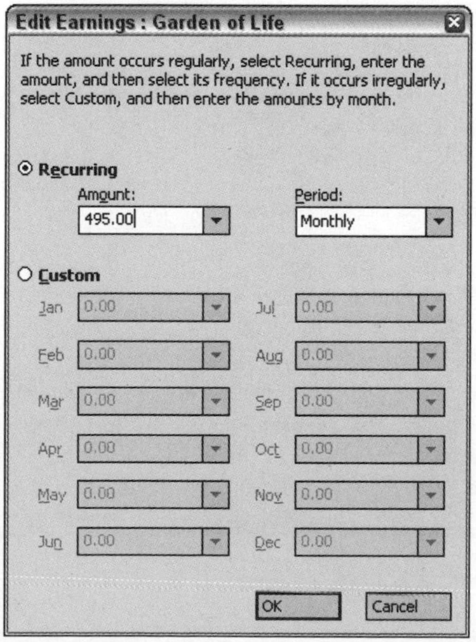

Figure 11-10:
Describe your income here if Money didn't estimate it correctly.

The Enter Your Income window also offers buttons for doing these chores:

- **Moving a category to a different budget group:** Click the Move button and choose the group in the Move dialog box.

- **Creating a new budget group:** Click the Add button and, in the Choose Categories dialog box (refer to Figure 11-9), choose the first option button and enter a name for the group in the first text box. Then click Next and choose categories and subcategories for the group.

- **Removing categories:** Click a category name and then click the Remove button.

Autobudgeting with Money

One way to take some of the tedium out of setting budget goals is to click the Autobudget button on the Enter Your Expenses window. An Autobudget is a bit like the 1040EZ tax form: It does the job as long as your finances are not particularly complicated and you don't have a lot of categories to budget for.

When you click the Autobudget button, you see the Autobudget dialog box. The dialog box analyzes your past spending (yeah, right) and lists the amounts it thinks that you should spend in most of your categories. Autobudget doesn't work, however, if you haven't entered at least a month's worth of transactions.

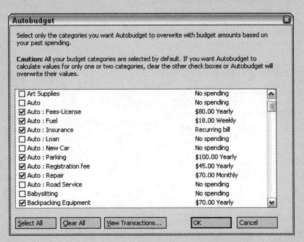

To enter new budget goals quickly, enter numbers from the Autobudget dialog box. To do that, click the Clear All button, click the check box next to each category and subcategory that you want to enter in your budget, and then click OK. The numbers from the Autobudget dialog box are transferred to the Enter Your Expenses window.

Enter your expenses: Budgeting your monthly expenses

Now comes the hard but interesting part — the Enter Your Expenses window, which is shown in Figure 11-11. Your task now, if you choose to accept it, is to enter category-by-category budget goals and tell Money how much you intend to spend in each category. This window is where you look long and hard at your spending habits to find out where you spend and how you can rein in your spending. If you've scheduled any bills in the Bills & Deposits window (see "Scheduling Bills So That They Are Paid On Time," earlier in this chapter), the monthly amounts of those bills are listed in the window already and are marked by an icon.

The buttons along the bottom of the window — Add, Move, Edit, Remove, and View Spending — work the same way on this window as the Enter Your Income window. Click the Add button to add a category or subcategory to the list. Select a category and click the Edit button to open the Edit dialog box (refer to Figure 11-10) and declare how much you spend monthly in a category. Tinker with the numbers until you formulate a budget that challenges you to spend more wisely.

Expense categories   Budget goals

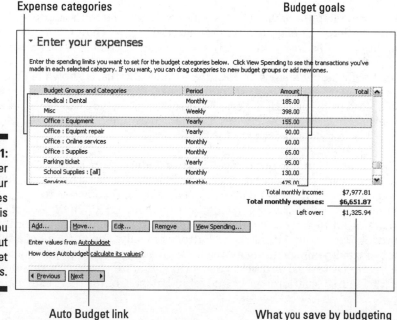

Figure 11-11: The Enter Your Expenses window is where you hammer out your budget goals.

Auto Budget link   What you save by budgeting

Entering category-by-category spending goals can be a tedious activity. Fortunately, Money offers a shortcut for doing the job a little faster — the Autobudget. Read the sidebar "Autobudgeting with Money" to find out how you can enter starting-point numbers for spending goals.

Savings goals: Declaring what to do with extra money

The Savings Goals window is for declaring what you will do with the money you save by budgeting. Click the Spend All Excess Income option button if you want to spend it, but if you are looking ahead to a vacation, car, or something else you want to save for, you can put its name in the Savings Goals window. In Budget reports, Money lists these goals and shows you in monetary terms how close or far away you are from attaining them.

Click the Add Another Goal button, enter a name for the goal, declare the date by which you hope to achieve it, and enter the amount you hope to save.

Budget summary and status

After you fill in the Savings goals window, you come to the Budget summary window. Scroll through the window, admire the pie charts, and marvel at how much you will save by sticking to your budget. Then click the Finish button.

The final window, Review Your Current Budget Status, is shown in Figure 11-12. It tells you whether you are meeting your budget goals this month. By choosing an option from the Budget Period drop-down menu, you can see whether your weekly or yearly income covers your budget expenses. Scroll down the list. Over-budgeted items are listed at the top.

The Review Your Current Budget Status window offers a couple of buttons for tinkering with the budget. Click the Reallocate Funds button if you have exceeded your spending limit in one category and you want to "borrow" money from another category to cover the overrun. Click the Add a One-Time Item button to enter a one-time expense such as a major car repair into the budget. Personally, I think these buttons are silly. The purpose of a budget is not to track your spending more closely. The purpose is to get a better sense of where you spend and how you can spend more wisely. These buttons are meant to help you force your budget to balance, but is that really necessary?

Figure 11-12:
The Status
window
shows
whether
your
average
monthly
income can
cover the
average
monthly
expenses
that you list
in the
budget.

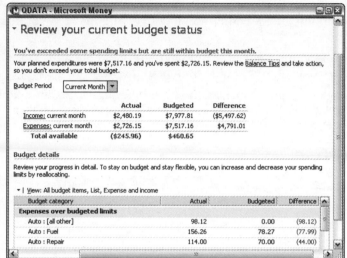

Seeing whether you met your budget goals

You've drawn up a budget, carefully recorded your income and expenses for a month or more, and now the moment of truth has arrived. It's time to see whether you've met your budget. The envelope, please. . . .

The best way to find out whether you met your budget is to create a budget graph or report, but Money gives you two other opportunities to see how well you are sticking to your budget:

- **Home Page:** You can customize the Home Page to make is show a small budget summary report (see Chapter 1).

- **Thermometers:** Click a transaction in a checking account register, and, if you have budgeted for the category, a small bar chart (Microsoft calls them "thermometers") appears at the bottom of the register. The bar chart clearly shows whether you met your budget goal for the category.

Follow these steps to create a budget report or graph and find out how well you did:

1. **Click the Reports button on the Navigation bar.**

   The Pick a Report or Chart window appears.

2. **If necessary, click the Income and Expenses button and then scroll to the Monthly Budget and Annual Budget buttons at the bottom of the window.**

3. **Select Monthly Budget or Annual Budget and click the Go to Report/Chart button at the bottom of the window.**

   You see a Budget report, as shown in Figure 11-13. It shows how your budget projections compare to your actual spending. Look in the Difference column to see whether you overspent or underspent your budget projections.

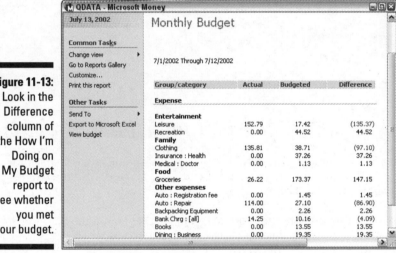

Figure 11-13: Look in the Difference column of the How I'm Doing on My Budget report to see whether you met your budget.

Care to see the report in chart form?

4. **Under "Common Tasks," click the Change View button and then choose Bar Chart from the pop-up menu.**

   A pair of bars corresponds to each category and subcategory in your budget. Gently slide the mouse pointer over the bars to read the category names and spending amounts. The Actual bar on the left shows what you spent, and the Budgeted bar on the right shows how much the budget called for you to spend. The Difference bar shows by how much the Actual and Budgeted figures differ.

If you drew up more than one budget . . .

You can formulate more than one budget. Some people formulate a pessimistic and an optimistic budget. Some formulate a gloomy and a hopeful budget.

In any case, if you have fashioned more than one budget, click the Archived Budget link in the Budget Planner window to tell Money which budget you want to work with. You see the Save or Open a Budget dialog box, shown in Figure 11-14. Select the budget you want and click the Load Budget button.

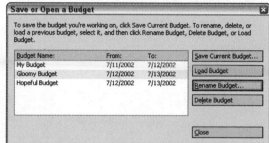

Figure 11-14:
Choosing
which
budget to
tinker with.

Tracking Your Frequent Flyer Miles

Some credit card companies entice their customers with frequent flyer miles or frequent flyer points. For every dollar you charge to your credit card, you are awarded miles or points to be redeemed at an airline ticket counter. These programs are a wonderful way to fly for free, and to make sure that you are being credited properly, you can track miles or points in a Frequent Flyer account.

Follow these steps to set up an account for tracking frequent flyer miles or points.

1. **Click the Account List button to go to the Account List window.**

2. **Click the Add a Frequent Flyer Plan button.**

   You will find this button under "Common Tasks." After you click it, you see the New Frequent Flyer dialog box.

3. **For tracking purposes, enter a name for the program and click Next.**

4. **Choose Track Miles or Track Points to describe how miles are earned; then click Next.**

5. **Enter how many miles or points you have already earned, if any; then click Next.**

6. **Declare how and when the program expires and click Next.**

7. **Click the Yes option button to link the program to a Money credit card account, and then choose the name of the account from the Account drop-down menu.**

The name for the frequent flyer program that you entered in Step 1 is added to the Account List window. To see how many miles or points you have earned, add more miles or points, or deduct miles or points, the name of the account in the Account List window. You see a Frequent Flyer screen like the one in Figure 11-15. From here, you can keep careful tabs on your miles or points and make sure that you get the trip to Hawaii.

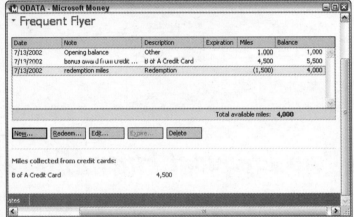

Figure 11-15:
Tracking
frequent
flyer miles.

Chapter 12

Planning for the Years Ahead

· ·

In This Chapter

▶ Being alerted to important financial events

▶ Projecting your cash flow

▶ Projecting your financial future with the Lifetime Planner

▶ Devising a plan to get out of debt

· ·

Most people don't like focusing on the future, and who can blame them? Retirement, children's college expenses, next year's taxes — who wants to think about that? Maybe it's better to live fast, die young, and leave a beautiful memory.

Actually, you would do well to plan ahead for, or at least give a moment's consideration to, your financial future. This chapter explains how to enlist Money's help in planning for your retirement and other long-term objectives. You also discover how to use Money as your executive secretary and have Money remind you when you need to make important financial decisions and considerations. This chapter even shows you how to use Money to gaze into the future and predict how full or empty your checking and savings accounts will be.

For reasons beyond my understanding, Microsoft includes the tools for planning ahead only in Money 2003 Deluxe. Unfortunately, that means that you can't use any of the features I describe in this chapter unless you run Money 2003 Deluxe.

Being Alerted to Important Events

Who doesn't need a wake-up call now and then? To keep from slumbering, you can make what Money calls *Advisor FYI alerts* appear on the Home Page, in Money Express, on the right side of the Money toolbar next to the More button, and in Monthly reports (if you generate Monthly reports). Clicking an alert takes you to the Review the Advisor FYI Details window, where you can find out why you are being alerted. Alerts are notices about upcoming financial events and dates. As part of the Advisor FYI feature, you can also get financial advice. Figure 12-1 shows an alert on the navigation bar, the Review the Advisor FYI Details window, and alerts in Money Express.

Click an advisory to go to the Advisor FYI Details window.

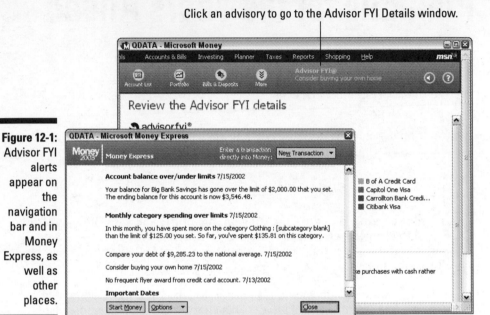

Figure 12-1: Advisor FYI alerts appear on the navigation bar and in Money Express, as well as other places.

To tell Money that you want to be alerted and what you want to be alerted about, choose Tools⇨Customize Advisor FYI or, in Money Express, click the Options button and choose Configure Advisor FYI Alerts in Money on the pop-up menu. You see the Advisor FYI Options dialog box, shown in Figure 12-2.

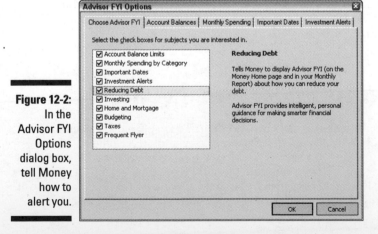

Figure 12-2: In the Advisor FYI Options dialog box, tell Money how to alert you.

Click check boxes beside the subjects that you deem important enough to be alerted about. If you have questions about what a subject is, read its description on the right side of the dialog box.

Notice that the first four alert check boxes also happen to be the names of tabs in the Advisor FYI Options dialog box. If you clicked one of the first four check boxes, visit its tab to tell Money precisely how to alert you:

✔ **Account Balances:** Choose an account and use the text boxes to tell Money to alert you when the balance rises above or falls below a certain level.

✔ **Monthly Spending:** Choose an expense category and enter an amount so that Money can warn you when you go over the amount (Chapter 11 explains this one in detail).

✔ **Important Dates:** Enter and describe a date. Money alerts you to important tax-filing dates. Click the New button and enter a date that means something to you — a birthday, for example.

✔ **Investment Alerts:** Have Money alert you when a security reaches a certain high or low (Chapter 19 explains this one in detail).

The last five check boxes on the Choose Advisor FYI tab are for getting articles and advice about debt reduction, investing, mortgages, budgeting, taxes, and your frequent flyer program, if you are enrolled in one (Chapter 11 explains that one).

Projecting Your Cash Flow

"Cash flow" is a business term that describes how much day-to-day money will be on hand in the future. Cash flow is a measure of a business's health. Thanks to the miracle of computing, you can look ahead to what your cash flow will be — sort of. Money permits you to peek into the future with the Cash Flow Review command, but for the command to do its job, you must have been using Money for a while and have a regular income. The Cash Flow Review command works best for people who make a monthly salary or earn roughly the same amount of money each month.

To make cash-flow projections, Money takes into account your present account balances, post-dated transactions in account registers, average increases and decreases in your primary checking and savings accounts, scheduled transactions (if you've scheduled any), and your budget (if you formulated a budget). Scheduling transactions, a subject of Chapter 11, does wonders for cash-flow projections because it gives Money more data to work with. You can view transactions in the Forecast Your Cash Flow window and the bottom of account registers. Money offers one or two ways to tinker with projections to make them more accurate.

Choose Accounts & Bills — Cash Flow Review or click the Cash Flow button to view the Forecast Your Cash Flow window, as shown in Figure 12-3. I hope the lines on your cash-flow chart are rising gloriously, not steeply falling. By choosing accounts on the Account drop-down menu and different time periods on the Time Period drop-down menu, you can peer into different time frames. How do you like this crystal ball?

If the cash-flow projections aren't reported correctly, try adding transactions to the list at the bottom of the window to describe your financial activity. Choose an option from the Time Period drop-down window to describe how often the activity takes places, click the Add button at the bottom of the window, and choose Withdrawal, Deposit, or Transfer from the pop-up menu. You'll see the Edit Transaction window, which looks and works like a transaction form. Enter a transaction and click OK. The transaction is entered on the list in the window. Scheduled transactions, if you've made any, already appear on the list. Choose the One-Time Item option on the pop-up menu to find out how one-time expenses or earnings — the purchase of a boat, a cash gift from Aunt Enid — affect your cash flow.

Choose an account.   Choose a time period.

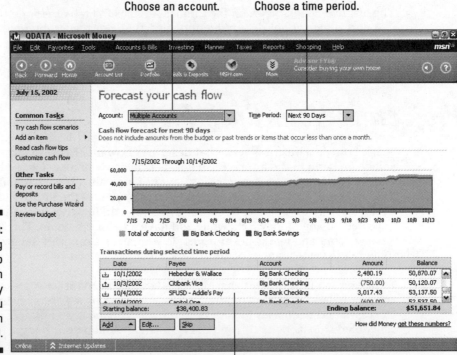

Figure 12-3:
Looking ahead to how much day-to-day cash you will have on hand.

Scheduled and added transactions.

Under "Common Tasks" on the left side of the window, Money offers techniques for adjusting cash-flow projections and playing what-if games. Check out these options to read the future more accurately:

- **Try Different Cash Flow Scenarios:** Takes you to the What-If Cash Flow window, where you can see what happens to projections if you spend or earn more.

- **Add an Item:** Offers the same options as the Add button.

- **Read Cash Flow Tips:** Takes you to a window where you can read "tips for cash flow optimization," courtesy of American Express.

- **Customize Cash Flow:** Takes you to the Customize Cash Flow window, where you can tell Money whether to include data from your budget (if you've formulated one) and your scheduled transactions (if you've scheduled any). Offers numerous options for fiddling with the projections.

Cash-flow projections for accounts appear at the bottom of account registers. If the projections aren't appearing there or you don't want them to appear, choose Tools⇨Options, select the Feedback tab in the Options dialog box, and click the Options button under "Personalized Feedback in the Account Register and Portfolio." The Personalized Feedback Options dialog box appears. Choose the first option button, Use As Much Window Space As Possible, if you want cash-flow projections to appear in account registers.

Introducing the Lifetime Planner

I call the Lifetime Planner a "monster" because if you want to — and if you have *a lot* of spare time on your hands — you can use it to map out your hopes and dreams for the future and find out whether your income will support your hopes and dreams. The Lifetime Planner is a sort of financial counselor in a can. Rather than visit the offices of a financial counselor (and be charged accordingly), you can try your hand with the Lifetime Planner.

To check out the Lifetime Planner, choose Planner⇨Lifetime Planner. You land in the LifeTime Planner window. Notice the buttons on the left side — About You, Income, Taxes & Inflation, and so on. By clicking those buttons and entering information in different windows, you tell Money how long you expect to live, what you expect your income to be, how you think taxes and inflation will affect your income, how much you expect your savings and investments to grow, what your assets are, how much debt you have, and what your living expenses are. (I show you how to do all these things shortly.)

When you finish prognosticating, you can go to the Summary window and generate a Bottom Line chart like the one in Figure 12-4, which shows how much money you will have when you retire. To generate the chart, Money looks at the balances in your accounts, makes projections about your future income, and compares your future income to how much you expect your living expenses and financial obligations to cost in the future.

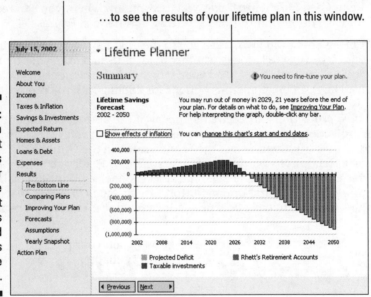

Answer these questions...

...to see the results of your lifetime plan in this window.

Figure 12-4:
The Bottom
Line chart
shows
whether
your income
will support
your goals
and
aspirations
over the
long term.

The fellow whose chart is shown in Figure 12-4 will retire in the year 2027 with accumulated wealth of about $75,000, start drawing on his savings and retirement income, fall deeply into debt, die in the year 2051, and leave behind approximately $900,000 in debt. The message `You need to fine-tune your plan` appears at the top of the chart. Most people have to fine-tune their plan, but that is the purpose of the Lifetime Planner — to make you think long and hard about the future.

Besides the Bottom Line chart, you can generate many other charts when you finish formulating your lifetime plan. The chart in Figure 12-5, for example, shows how a couple's combined salaries will grow over time. To forecast the future in a chart, select a question from the Pick a Question drop-down list.

Figure 12-5:
Select
questions
from the
Pick a
Question
drop-down
list on the
Forecasts
screen to
learn more
about your
lifetime
plan.

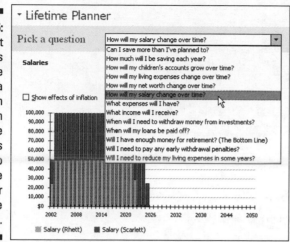

The Lifetime Planner makes its projections in today's dollars, not the inflated dollars of tomorrow. Most of the Lifetime Planner screens, however, have check boxes called Show Effect of Inflation that you can check to change the dollar figures to tomorrow's dollars.

After you have finished devising your lifetime plan, you can always update it by returning to the Lifetime Planner and clicking the Get Going on Your Plan button. You can also try out different scenarios on your plan, as "Playing 'what if' with your future" explains later in this chapter.

About you: Telling Money about yourself and your dependents

The first step in using the Lifetime Planner is to choose Planner⇨Lifetime Planner to get to the appropriate window, and then click the Get Going On Your Plan button. You land in the Tell Us about Yourself window, shown in Figure 12-6. Money uses the data you enter here to make long-term projections. For example, between your retirement age and your life expectancy age (read: "the age you want to die"), you will draw from the money you saved for retirement. Money uses that data to determine how much you need to save for retirement.

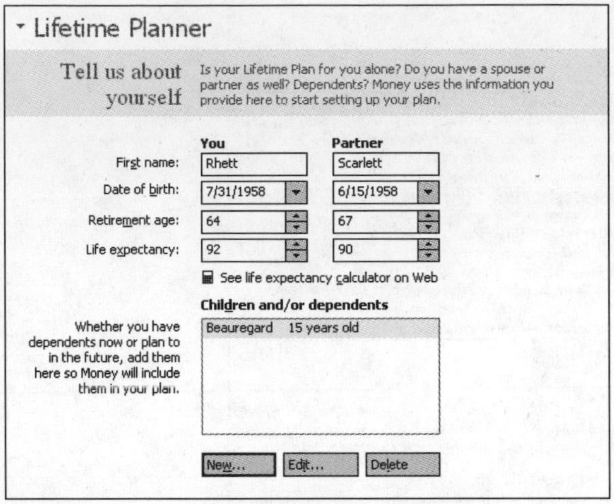

Lifetime Planner

Tell us about yourself

Is your Lifetime Plan for you alone? Do you have a spouse or partner as well? Dependents? Money uses the information you provide here to start setting up your plan.

	You	**Partner**
First name:	Rhett	Scarlett
Date of birth:	7/31/1958	6/15/1958
Retirement age:	64	67
Life expectancy:	92	90

See life expectancy calculator on Web

Children and/or dependents

Whether you have dependents now or plan to in the future, add them here so Money will include them in your plan.

Beauregard   15 years old

New...   Edit...   Delete

Figure 12-6:
Describe
yourself.

If you have dependents or a spouse, enter their data as well in the bottom half of the window. Click the New button and fill in the Add Person dialog box to describe a dependent. Money needs information about dependents because, with you as their sole support, they draw upon your income now and in the future. Click the Edit button to change the information about a dependent or the Delete button to delete a dependent from the list.

Income: Describing your present and future income

The next step is to click the Income button (or click Next) and tell the planner what your income is and how you expect it to increase (I certainly hope it increases) over time. The Lifetime Planner needs to know this information so that it can determine whether you will have enough income to meet your goals.

On the Career screen, enter your gross annual salary or wage income (what you make before taxes). Notice the following gizmos on this screen that you can use to help describe your future income:

✔ **Annual Raises button:** Money assumes that your salary or wage income will increase by 3 percent each year until age 50, at which time society will cruelly stop giving you pay raises. To change these assumptions, click the Annual Raises button and make entries in the Annual Raises dialog box.

✔ **Events:** On this screen, "events" are changes that affect income, such as changing jobs, taking time off, working fewer hours. If an event is looming in your future, click the New button and describe it in the New Career Event dialog boxes.

If you have a spouse or partner and you are tracking his or her income in Money, fill in the second Career screen as well. Then click the Other Income button to go to the Other Income screen.

On the Other Income screen, you describe income from pensions, Social Security, inheritances, alimony, and other such income sources. Click the New Income button and make choices in the dialog boxes to describe this extra income.

Taxes & Inflation: Describing the tax and inflation rate

When you click the Taxes & Inflation button (or click Next), you come to a window for describing the two things that eat away at your income: taxes and inflation. Tell Money what the tax rate in your state is and what you think the annual inflation rate will be:

✔ **Tax rate:** Select your home state from the Enter Your State drop-down list to let Money determine the tax rate. You can also select the radio button called Adjust the Effective Tax Rate Myself and then drag the slider to the rate that you think is correct.

✔ **Inflation rate:** Money assumes that the inflation rate will be 3 percent, but if you disagree, click the Change Inflation Rate button and enter a different rate.

Savings & Investments: Describing your retirement savings

The next step is to click the Savings & Investments button on the Lifetime Planner window and tell Money which of your accounts are meant for retirement savings. When you click this button, you see the window shown in Figure 12-7. The amounts in the Account Value column come directly from your account registers.

On this and the other two Savings & Investments windows, you tell Money whether to include an account in future projections, how much you will contribute to these accounts in the years ahead, and by what rate you expect the accounts to grow:

✔ **Accounts window:** Checking and savings accounts for day-to-day expenses do not belong in projections. To exclude an account, click its name and then click the Exclude from Lifetime Plan check box (you'll find it in the lower-right corner of the window). Click the New Account button to describe an account that isn't on the list.

✔ **Savings Contributions window:** Click the New Contribution button and fill in the dialog boxes to describe how much you will contribute to your retirement, savings, and investment accounts over the years. When you click a contribution on the Contribution Name list, its particulars appear on the bottom part of the window. To change a particular, click a hyperlink on the bottom of the screen and fill in the dialog box that appears.

✔ **Life Insurance window:** Click the Add Policy button and describe any life insurance policies that you and your partner have, if you have a partner, in the dialog boxes. The Lifetime Planner uses the value of the policy as a means of calculating future income.

Expected Return: Describing how your money will grow

Money has preconceived ideas about how much accounts will grow in value (by 9 percent before retirement and 7 percent after retirement). If you don't care for Money's estimates, click the Use Custom Rate radio button or Use the Rate Money Estimates radio button. If you want to use a custom rate, click the Simple Change link to enter a rate for all your retirement accounts, or click the Details Change link to enter rates for each account.

Homes & Assets: Describing things of value that you own or will own

Houses, property, and businesses that you own count as assets that will grow in value over the years. As such, they can be included in wealth projections. You can also count jewelry, antiques, and collectibles as assets. To include assets in projections, click the Homes & Assets button.

To tell Money about an asset, click the Add Asset button and fill in the dialog boxes. Assets appear on the Name of Asset or Asset Account list. To change the particulars of an asset — its value, appreciation rate, and so on — click the asset on the list and then click a hyperlink at the bottom of the screen. You see a dialog box for changing the particulars.

Do not count things that *depreciate* (decrease in value over the years), such as equipment or cars, as assets.

Loans & Debt: Describing current and future loans

No projection can be accurate unless it includes information about loans and debts. Click the Loans & Debt button to describe the money you owe and will owe for future debts, loans, and mortgages.

Loan and mortgage accounts that you set up already (see Chapter 16) appear on the Loans & Debt window, as do the projections of your debt reduction plan if you make one (see "Planning to Get Out of Debt," later in this chapter).

To describe a future debt or loan, click the New Loan button and fill in the dialog boxes. Be sure to click the No, I Plan to Open This Loan in The Future radio button — if you don't, you go to the Loan wizard, where you set up a new Loan account.

To change the particulars of a loan or debt on this screen, click its name, click the Edit button, and then change the particulars in the Edit Loan dialog boxes.

Expenses: Describing the cost of living

When you click the Expenses button, you see the Living Expenses screen, shown in Figure 12-8. Here you describe how much it costs for you and anyone you support to live. The names of people on this list come from the About You screen.

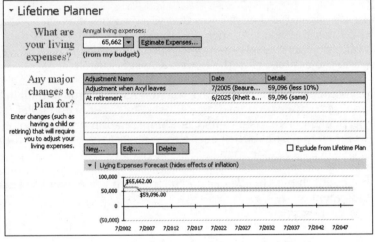

Figure 12-8: The Living Expenses screen is where you tell Money what you expect your annual living expenses to be.

Money gets the annual living expenses figure at the top of the screen by deducting taxes, savings contributions, and loan payments from your annual income. If you want to get the figure from your budget (if you created a budget), click the Estimate Expenses button and, in the dialog box that appears, select the Use the Annual Budget estimate check box to get the number from your budget (Chapter 11 describes budgeting).

Adjustments to your living expenses — caring for an elderly person, having a child — appear on the list. Click the New button and fill in the New Living Expense Adjustment dialog box if an event in your future will affect your living expenses. Similarly, you can select an adjustment on the list and click the Edit button to adjust its cost or duration.

The College & Other window is for taking account of college expenses, trips to Madagascar, and other expensive interludes. Click the New Expense button and fill in the dialog boxes to describe these expenses.

Results: Reading your financial future

At last, you can click the Results button and examine your plan to see whether you will be financially sound in the years to come. You can discover the following about your future by clicking these buttons:

- ✔ **The Bottom Line:** A chart that shows how much wealth you will have in the years to come and how well your savings will support you in retirement (refer to Figure 12-4).

- ✔ **Improving Your Plan:** Practical advice for improving your financial future, and links to Web sites where you can get financial advice.

- ✔ **Forecasts:** Charts that clearly show how much you will save each year, how your salary will increase, and when loans will be paid off, among other things. Choose a question from the Pick a Question drop-down list to generate a new chart (refer to Figure 12-5).

- ✔ **Assumptions:** A summary of all the choices and entries you made in the Lifetime Planner windows. Money uses this data for its financial projections.

- ✔ **Yearly Snapshot:** A report on the state of your future finances. Drag the Pick a Year slider or enter a new year to see what your financial picture will be in the years to come.

Action Plan: What you should do next

Click the Action Plan button to receive a ream of advice about improving your financial position. Microsoft calls this "a complete, credible financial plan to help you achieve your long-term financial goals such as retirement, college, or buying a home."

Playing "what if" with your future

After you have gone to the significant trouble of formulating a lifetime plan, you can use the plan as a means of playing "what if" with your future. What if you retire early — how well would your retirement savings and investments support you? Suppose that you decide to take a sabbatical from work — can you afford it? You can ask questions like these and see what happens to your lifetime plan. Figure 12-9 answers the question, "What would happen to my retirement savings and investments if the stock market fell, *gulp!,* by 50 percent?"

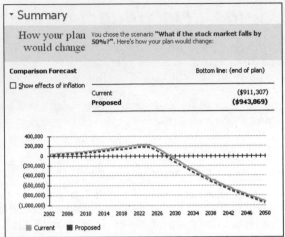

Figure 12-9:
Use the
Financial
Event
Modeler to
find out how
different
events
would affect
your lifetime
plan.

Follow these steps to test different scenarios on your lifetime plan:

1. **Choose Planner⇨Financial Event Modeler.**

   After you click the button, you see the Welcome to the Financial Event Modeler window.

2. **Click the Start Exploring button.**

3. **In the Goal window, choose a question from the Scenario drop-down menu, and enter other information as necessary.**

   Depending on the question you pose, you are asked for different types of information.

4. **Click the Compare My Plan button.**

   A chart shows how your lifetime plan is altered by the what-if scenario you chose.

Click the Try New Scenario button to return to the Goal window and test another scenario. To make the scenario a part of your lifetime plan, click the Accept Changes button.

Planning to Get Out of Debt

Paying off your credit card debt may be the single most important step you can take to improve your financial picture. Credit card issuers charge outrageous rates of interest, and you have to pay them every month if you don't pay off, or at least pay down, the balance that you owe on your credit cards.

To help you get the discipline to pay off credit card debt, Money offers the Debt Reduction Planner. With this gizmo, you decide how much you can devote to reducing debt each month, and then you schedule an extra payment to help ensure that the debts are paid each month (Chapter 11 explains scheduling payments).

Follow these steps to devise a debt-reduction plan:

1. **Choose Planner⇨Debt Reduction Planner.**

   You go to the Debt Reduction Planner window.

2. **Click the Start Creating Your Personalized Debt Plan button.**

   You see the Include Debt Accounts in Your Plan window, which lists all the credit card, liability, line of credit, loan, and mortgage accounts you set up with Money (Chapter 16 explains loan and mortgage accounts), as well as how much you owe on each account, the interest rate, and other information.

   Your next step is to tell Money which accounts you want to pay off, but you shouldn't include loan and mortgage accounts in the plan. The interest rates on these types of accounts are not high, or they are at least reasonable, and the interest on some of them is tax deductible as well. To reduce your debt, your first job is to pay down credit card and line of credit debt.

3. **Tell Money which accounts to include in your plan by selecting an account, clicking the Move Into Plan button, and filling in the dialog boxes to describe how much you owe and how much you have to pay each month on the debt.**

   Describe the interest rate, payment frequency, and other particulars of the plan. If you need to change the particulars of a loan or credit card account that is listed in the window, click it, click the Edit Debt Info button, and change the particulars in the Details dialog box.

   Select an account and click the Move Out of Plan button if you need to move it out of the plan.

4. **Click the Next button to move to the Define Your Payment Plan window.**

   Under Status, in the lower-left corner of the window, you see how much you owe, how much you spend to service your debts, and when you will be out of debt at the rate you are paying now, as shown in Figure 12-10.

5. **Either enter how much extra money you want to pay each month to get out of debt in the text box, or click the radio button called The Date I Want to Be Out of Debt, and drag the slider to choose a new target date; then, click the Next button.**

   You see the View Your Debt Plan graph, which shows how your debt is reduced over time.

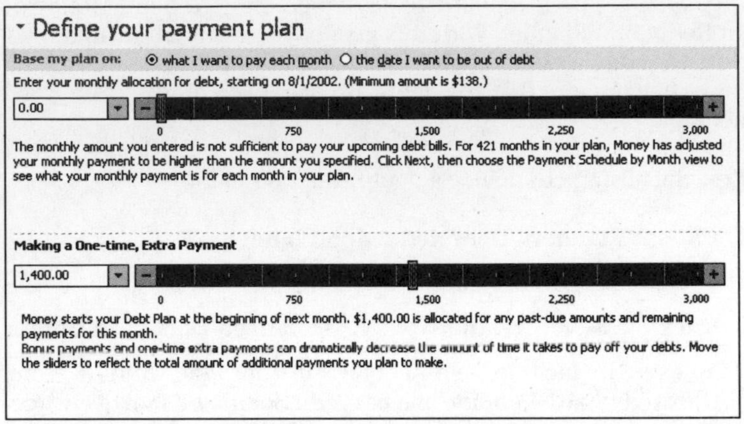

Figure 12-10:
Telling
Money
when you
want to pay
off your
high-
interest
debts.

6. **Click the Next button.**

   You see the Take Action & Reduce Your Debt window. It offers some gratuitous advice about reducing debt. If you want to schedule debt payments, click an item in the box and see Chapter 11 to see how scheduling works.

7. **Click the Finish button.**

   You land on the Home Page.

Chapter 13

Preparing for Tax Time

. . . .

In This Chapter

▶ Estimating how much you will owe in taxes

▶ Scheduling tax dates

▶ Discovering tax-deductible expenses

▶ Calculating how much to withhold for taxes

▶ Estimating capital gains taxes

▶ Generating tax reports

▶ Exporting Money data to a tax-preparation software package

. . . .

*B*enjamin Franklin wrote, "In this world, nothing is certain but death and taxes." This chapter explains how to do your best by one of these certainties. As for the other, all you can do about it is to eat right, get enough sleep and exercise, and hope for the best.

In this chapter, you discover how to estimate your next tax bill, get Money's help finding tax-deductible expenses, and determine how much to withhold from your paycheck for taxes. You also find out how to determine capital gains taxes on the sale of a security, generate tax reports, and prepare Money data so that you can use it in a tax-preparation software package.

Estimating Your Tax Bill

Knowing what you will owe in taxes next year never hurts, especially if you don't like surprises. Money offers the Tax Estimator to help you estimate what you owe for last year and what you will owe for this year. Notice, however, that the thing is called the Tax Estimator, not the Tax Accountant. The Tax Estimator can give you a rough idea of what you owe or will owe the IRS, but it can't take the place of a tax accountant and do your income taxes for you.

Finding out the tax rates

Built into the Money 2003 Tax Estimator are accurate tax rates for the year 2002. But suppose that you are trying to estimate your income taxes for the year 2003 or 2004. How can you obtain the correct tax rates for those years?

Follow these steps to download the latest tax rates from Microsoft:

1. **Choose Taxes⇨Tax Settings to go to the Set Up Your File for Tax Tracking window.**

2. **Click the Download the Latest Tax Data from the Web button.**

Your machine connects to the Internet, you see the Call Progress dialog box, and the latest tax rates are downloaded to your computer.

3. **While you're on the Set Up Your File for Tax Tracking window, click the second-to-last link, Set Your Filing Status and View Tax Rates by Income Bracket.**

A window appears and shows you the latest tax rates.

Set your filing status and see tax rates

Show rates for tax year:		2002 Tax Year in Progress ▼			
Show rates for filing status:		Married Filing Jointly ▼			
Income:	0.00 --	12,000.00	is taxed at	10	%.
Income:	12,001.00 --	46,700.00	is taxed at	15	%.
Income:	46,701.00 --	112,850.00	is taxed at	27	%.
Income:	112,851.00 --	171,950.00	is taxed at	30	%.
Income:	171,951.00 --	171,950.00	is taxed at	35	%.
Income:	171,951.00 -- up		is taxed at	38.6	%.
	Long-Term Capital Gains taxed at a maximum rate of			20	%.

Standard Deduction:	7,850.00	Blind:	900.00
Exemption Amount:	3,000.00	Over 65:	900.00
Exemption Cutoff:	206,000.00	Deduction Cutoff:	137,300.00
Maximum Capital Loss:	3,000.00 ▼		

Choose Taxes⇨Tax Estimator to find out what your tax bill is for last year or maybe for the coming year. After you choose the command, you land in the Welcome to the Tax Estimator window. Clicking the Next button as you go along, you answer Money's survey questions about you, your income, adjustments to your income, deductions, and tax credits. These questions are the very same ones that tax accountants ask when they determine how to lower your taxes. By the time you reach the Summary window, Money will have prepared an estimated tax return for you like the one in Figure 13-1. Either click the Next button or click Tax Estimator Steps buttons on the left side of the Money screen to get from window to window.

Click to go from window to window.

Figure 13-1:
Answer the
questions
and get a
mini tax
return.

QDATA - Microsoft Money		

July 15, 2002

Estimated tax summary

Tax Estimator Steps

Welcome

Getting Started

Income

Adjustments

Deductions

Credits

Summary

Related Tasks ▶

	Completed Tax Year 2001	Current Tax Year 2002
Filing status:	Single	Single
Marginal tax rate:	27.0	15.0
Wages & salary:	$112,020.47	$70,766.23
Capital gains & losses:	$0.00	$0.00
Interest / dividend income:	$140.14	$128.42
Other income:	$450.12	$312.87
Total income:	$112,610.73	$71,207.52
Total adjustments:	$12,958.00	$9,993.50
Adjusted gross income:	$99,652.73	$61,214.02
Deductions:	$23,319.44	$22,981.00
Nonrefundable credits:	$360.00	$800.00
Refundable credits:	$90.00	$200.00
Total exemptions:	$11,200.00	$11,200.00
Taxable income:	$65,133.29	$27,033.02
Estimated taxes:	$19,971.99	$8,241.95
Estimated taxes paid:	$22,257.00	$2,234.69

◀ Previous   Done

Here's some good news: Some of the information is already entered in these windows because Money grabbed it from the data file. If you enter your own numbers and regret doing so, you can get the numbers from Money by clicking the Reset Value button along the bottom of a window and choosing an option on the pop-up menu that describes how you want Money to plug in its numbers.

Describe your tax situation in these six windows:

✔ **Getting Started — Enter Your Personal Information:** In the first window, declare your filing status, number of dependents, and whether you are blind and over age 65. Question 5, Estimated Taxes Paid and Withheld, should already be entered. Money gets this information from Tax categories. It is very likely quite correct, but you can enter your own numbers if you want.

✔ **Income — Enter Your Income:** Describe your income from salaries, wages, alimony, unemployment, and so on. Once again, many of these values come straight from the data file. Do your best to estimate these numbers.

✔ **Adjustments — Enter Your Adjustments to Income:** Describe adjustments to your income — for contributions to IRAs and SEPs, health insurance payments, and so on. The numbers you enter here lower your tax bill.

✔ **Deductions — Enter Your Itemized Deductions:** Describe the payments you made that can be deducted from your gross income — payments for medical and dental work, taxes, mortgage interest, charitable contributions, and so on.

✔ **Credits — Enter Your Tax Credit Information:** Describe credits for childcare, education, and so on. Click the Detail links in this window to find out whether you are eligible for any of these credits.

✔ **Summary — Estimated Tax Summary:** There it is — a mini tax return that shows your taxable income and roughly what you will owe in taxes (refer to Figure 13-1). If a number needs adjusting, click a link to return to the window where the number came from and make an adjustment.

Scheduling Important Tax Dates

Especially if you are self-employed and you pay quarterly tax estimates, certain dates are sacrosanct. Quarterly tax estimates are due on June 15, September 15, January 15, and April 15. Miss those dates at your peril!

As Chapter 12 explains in detail, you can get the help of the FYI Advisor to remember these dates. Choose Tools➪Customize Advisor FYI to view the Advisor FYI Options dialog box, and click the Important Dates tab. Make sure that the quarterly estimated tax payment check boxes on the tab are selected. This way, the dates will appear on the Home Page, in Money Express, and on the right side of the Money toolbar to remind you that the IRS needs feeding.

Another way to keep abreast of your tax responsibilities is to change to Tax view on the Home Page. Click the Home button to go to the Home Page and then choose Tax on the Choose a View drop-down menu.

Getting Help for Lowering Your Tax Bill

If you itemize deductions on income tax reports or you use Money to track business expenses, you owe it to yourself to find every tax-deductible expense you can claim on income tax forms. Money offers a way to do that.

To get Money's help to locate tax-deductible expenses, choose Taxes➪ Deduction Finder. In the What Deductions Are You Eligible For? window, click the Get Started button. Very shortly, you land in the Tax Deduction Finder form, a questionnaire you fill out. Keep answering the questions and clicking the Continue button. These questions are the very same ones that tax accountants ask when they determine how to lower your taxes. When you're done, the Deductions You May Qualify For window explains in detail all the different deductions for which you are eligible.

Determining How Much to Withhold

How much should you withhold from your paycheck for taxes? This question has puzzled philosophers for centuries. Being told on April 15 that you didn't withhold enough and you owe in taxes is very unpleasant. Most people like to be told that they are due a refund because they withheld too much in taxes from their paycheck. To help you determine how much to withhold, Money offers the Tax Withholding Estimator. With this gizmo, you declare your income, state whether you want a tax refund, and find out precisely how much to withhold.

You must have used the Tax Estimator to estimate what you owe in taxes before you can take the Tax Withholding Estimator for a spin. Money uses information you entered in the Tax Estimator to determine how much to withhold.

To try out the Tax Withholding Estimator, choose Taxes⇨Tax Withholding Estimator. You see the Estimate My Withholding window shown in Figure 13-2. Answer the questions on this and the subsequent window. When you are done, Money tells you the total amount to withhold per paycheck to reach your refund goal.

Estimate my withholding

Based on your entries in the Tax Estimator, you will owe a tax payment of $5,887.21. You can adjust this amount by completing the information on this screen. Money will estimate how many allowances you should claim on your Form W-4 to reach your target refund or payment.

Choose a target tax refund or payment

What do you want to do with your taxes? ⦿ Receive a refund
                                          ○ Owe taxes

Select the amount of your target refund or tax payment at the end of the year.   350.00

Enter your paycheck information

	Self	Spouse
1. Taxable portion of paycheck Enter gross wages minus any pre-tax items, such as 401(k) deductions.	6,582.41	0.00
2. Paycheck frequency	Monthly	Monthly
3. Date of next paycheck this year	7/15/2002	7/15/2002

Next

Figure 13-2:
To get a tax refund, how much should you withhold?

Estimating Capital Gains Taxes

Estimating the capital gains taxes on the sale of a security can be difficult, so Money offers the Capital Gains Estimator. In the Capital Gains Estimator, you tell Money the rate you are taxed, select one of the securities you own, enter how much you propose to sell your shares for, and find out how much you stand to profit and how much capital gains tax you have to pay on your profits.

Use the Capital Gains Estimator before you sell a security to see whether selling it is worthwhile, given the taxes you have to pay on the profits. In order to use the Estimator, you must have set up an investment account and recorded the purchase of the security in the account (see Chapter 19).

To estimate capital gains taxes, choose Taxes⇨Capital Gains Estimator. You land in the Welcome to the Capital Gains Estimator window. Click Get Started and provide information about your tax situation and the security in these four windows:

- **Set Tax Rates:** Describe your filing status, your income bracket, and whether you want to estimate state as well as federal capital gains taxes. The Capital Loss Carryover text boxes are for declaring a capital loss from the previous year that you have carried into the current year. You can deduct up to $3,000 per year in capital losses.

- **Select Accounts:** Choose the name of the investment account where you track the security.

- **Estimate Capital Gains Tax:** Select the security you propose to sell and update its price by clicking the Update Prices button under Common Tasks. Then enter the sale price and the quantity of shares you want to sell, as shown in Figure 13-3.

  If you bought the security in more than one lot, choose an option from the Distribution Method drop-down menu to describe which shares you want to sell. A lot is a group of securities purchased at the same time and at the same price. FIFO means "first in, first out" and LIFO is "last in, first out." Choosing FIFO sells the oldest shares, no matter which lot they belong to; LIFO sells the newest shares. Choosing Max Gain or Min Gain tells Money to sell shares from whichever lot will earn the most or the least money. Choose Custom to pick and choose shares from different lots.

- **View Action Plan:** Read the summary information about how much you stand to lose or gain by selling the security.

After you go to the trouble to investigate the capital gains implications of selling a security, you can save the information you entered in a "scenario." To examine the sale later on, you can simply call up its scenario without going to the trouble of entering the stock sale information again. To save a scenario, click the Scenarios button under Common Tasks, choose Save This Scenario, and enter a name in the Save This Capital Gains Scenario text box. To call on the scenario, click the Scenarios button and choose its name on the submenu.

Enter the sale price and quantity.

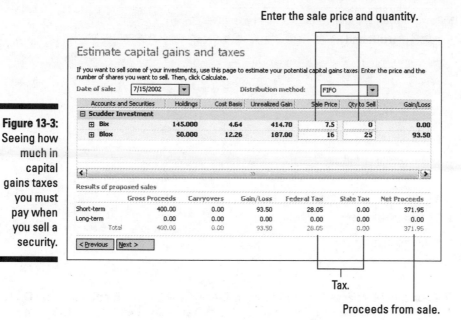

Figure 13-3:
Seeing how much in capital gains taxes you must pay when you sell a security.

Tax.

Proceeds from sale.

Looking at Line-Item Income and Expenses

Chapter 4 explained how to assign categories to line items on tax forms (W-2, Schedule A, Schedule C, and so on). To refresh your memory, you go to the Categories window, click the Set Up Categories button, choose a category, and select a tax form and form line for reporting income or expenses in the category.

As long as you went to the trouble to assign line items to different categories, you can find out very quickly what your tax-related income and expenses are as reported on tax forms. Choose Taxes➪Tax Line Manager. You see the Review Your Tax-Related Income and Expenses window, shown in Figure 13-4. If you have the wherewithal to do your own taxes, you can plug these numbers right into your tax return. In fact, this window is modeled after a tax form to make plugging in the numbers easier.

The View menu offers some nifty commands for examining tax lines. Choose Tax Lines that Have Been Used to see only the lines that pertain to your income and expenses in the window.

Review your tax-related income and expenses

Review the following income and expense totals from your Money file. To see the transactions included in a total, click the line, and then click Go to Details.

▾ | View: Tax lines that have been used, 2002 Tax Year in Progress

Tax Form Line	Year to Date	Projected Total
W-2		
Your salary	4,960.38	29,762.28
Your federal tax withholding	(1,200.00)	(2,223.35)
Your Social Security tax withholding	0.00	0.00
Your Medicare tax withholding	0.00	0.00
Your state tax withholding	(200.00)	(370.56)
W-2 (Spouse)		
Your spouse's salary	25,916.80	41,003.95
Your spouse's federal tax withholding	0.00	0.00
Your spouse's Social Security tax withholding	0.00	0.00
Your spouse's Medicare tax withholding	0.00	0.00
Your spouse's state tax withholding	0.00	0.00
Form 1040		
Your IRA contributions	698.00	816.80
Your spouse's IRA contributions	0.00	0.00
Your non-working spouse's IRA contributions	0.00	0.00

[Go to Details] [Add Tax Line...]

Figure 13-4:
You can plug these numbers straight into a tax form.

To remove or change a line item from the window, select it and click the Go to Details button. You land in a window for deleting line items (click the Remove button) and changing income and expense figures (click the Edit button).

Tagging Tax Categories So That You Can Generate Tax Reports

Chapter 4 explained how to tag categories so that your income and expenses that pertain to taxes are figured in tax reports. Especially if you itemize deductions on tax returns, tagging tax-related income categories and expense categories is absolutely necessary. To save you the trouble of turning to Chapter 4, here are shorthand instructions for tagging tax-related categories:

1. **Choose Accounts & Bills⇨Categories and Payees to go to the Set Up Your Categories window.**

2. **Click the Set Up Tax Categories button.**

3. **You land in the Associate Money Categories with Tax Form Lines window.**

4. **Scroll down the list until you find a category or subcategory whose tax status needs changing, and then click the category or subcategory to select it.**

5. **Select the Include on Tax Reports check box.**

You can also get to the Associate Money Categories with Tax Form Lines window by choosing Taxes⇨Tax Settings and choosing Assign Money Categories to Match Lines on a Tax Form in the window that appears.

Generating Tax Reports

Money tax reports are very convenient indeed. Instead of scouring an account register for tax-related income and expenses, you can simply generate a report. You know right away what your income is and how many adjustments and deductions you can make.

The fastest way to generate a tax report is to choose Taxes⇨Tax Reports. You land in the Pick a Report or Chart window, where you can generate one of these reports:

- ✔ **Tax-Related Transactions:** Shows category by category what your income and expenses are in tax-related categories. Use this report to calculate income and tax-deductible expenses for tax returns.

- ✔ **Capital Gains:** Shows capital gains and losses for the securities you sold or purchased this year. Use this report to calculate and tabulate capital gains and losses.

- ✔ **Loan Interest:** Shows how much of your loan payments went to servicing interest. Use this report to calculate tax-deductible interest payments. You must have set up a loan account to generate this report (see Chapter 16).

- ✔ **Tax Software Report:** Shows your total income and expenses as they are to be reported on tax lines on various tax forms. Use this report to gather data for tax software programs.

Chapter 14 explains reports and charts in detail, including how to customize them and change their reporting dates.

Exporting Money Data to a Tax-Preparation Program

As of this writing, the TaxCut Deluxe tax-preparation program accepts data from Money files. In other words, you can draw on data from Money as you prepare your taxes with TaxCut. To provide tax information to TaxCut, you save your Money data in a TXF file, open TaxCut, and import the TXF file into the tax-preparation program. Money has a special command for saving data in a TXF file. Before you create the TXF file, however, you need to tell Money which accounts to include in the file.

Follow these steps to tell Money which accounts hold tax data:

1. **Choose Taxes⇨Tax Settings.**

   You go to the Set Up Your File for Tax Tracking window.

2. **Click the link called <u>Choose Accounts to Include in Tax Return Information</u>.**

   The Choose Accounts for Tax Preparation dialog box appears.

3. **Check the names of accounts where you keep tax data and click OK.**

   I find it easiest to click the Clear All button to remove all the check marks and then check off the handful of accounts where tax data is kept.

Now you're ready to create the TXF file for the TaxCut tax-preparation package. Go to it:

1. **Choose <u>F</u>ile⇨Export to <u>T</u>ax Software.**

   You land in the Prepare to Export Tax Information window. You can also give the command by choosing Taxes⇨Export to TaxCut.

2. **Choose a year from the <u>R</u>eview Taxes For drop-down menu.**

3. **If necessary, enter a data in the Enter Start <u>D</u>ate of Tax Year text box; then click the <u>C</u>ontinue button.**

   As shown in Figure 13-5, the next window asks which line items to include in the file.

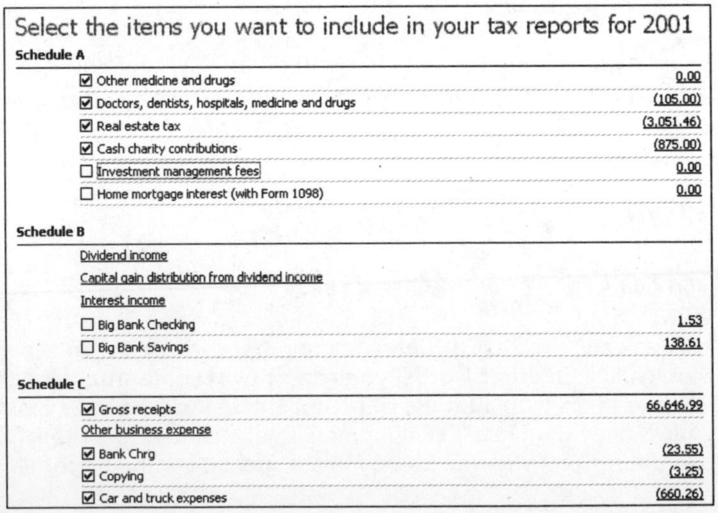

Figure 13-5: Choosing line items for a TXF tax-preparation file.

Select the items you want to include in your tax reports for 2001

Schedule A

☑ Other medicine and drugs	0.00
☑ Doctors, dentists, hospitals, medicine and drugs	(105.00)
☑ Real estate tax	(3,051.46)
☑ Cash charity contributions	(875.00)
☐ Investment management fees	0.00
☐ Home mortgage interest (with Form 1098)	0.00

Schedule B

Dividend income

Capital gain distribution from dividend income

Interest income

☐ Big Bank Checking	1.53
☐ Big Bank Savings	138.61

Schedule C

☑ Gross receipts	66,646.99

Other business expense

☑ Bank Chrg	(23.55)
☑ Copying	(3.25)
☑ Car and truck expenses	(660.26)

4. **Go down the list and check off line items that pertain to your tax situation; then click the Continue button.**

   Very likely, the line items that pertain to you are the ones with monetary figures in them.

   After you click the Continue button, you come to Prepare Your Taxes Using Software window.

5. **Choose Export Your Tax Information as a Data File.**

   The Export Tax dialog box appears.

6. **Name and save the file.**

   Don't forget what you named it and where you saved it. TaxCut or the other tax-preparation software you use will ask where to get this file.

As I write this, only TaxCut accepts TXF files from Money, but if your taxes aren't complicated, you can use other programs for tax reporting by generating a Tax Software report and entering the numbers by hand in the tax-preparation program. The previous section in this chapter explains how to generate a Tax Software report. Table 13-1 describes the leading tax-preparation software packages.

Table 13-1	Tax-Preparation Software Packages	
Program	*Cost*	*Imports Directly from Money?*
TaxAct Deluxe	$29.95	No
TaxCut Deluxe	$39.95	Yes
TurboTax Deluxe	$39.95	No

*Prices listed here are current as of August 2002.

For reviews and information about software, including tax-preparation programs, go to www.cnet.com on the Internet, type **tax** in the Search box, and click the Go button. Cnet.com offers detailed information about software, and you can purchase software from Cnet.com as well.

Getting Tax Help on the Internet

The Money Central Web site offers advice about tax planning and preparation. Here are a handful of other Web sites that are useful to taxpayers:

- ✔ **The Digital Daily:** The Digital Daily is the official home page of the Internal Revenue Service. The site offers tax information as well as a means of downloading any tax form (click the <u>Forms & Pubs</u> hyperlink). Address: www.irs.gov

- ✔ **Federal Forms and Publications:** Save yourself a trip to the post office by going to this Web site. From here, you can download tax-reporting forms, schedules, and publications. Address: www.irs.gov/forms_pubs/forms.html

- ✔ **State Forms and Publications:** From here, you can click a link, go to your state's tax Web site, and download forms, schedules, and publications for reporting state income taxes. Address: www.taxadmin.org/fta/forms.ss1

- ✔ **Quicken Tax Center:** Offers advice for taxpayers as well as tax estimators and evaluators that you can use online to determine what you owe in taxes. Address: www.quicken.com/taxes

- ✔ **TaxPlanet:** Gives information about everything you care to know about new tax laws. Address: www.taxplanet.com

- ✔ **Yahoo! Tax Center:** Offers tax tips as well as information about estimating and lowering tax bills. Address: taxes.yahoo.com

Part IV
Improving Your Financial Picture

The 5th Wave — By Rich Tennant

"I've been in hardware all of my life, and all of a sudden it's software that'll make me rich."

In this part . . .

Is your financial picture out of focus? Can't tell how much you're earning or where you're spending all that money? Can't see what your financial future looks like?

Start reading. This part of the book explains how to use Money to generate reports and graphs, plan for your retirement, and do other tasks to bring your financial picture into sharp focus.

Chapter 14

Reports and Charts for Seeing Where You Stand Financially

*R*eports and charts are two of my favorite things in Money 2003. Reports and charts determine right away what your financial standing is. Until I discovered the Tax-related Transactions report, I used to spend hours and hours on April 14 tabulating tax-deductible expenses for my income tax report. Until I discovered the Spending by Category chart, I had no idea where I spent all that money. Until I spent a night in the Sierra Mountains, I didn't know that the sky has so many stars, but that's another story.

Maybe you want to create a report or chart to prove to a loan officer how credit-worthy you are. Maybe you want to find out how much it cost to drive your car last year. Maybe you want to see how a stock price fluctuated to find out whether the price fluctuation really resembled a rollercoaster ride. Whatever you need, Money can help.

This chapter tells you about the 38 types of reports and the 26 kinds of charts that you can create with Money; how to customize a report or chart so that it yields precisely the information that you want it to yield; how to print reports and charts; and how to export the reports to other computer programs.

A Look at the Pick a Report or Chart Window

To create a report or chart, you start from the Pick a Report or Chart window, shown in Figure 14-1. Click the Reports button on the Navigation bar or choose Reports⇨Reports Gallery to get to the Pick a Report or Chart window.

On the left side of the gallery are the eight categories of reports and charts. By clicking a category name, you can see the reports and charts that are available in the category. In Figure 14-1, for example, the Income and Expenses category has been selected, so the window lists the reports and charts in the Spending Habits category.

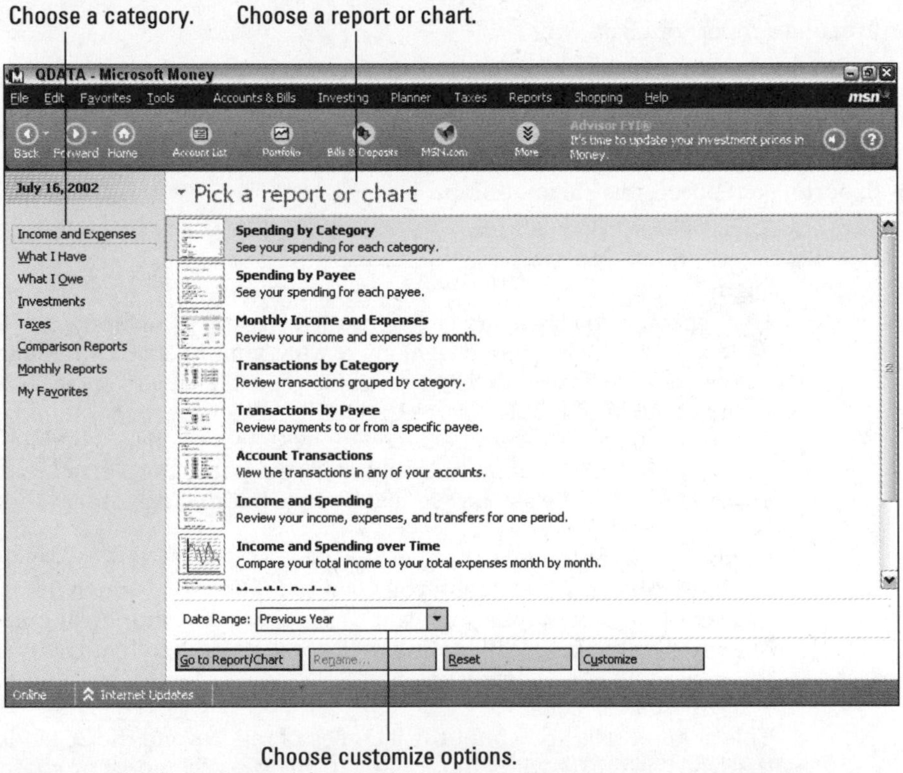

Choose a category.   Choose a report or chart.

Figure 14-1:
The Pick a
Report or
Chart
window is
the starting
point for
creating a
report or
chart.

Choose customize options.

REMEMBER

By now you must be wondering, "But how can I tell which of these names are reports and which are charts?" Good question. The answer is that you can make a report or a chart from almost every name in the Pick a Report or Chart window. For example, Figure 14-2 shows both the report and the chart that you can create with the Spending by Category option in the Income and Expenses category. On the left side of Figure 14-2 is a Spending by Category report; on the right side is a Spending by Category pie chart.

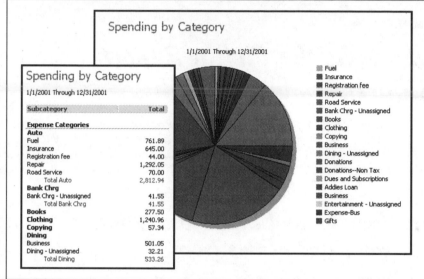

Figure 14-2:
You can create a report (left) or a chart (right) with almost any option in the Pick a Report or Chart window.

Miscellaneous reports and charts

The Pick a Report or Chart window isn't the only place where you can get a report or chart that describes your financial picture. You can also get reports and charts from the following places:

✔ **Home Page:** If you so choose, you can make the Chart of the Day appear on the home page. This chart changes day by day and sheds light on a different part of your finances.

✔ **A register:** While you are staring at a register, click the Analyze Spending button and choose an option from the menu to generate a report or chart that illuminates activity in the account.

✔ **Categories window:** Click a category name on the Categories window and click the Go to Category button to see a chart that shows how much you spent in the category in each of the past six months. Click a Payee name in the Payees window and click the Go to Payee button to see a mini register that shows what you paid the payee.

✔ **Bills and Deposits window:** Click the Forecast Cash Flow button to see a chart that shows how the bills you have scheduled affect account balances.

✔ **Find and Replace dialog box:** On the Search Results screen of the Find and Replace dialog box is a button called Create Report. Click it and you get an Account Transactions report that shows when and where the transactions you were looking for were entered.

TIP

After you generate a report or chart for the first time, a report or chart icon appears beside the report or chart's name in the Pick a Report or Chart window. Which icon you see — the one for a mini-report or for a mini-chart — depends on which one you generated. Double-click the icon to generate a report or chart.

Looking at the Pick a Report or Chart Window

Money offers no fewer than 38 types of reports and 26 types of charts. As fast as I can — because I know that you're in a hurry — I briefly tell you in the following sections what the different reports and charts are. Turn to these pages when you are looking for a report or chart to illuminate your financial picture.

Income and Expenses: Where the money goes and comes from

By clicking the Income and Expenses link on the Pick a Report or Chart window, you can create these reports and charts:

Report/Chart	What It Tells You	Use
Spending by Category	How much you spend by category, ranked from largest expense to smallest (refer to Figure 14-2).	To find out your biggest expenses.
Spending by Payee	The names of payees to whom you paid money, and the amounts you paid.	To find out where you shop most often and perhaps where you should stop shopping so often.
Monthly Income and Expenses	How much you spent and how much you earned in the past three months, by category, in your bank and credit card accounts.	To find out what your expenses and sources of income were.
Transactions by Category	A report that lists, under each expense category, the spending transactions you entered so far this year.	To examine your spending habits.

Report/Chart	What It Tells You	Use
Transactions by Payee	A report that lists, under each category, who you paid money to or received money from.	To examine sources of income and expenses.
Account Transactions	A report that lists all the transactions in an account by month, or a line chart that shows a running account balance of the history of the account.	To find transactions in an account or to list and print part of an account register.
Income and Spending	Your expenses by category and your income by category.	To compare your income to your expenses and find out how much you are saving or going into the red.
Monthly Budget	Your monthly your budget goals.	To help review find out whether you met your budget.
Annual Budget	Your annual your budget goals.	To help you find out whether you met your budget.

What I Have: A look at assets and liabilities

The following reports and charts fall under the What I Have category on the Pick a Report or Chart window:

Report/Chart	What It Tells You	Use
Net Worth	How the value of your assets and liabilities compare to one another.	To find out your net worth.
Net Worth Less Capital Gains	How the value of your assets and liabilities is affected by capital gains taxes.	To get a better look at your net worth.

(continued)

Report/Chart	What It Tells You	Use
Net Worth over Time	How the value of your assets and liabilities compare over a certain time period. (Use the Date Range drop-down list to select a time period.)	To examine your net worth over time.
Net Worth Over Time Less Capital Gains	How the value of your assets and liabilities, affected by capital gains taxes, change over time.	To get a focused picture of your net worth.
Account Balances	How much money is in your bank and other kinds of accounts at present.	To find out how much money is on hand.
Account Balance History	How the balance and value of all your accounts has changed over time. (Choose an option from the Accounts drop-down menu if you want to select a single account.) Figure 14-3 shows an Account Balance History chart.	To see how fickle time, fate, and one's spending habits are.
Account Balances with Details	The information about your accounts that is kept on the Account Details window — the account number, opening balance, and so on.	To quickly look up account numbers and other information.
Asset Allocation	A description of how diversified your investments are.	To see whether all your eggs are in one basket.
Frequent Flyer Miles	Information about the frequent flyer points or miles you've earned.	To see whether you have enough miles or points for a vacation you've been planning.

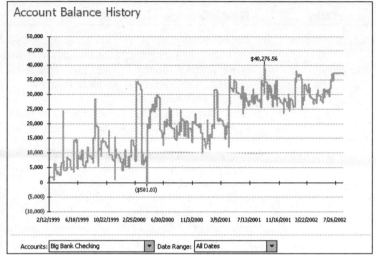

Figure 14-3:
An Account
Balance
History
chart.

What I Owe: A look at debts and upcoming bills

Look to the What I Owe category in the Pick a Report or Chart window to generate these reports and charts:

Report/Chart	What It Tells You	Use
Scheduled Bills	Which bills you have scheduled in the Bills and Deposits window.	
Upcoming Bills	Which bills in the Bills and Deposits window are supposed to be paid in the coming month.	To find out which bills are overdue or due 31 days in advance.
Upcoming Bills and Deposits This Month	Which bills and deposits in the Bills and Deposits window are due this month.	To compare your income to your expenses so that you can decide which bills to pay.
Credit Card Debt	Your total credit card debt.	To suffer despair over credit card debt and see which one you owe the most on.

(continued)

Report/Chart	What It Tells You	Use
Loan Terms	The information about your loans that is kept in the Payment Terms window — the loan amount, remaining balance, interest rate, and so on.	Print this report if you apply for a new loan so that you can give the lender details about your other loans.
Loan Amortization	How much of each loan payment goes toward servicing interest, how much goes toward reducing the principal, and a running balance of how much you owe. (You must have set up a loan account in Money, as described in Chapter 16, to run this report.) Choose a new loan or mortgage from the Accounts drop-down list.	To see how principal and interest payments on a loan break down.

Investments: Examining your portfolio's performance

The Investments category on the Pick a Report or Chart window offers these reports and charts for finding out how skilled an investor you are:

Report/Chart	What It Tells You	Use
Portfolio Value by Investment Account	The value of each of your investment accounts, as well as each security in the accounts.	To see changes in the monetary value of your securities.
Portfolio Value by Investment Type	What percentage of your investments are in mutual funds, stocks, and so on.	To find out how diversified your investments are.
Performance by Investment Account	The gain or loss in monetary terms and the gain or loss as a percentage of the security's total value in the past year of each security you own.	To compare investments to determine which is performing the best.

Report/Chart	What It Tells You	Use
Performance by Investment Type	The gain or loss in monetary terms and by percentage for each of your securities, with securities grouped by investment type.	To compare types of investments — stocks, mutual funds, and so on — to see which type performs best.
Price History	The up-and-down performance of individual stocks and other securities this year so far, as shown in Figure 14-4. Choose a type of investment from the Investments drop-down list.	To exercise your eyeballs and make them move up and down.
Investment Transactions	The investment transactions you entered in investment registers.	To review activity in investment accounts.
Asset Allocation	How diversified your investment portfolio is.	To find out whether all your eggs are in one basket.
Bond Summary	The value and latest price, as well as other details, of the bonds you own.	To examine your bond investments.
Bond Performance	Performance data concerning the bonds you own, including the percentage price gain and annual return.	To see how well your bond investments are performing.

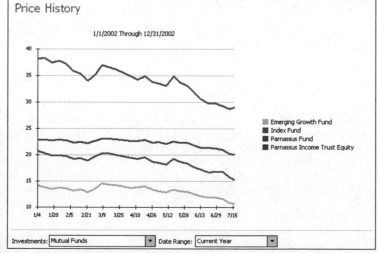

Figure 14-4: The Price History line chart traces the performance of stocks and securities.

Taxes: A look at tax-related transactions and capital gains

As tax time draws nigh, click the Taxes link in the Pick a Report or Chart window and create a handful of these reports. This window produces reports only:

Report	What It Tells You	Use
Tax-Related Transactions	Category by category, your total income and expenses in tax-related categories.	For calculating income and tax-deductible expenses on tax returns.
Capital Gains	Capital gains and losses for each security you own or owned.	For calculating capital gains and losses.
Loan Interest	How much of your loan payments go each month and year toward servicing interest.	For determining what your loan interest payments were. Some loan interest payments are tax deductible.
Tax Software Report	Your total income and expenses as can be reported on the tax lines on various tax forms.	For gathering data so that you can plug it into tax-preparation software programs.

Comparison Reports: For comparing the past with the present

Are you better off than you were four years ago? You can find out very quickly by clicking the Comparison Reports link in the Pick a Report or Chart window and choosing one of these reports:

Report	What It Tells You	Use
Spending by Category Comparison	How you spent in different categories in two different time periods. Choose time periods from the drop-down menus.	For understanding your spending habits better.

Report	What It Tells You	Use
Spending by Payee Comparison	Your income in two different time periods. Choose time periods from the drop-down menus.	For comparing your earnings from year to year.
Income and Spending Comparison	Your expenses and earnings presented by category in different time periods.	For comparing what was with what is.

Monthly Reports: Seeing how you fared this month

Money creates monthly reports automatically. The reports show where you spent money and your net worth, among other things. To see a report from your economic past, go to this window and double-click it.

My Favorites

The My Favorites category on the Pick a Report or Chart window is for you and you alone. The "Adding a customized report or chart to the Favorites menu" section, later in this chapter, explains how you can keep your own customized reports in the My Favorites category and draw upon them whenever you please.

Creating a Report or Chart

To create a report or chart, you need to be familiar with the different types that Money offers. (Refer to the section "A Look at the Pick a Report or Chart Window," earlier in this chapter.) You may be interested to know that you can usually turn a report into a chart and a chart into a report. Too bad life isn't always that easy.

Generating the report or chart

Follow these steps to create a report or chart:

1. **Click the Reports button on the Navigation bar or choose Reports⇨Reports Gallery.**

The Pick a Report or Chart window appears (refer to Figure 14-1).

2. **Click a category name on the left side of the window.**

   The first category is Income and Expenses; the last is My Favorites. The "Adding a customized report or chart to the Favorites menu" section, later in this chapter, explains how to put customized reports and charts in the My Favorites category or on the Favorites menu so that you can generate them faster.

3. **Click a report or chart name in the Pick a Report or Chart window.**

   Depending on the report or chart you select, a drop-down list or two appears along the bottom of the window. Make a selection from a drop-down list to make your report or chart show exactly what you want it to show.

4. **Double-click the name or click the <u>G</u>o to Report/Chart button.**

What you see next depends on which report or chart you created. Sometimes you get a chart and sometimes you get a report. Sometimes the report or chart covers the right time period; sometimes it doesn't. Read on to find out how to turn a report into a chart or a chart into a report. Later in this chapter, the "Customizing Reports and Charts" section explains how to change the appearance and parameters of a report or chart.

In the meantime, click the Reports button or the Back button to return to the Pick a Report or Chart window.

To create a report or chart in one mighty stroke, click the down arrow that appears next to the word *Pick* in the upper-left corner of the window, select a category from the drop-down list, and then select a report/chart name, as shown in Figure 14-5.

Figure 14-5:
The speedy way to create a report or chart.

Pick a report or chart	
Income and Expenses ▶ egory	
What I Have ▶ or each category.	
What I Owe ▶	
Investments ▶	Portfolio Value by Investment Account
Taxes ▶	Portfolio Value by Investment Type
Comparison Reports ▶	Performance by Investment Account
Monthly Reports ▶	Performance by Investment Type
Transactions by	Price History
Review transaction	Investment Transactions
	Asset Allocation
Transactions by	Bond Summary
Review payments t	Bond Performance
Account Transactions	
View the transactions in any of your accounts.	

Turning reports into charts and charts into reports

When you create a report or chart from the Pick a Report or Chart window, Money does its best to give you the report or chart you want, but often it makes the wrong choice. Frequently, the program gives you a chart when you wanted a report or a report when you wanted a chart. And sometimes the program gives you the wrong kind of chart.

You can fix that dilemma by clicking the Change View link, the first link under "Common Tasks," and choosing an option from the submenu. To turn a report into a chart, for example, choose Bar Chart or Line Chart on the submenu.

Some charts can't be turned into reports, and when that's the case, the Change View button is dimmed and nothing happens when you click it.

Investigating the figures from which a chart or report is constructed

The figures on reports and the lines on charts are constructed from numbers that you entered in your account registers. Suppose that you get curious about a number on a report or pie slice in a pie chart. Maybe you want to know why a number is so high or a pie slice is so fat. Maybe you can't believe that you spent so much or profited so little. You can move the mouse pointer over the number or pie slice and do some investigating.

In Figure 14-6, a pie slice on the right side of the chart is awfully large. Suppose that you want to know why it's so large. As the figure shows, you can move the pointer over part of a chart and see a box with a figure that shows you what the chart segment represents in monetary terms. In the figure, you can see that this person spent a whopping $18,692.34 on home repairs. That must have been a big hailstorm.

In reports and charts, the pointer turns into a magnifying glass when you move it over a summary figure, pie slice, bar, or whatnot. It does that, I should say, if you can double-click to see the figures from which the chart was constructed. By double-clicking when the pointer looks like a magnifying glass, you can see the account transactions from which the part of the chart or report was constructed.

Figure 14-6:
Move the
pointer over
part of a
chart to see
what it
represents,
and then
double-click
to see the
transactions
from which
it was
constructed.

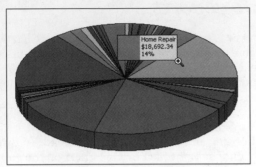

Customizing Reports and Charts

Chances are, the report or chart you created doesn't meet your high expectations. Perhaps it doesn't look right or it covers the wrong time period. Perhaps you want to remove data from one or two accounts in a report to keep the report's figures from being skewed. Maybe you want to change a chart's title.

When you want to change anything about a report or chart, click the Customize link. Whether you are dealing with a report or a chart, you see the Customize Report dialog box, shown in Figure 14-7.

Figure 14-7:
Customize
charts and
reports
in the
Customize
Report
dialog box.

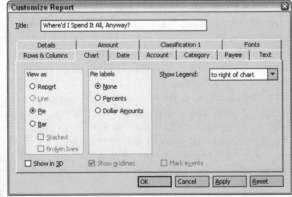

✔ **Apply:** Applies the changes you've made but does not close the dialog box. Click the Apply button after you make a change but you aren't sure whether you want it to be permanent. After your improvements have been applied, drag the Customize Report dialog box to a corner of the screen and look at the damage you did. If you don't like what you see, select different options in the dialog box.

✔ **Reset:** Unravels all the work you did to the report or chart and applies the default settings that you had to begin with.

✔ **Cancel:** Closes the dialog box. Click this button if you decide not to customize.

Maybe the biggest change you want to make to a chart or report is to its title. Change it by typing a new name in the Title box. Beyond that, read on to find out how to customize charts and reports with the ten tabs in the Customize Report dialog box.

Rows & Columns tab: Changing the rows and columns

The Rows & Columns tab in the Customize Report dialog box is for changing the rows (legend items, if you are customizing a chart) and columns (labels, if you are dealing with a chart):

✔ **Rows:** The Rows drop-down list is for selecting how items on the report or chart are grouped. In the case of reports, you specify which items appear as row headings along the left side. In the case of charts, you decide which items comprise the bars, pie slices, or Y-axis values in a line chart.

✔ **Columns:** The Columns drop-down list offers a number of different choices. For reports, select the items that are to appear along the top of the report as column headings. For charts, select the X-axis values.

✔ **Combine All Values Under % of Total:** Rather than include every scrap of data in a report or chart, you can bundle the smaller amounts into a single row, pie slice, or whatever. Enter a percentage in this box to tell Money where to draw the line between amounts that get bundled and items that don't get bundled. This option cleans up pie charts and makes them look much better.

✔ **Sort by:** Usually, items are sorted by amount from highest to lowest, but you can arrange items in different ways from this drop-down menu.

✔ **Include Abbreviations:** If you entered abbreviations for categories in the Details window, clicking this check box makes abbreviations as well as category names appear on reports and charts.

Chart tab: Choosing chart types and other chart options

The options on the Chart tab for changing the look of a chart are self-explanatory, I think. True, it's difficult to figure out what the bar chart's Stacked option is, but all you have to do to find out is click one of the options, click the Apply button, and peek at your bar chart.

On the other hand, in case you really need an explanation, here are descriptions of the options for changing the look of a chart:

- ✔ **View As:** Click the appropriate radio button to change the chart to a bar chart, a line chart, or a pie chart, or to turn a chart into a report.

- ✔ **Stacked option:** When you are working with a bar chart, click Stacked to put the bars one on top of the other and show total amounts.

- ✔ **Broken bars:** Select this option to make breaks appear in bars when they have reached important thresholds.

- ✔ **Pie Labels:** Select None to keep labels off the chart, percents to display a percentage figure that shows how fat each pie slice is, or Dollar amounts to list dollar figures rather than percentage figures next to each pie slice.

- ✔ **Show in 3D:** Select this option to give the chart a third dimension. Line charts look especially good in three dimensions. Three-dimensional charts look great (refer to Figure 14-6).

- ✔ **Show Gridlines:** Click this option to draw or remove *gridlines* — the lines on bar and line charts that show roughly how big or small a value is — on the chart.

- ✔ **Show Legend:** Select this option to tell Money where to place the *legend*, the key that tells what the pie slices, bars, or lines mean, and whether to show the option at all.

Date tab: Changing the date range

To change the time period that the report or chart covers, select an option from the Range drop-down list or enter a beginning and ending date of your own in the From and To text boxes.

Account tab: Choosing accounts for the report or chart

To start with, your report or chart gathers data from all your accounts, but perhaps you want it to focus on two, three, or four. To decide which accounts get covered, click the Clear All button on the Account tab and then check each account whose data you want to include in the report or chart. You can also click the All Open Accounts button to gather data only from accounts that are open.

Category tab: Excluding categories from reports and charts

To begin with, reports and charts gather data from all categories and subcategories, but you can exclude categories by way of the Category tab. Click a button to generate a report solely with Income, Expense, or Tax-related categories, or else click the Clear All button and check each category on the list from which the report is to draw data. Uncheck the Show Subcatgories check box to keep subcategories from appearing on reports and charts.

Payee tab: Excluding payees and income sources

If you want to get really picky, you can even exclude certain payees and sources of income from reports and charts. Perhaps including a certain payee or income source would skew a report or chart and render it invalid. In that case, go to the Payee tab and click to remove the checkmark beside the name of the payee or income source.

Text tab: Using text criteria to gather data

This odd tab is for gathering data on the basis of the words in transactions. For example, entering *Bills* in the text box results in having data gathered only from transactions in which the word *Bills* appears, be it in the Payee field, the Category field, or the Memo field.

Be sure to click the Apply button if you use this tab. Gathering data this way can have weird consequences.

Details tab: Gathering data on the basis of type and status

Use the Type drop-down list on the Details tab to generate reports about payments, deposits, unprinted checks, online bill payments that were not sent, or transfers, and whether or not these transaction types have been reconciled. You can also generate reports around check numbers from this tab.

Amount tab: Querying by amount

On the Amount tab, you can fish in your records for amounts of a certain amount or within a certain range.

Classification tab: Including classes and sub-classes in reports

If you track your spending and income with classes as well as categories, your Customize Report dialog box includes a Classification tab (it is named after the classification you created). From this tab, you can exclude classes and subclasses from reports and charts.

Fonts tab: Changing how reports and charts look

To change the way the letters look on reports and graphs, go to the Fonts tab and choose a new font and type size. You can also make columns on reports wider or narrower from this tab, but be sure to click the Apply button first. Changing fonts and especially font sizes has a way of throwing everything out of whack on a report or chart. You can always click the Reset button if you create too much chaos.

Adding a customized report or chart to the Favorites menu

After you go to the trouble of customizing a report or chart, you may as well put it in the My Favorites category of the Pick a Report or Chart window. That way, you can generate it again without having to tinker with the settings in the Customize Report dialog box.

Follow these steps to add a report or chart to the My Favorites category:

1. **Create and customize the report or chart.**

2. **Choose Favorites⇨Add to Favorites, or right-click the report or chart and choose Add to Favorites from the shortcut menu.**

   You see the Add to Favorites dialog box.

3. **Enter a descriptive name in the Report Name text box.**

4. **Click OK.**

Besides landing in the My Favorites category of the Pick a Report or Chart window, the name of your customized report or chart also appears on the Favorites⇨Favorite Reports menu. You can select it there, too.

To remove a customized report from the Pick a Report or Chart window, click the My Favorites link, click the name of the report or chart, click the Delete button along the bottom of the window, and click Yes in the confirmation box.

Printing Reports and Charts

Before you print a report or chart, I strongly recommend visiting the Report and Chart Setup dialog box, where you tell Money what kind of printer you use and whether you want to print in portrait or landscape style. The following pages reveal intimate secrets that I got from a tabloid about the Report and Chart Setup dialog box. They also tell you how to print a report or chart.

Getting ready to print a report or chart

Follow these steps to tell Money how you want to print your report or chart:

1. **Choose File⇨Print Setup⇨Report and Chart Setup.**

   You see the Report and Chart Setup dialog box.

2. **From the Printer drop-down list, select the name of the printer with which you will print, if you print on more than one printer.**

3. **Under Orientation, select the Landscape option if you want to print lengthwise on the paper.**

Wide reports and charts fit on the page better when they are printed in landscape fashion. With the Landscape option, the page is turned on its side and it is longer on the top and bottom, like a landscape painting.

4. **Click OK.**

If you are printing a detailed chart and you want it to look especially good, click the Options button in the Report and Chart Setup dialog box. The Option button opens the Printer Properties dialog box, where you can choose options for changing the resolution of your printer, if your printer permits resolution options to be changed.

Printing the report or chart

To make a hard copy of your report or chart so that you can send it to the hard-hitting *Hard Copy* television show, follow these steps:

1. **Put the report or chart on your computer screen.**

2. **Press Ctrl+P or choose File⇨Print.**

You see the Print Report or Print Chart dialog box.

3. **In the Copies box, enter the number of copies you want, if you want more than one copy.**

4. **Click OK.**

Exporting a Report or Chart

The wonderful report or chart that you created is not trapped inside the Money program. No indeed. You can export it to other programs so that you can include it in an annual report or a slide presentation, for example. Follow these steps to export a report and help improve the trade deficit:

1. **With the report or chart on-screen, choose Edit⇨Copy (or press Ctrl+C).**

Doing so copies the report or chart to the Windows Clipboard.

2. **Move to the program to which you want to make the copy and choose Edit⇨Paste (or press Ctrl+V).**

After a chart is copied, it lands in the other program in the form of a vector graphic. You can change the shape of a vector graphic by pulling and tugging at its perimeters.

After a report is copied, it lands in the other program in the form of a *tab-delimited text file,* a list in which each component is separated from the next by a tab space. That's no big deal, however, because most spreadsheet and word processing programs can handle tab-delimited text files. The only thing you have to worry about is reformatting your report after it lands in the other program.

To format a report in Microsoft Word, remove all empty rows from the report and then select the table part of the file — that is, select everything except the title, date, and so on. To do that, click to the left of the first row in the report (the row with the column headings), hold down the mouse button, and drag down the screen until the last row is selected. Then choose Table➪ Convert Text to Table and click OK in the Convert Text to Table dialog box. If you need help formatting the table, get a good book on Word. May I suggest *Word 2002 For Dummies Quick Reference*, by Peter Weverka (published by Hungry Minds, Inc.). It's a classic.

Exporting reports for use in spreadsheet programs

To export a Money report to a spreadsheet program, save the report as a file. From there, you can use the spreadsheet program's commands to import the report. Follow these steps to save a report as a file:

1. **Right-click the report and choose Export from the shortcut menu.**

   You see the Export Report dialog box.

2. **In the File Name text box, enter a descriptive name for your report.**

3. **Select the folder in which to save your report.**

4. **Click OK.**

   The report is saved as a tab-delimited text file. If the spreadsheet program asks what kind of file you are importing, cover your ears and shout, "Tab-Delimited Text File!"

Chapter 15

Money for Homeowners

- -

In This Chapter

▶ Finding out how high a loan or mortgage you can afford and what the monthly payments will be

▶ Calculating the total costs of purchasing a home

▶ Comparing one loan or mortgage to another

▶ Determining what houses cost in a neighborhood

▶ Deciding whether to refinance a loan

▶ Cataloguing the items that you own

- -

*T*his chapter looks into all the features that Money offers homeowners and people who are thinking about buying a house. Curiously, these features are stashed away on the Home page where no one is likely to find them. I stumbled over them by accident late one night while taking out the cat, and it's a good thing I did, because I wouldn't have found them otherwise.

If you are shopping for a home loan, this chapter is especially useful. I'll bet my bottom dollar that you are confused by terms such as *points* and *closing costs*. With Money 2003 Deluxe, you can analyze different kinds of mortgages or loans and cut through the mumbo-jumbo. You can find out exactly how much borrowing costs — that is, you can find out exactly what the monthly mortgage payments on a loan will be. You can also find out how much you can afford to borrow and whether refinancing a loan is worthwhile.

This chapter explains how to compare and contrast loans and mortgages, find out what property costs in a certain neighborhood, and catalogue the items that you own.

A Quick Look at What Money Offers Homeowners

Before you start rummaging in this chapter for things that are of interest to you, take a look at Table 15-1. It briefly explains the different Money features that pertain to homeowners and people who are shopping for a house. These features are available in House view in the Money Home Page window. Follow these steps to switch to House view:

1. **Click the Home button on the Navigation bar to go to the Home page.**

2. **Choose House on the Choose a View drop-down menu.**

   Figure 15-1 shows the Home Page in House view. Click a link on the Home page to explore a different aspect of Home ownership. Table 15-1 describes what these links do. Links marked with an asterisk (*) in the table take you to a Web site at Homeadvisor.com, Mortgageselect.com, or Money Central.

Choose House.   Click a link.

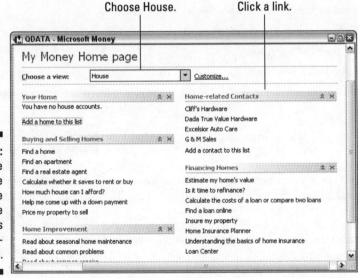

Figure 15-1: Go to House view on the Home Page to test-drive features for home-owners.

Table 15-1	Money Features for Homeowners
Home Page Link	*What You Can Do*
Add a Home to this List	Create a Home account for tracking the equity in your house. See Chapter 16.
Home-Related Contacts	Make a list of tradespeople — plumbers, electricians, and so on — whose help you may need someday. The names come from your Payee list. Click a name and you go to the Details window, where you can find telephone numbers and addresses.

Home Page Link	What You Can Do
Find a Home*	Study house prices in any city in the United States or Canada. You can also compare house prices in different areas. See "Finding Out What Houses Cost," in this chapter.
Find an Apartment*	Examine rental rates in different cities.
Find a Real Estate Agent*	Search for real estate agents by city or ZIP code. Agents are members of LendingTree, Inc., an affiliation of 650 real estate companies.
Calculate Whether It Saves to Rent or Buy*	Compare the cost of renting to the after-tax cost of buying a house.
How Much House Can I Afford*	See how much you can pay for a house, given how much of your monthly income you can devote to mortgage payments and how much you can borrow. See "Finding Out Roughly What You Can Pay for a House," in this chapter.
Help Me Come Up with a Down Payment	Use the Purchase Wizard window to devise a plan for saving for a down payment on a house or other big-ticket item. You can also choose Planner⇨Purchase Wizard to operate the Purchase Wizard. See Chapter 11.
Price My Property to Sell*	Read advice about determining the market value of a house you want to sell.
Estimate My Home's Value*	Find out what a house is worth according to Freddie Mac (these are rough estimates at best). You can also find out the sale prices of houses near the one you are investigating. See Chapter 16.
Is It Time to Refinance?*	Find out what it costs for a loan so that you can compare the cost to a loan or mortgage you already have. ("Determining Whether Refinancing Is Worthwhile," in this chapter, explains a better way to compare loans.)
Calculate the Costs of a Loan or Compare Two Loans	Compare one loan or mortgage to another. See "Calculating and Comparing the Costs of a Loan," in this chapter.

(continued)

Table 15-1 *(continued)*

Home Page Link	What You Can Do
Find a Loan Online*	Read articles about obtaining home loans and, if you so desire, apply for a loan from MortgageSelect.com.
Insure My Property*	Read articles about shopping for home, auto, life, and health insurance.
Home Insurance Planner*	Take a survey and, on the basis of your answers, find out how much life, auto, home, and health insurance you need.
Understanding the Basics of Home Insurance*	Read articles about home insurance, how much you need, and where to obtain it.
Loan Center*	Read about and start shopping for life, auto, home, and health insurance.
Home Inventory	Catalogue different items you own so that you can keep track of their value and where they are. See "Cataloguing the Items in Your Household," in this chapter.
Home Improvement*	Read various articles about maintaining and making repairs to your home.

Clicking this link goes to a Web site on the Internet — Homeadvisor.com, Mortgageselect.com, or Money Central.

Finding Out Roughly What You Can Pay for a House

A lot of factors go into figuring out how expensive a house you can afford. You have to determine the monthly mortgage payment that you can make comfortably. You have to drive around strange neighborhoods with real estate agents and imagine yourself living in houses that would be okay if not for the threadbare carpets and all that cottage cheese on the ceilings.

Money can't help you locate a dream house, but it can help you crunch the numbers and find out how much money you can borrow comfortably and how much of a down payment you can afford, given the amount you need to borrow. Follow these steps to get a rough estimate of how much you can pay for a house or other property:

1. **Go to the Home Page and switch to House view.**

   You can do that by choosing House on the Choose a View drop-down menu.

2. **Click the <u>How Much House Can I Afford</u>? link.**

   Strange to think of a house as a quantity, but the link does say "how much?" Anyhow, you soon land on a Web page with a gizmo called the Loan Calculator, as shown in Figure 15-2.

Drag a slider to enter the figures.

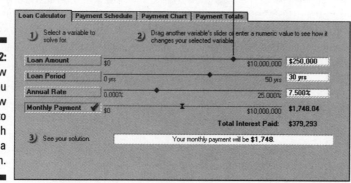

Figure 15-2:
See how much you can borrow or afford to pay each month on a loan.

3. **Click a button to tell the Calculator what you want to find out.**

   That probably means clicking either the Loan Amount or the Monthly Payment button.

   - Click the Loan Amount button to find out how much you can borrow given the payment you can comfortably afford to make each month to service the loan. For example, if you can pay $1,500 a month and you want to know how much you can borrow at that amount, click the Loan Amount button.

   - Click the Monthly Payment button to find out how much you need to pay each month on a given loan. For example, if you want to borrow $130,000 but you want to know what the monthly payments to service that loan would be, click the Monthly Payment button.

4. **Enter the number of years you will pay off the loan in the Loan Period text box.**

   In a typical home loan, the number is 30 years.

5. **Enter the interest rate on the loan.**

6. **Look in the See Your Solution box.**

It tells you how much your monthly payment is or how much you can afford to borrow. To tinker with the numbers, try dragging a slider on the calculator.

While you're here, try clicking the Payment Chart and Payment Totals tabs in the Loan Calculator. They reveal some interesting numbers. The Payment Chart tab shows, over the length of the loan, how much of each payment is devoted to paying off the principal and how much is devoted to servicing the debt. As shown in Figure 15-3, the Payment Totals tab shows how much you will pay over the course of the loan to service debt and pay off the principal. In the figure, for example, a $250,000 loan costs $629,293.04 altogether over the 30-year period ($379.293.06 + 249,999.98). Better start saving your pennies! For that matter, make an extra payment now and then to reduce the principal you owe on the loan. Even a modest extra payment in each month will reduce significantly the total amount you have to pay.

The next section in this chapter describes a more sophisticated way to calculate the price of a loan or mortgage.

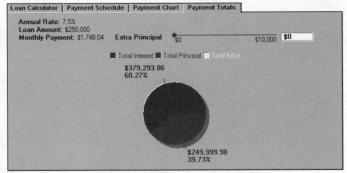

Figure 15-3:
The total cost of a loan is shown on the Payment Totals tab.

Calculating and Comparing the Costs of a Loan

When you are shopping for a loan or mortgage, the two most important questions to ask yourself are "How large of a loan can I afford?" and "How much will my monthly payments be?" The Loan Worksheet can help answer these questions, as well as show how interest rates affect loans and how long paying off a loan will take.

Use the Loan Worksheet to compare loans or mortgages or find out what a loan or mortgage costs. The Loan Worksheet cannot come to your aid as fast as the Lone Ranger, but it can help with the following difficult tasks:

- Finding out how much money you can afford to borrow
- Finding out how high the payments on a loan are
- Finding out how long it takes to pay off a loan
- Finding out how interest rates affect loan payments
- Comparing one loan or mortgage to another to see which is the better deal
- Comparing a mortgage that you are paying now to another mortgage to see whether refinancing is worthwhile

Follow these steps to use the Loan Worksheet as you agonize over whether you should buy a house, new car, or other expensive item that requires taking out a loan:

1. **Go to the Home Page and switch to House view.**

   To do that, choose House on the Choose a View drop-down menu.

2. **Click the Calculate the Costs of a Loan or Compare Two Loans link.**

   You see the introductory page of the Loan Worksheet. To calculate the cost of a loan or mortgage that you want to analyze, you fill out one, two, or three tabs, depending on what you want to know: Initial Costs, Loan Terms, or Variable Rate. After you fill out one page, click a tab to move to the next one.

3. **Click the Loan Terms tab.**

   You see the Loan Terms window, shown in Figure 15-4. On this page, you tell Money what you want to know about the loan and provide all the particulars that you do know.

   You can ignore the boxes under Loan B. Those boxes are for comparing one loan or mortgage to another, which you can read about in the "Comparing One Loan or Mortgage to Another" section, later in this chapter.

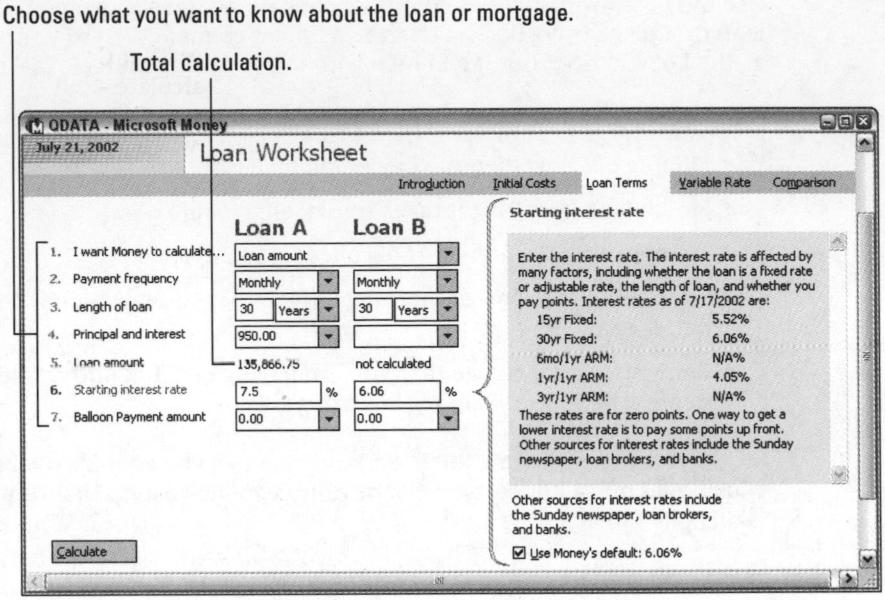

Choose what you want to know about the loan or mortgage.

Total calculation.

Figure 15-4:
On the Loan Terms tab, tell Money what you want to know about the loan or mortgage.

4. Click box 1, I Want Money to Calculate, and select the option from the drop-down list that describes what you want to know about the loan or mortgage in question.

This table explains the options in the I Want Money to Calculate box:

Option	Question That You Want Money to Answer
Length of Loan	How long will it take to pay off this loan?
Principal & Interest	How much can I afford to pay each month (or other time period)?
Loan Amount	How much can I afford to borrow altogether?
Starting Interest Rate	How will the interest rates change if I pay points up front or pay some of the closing costs out of my own pocket?
Balloon Payment Amount	If I make a lump-sum payment at the end of the loan, how will the principal, interest, and other loan particulars be affected?

5. **Fill in boxes 2 through 7 to describe the loan you are considering.**

   You can't fill in one of the boxes. One box says "Not Calculated" because it names the thing that you want Money to calculate — the thing you chose in Step 4. The answer to your question about your loan or mortgage appears where "Not Calculated" is now when you are done filling in the Loan Terms page.

   In Figure 15-4, I chose Loan Amount and asked Money how much I can afford to borrow on a 30-year mortgage, given that $950 per month is the amount I can pay comfortably and the interest rate on the loan is 7.5 percent.

   If you can't understand what Money wants you to enter in one of the boxes in the Loan Planner worksheet, click in the box and then read the explanation on the right side of the window.

6. **Click the Calculate button.**

   The answer to the question that you put to Money in Step 4 is listed next to the appropriate category and at the bottom of the window. In Figure 15-1, Money tells me that I can afford to borrow $135,866.75.

   You're done — unless you intend to pay initial costs for the loan or mortgage you are wrestling with, or the loan or mortgage charges a variable interest rate, not a fixed interest rate (see the following sections).

Investigating how initial costs alter the costs of a mortgage or loan

By "initial costs," Money refers to a down payment you make at the start of the loan, closing costs, discount points, and other such fees. *Closing costs* are appraisal fees, sales commissions, and other fees that you are charged when you take out a loan. Closing costs are expressed as a percentage of the purchase price of the item you want to buy with the loan.

When you take out a mortgage to buy a house, you are charged *discount points,* also known simply as *points.* Like closing costs, points are expressed as a percentage of the amount you borrow.

To tell Money about the closing costs, points, and down payment you intend to make on a loan, follow these steps after you have filled out the Loan Terms page of the Loan Planner worksheet (see the preceding section of this chapter):

1. **Click the Initial Costs tab.**

   You see the Initial Costs tab, shown in Figure 15-5.

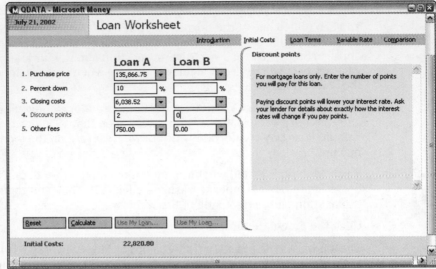

Figure 15-5:
Tell Money the amount of the up-front fees and down payment for the loan.

2. **Fill in the blanks on the Initial Costs tab.**

   Again, unless you are comparing two loans (which I discuss later in this chapter), just fill out the Loan A column.

3. **After you are done, click the Calculate button.**

   Money produces the Initial Costs total at the bottom of the window. In Figure 15-5, the figure is $22,820.80.

4. **Click the Loan Terms tab to return to the Loan Terms page, where you see how the particulars of the loan are affected by initial costs.**

   For example, if you entered a number in the Percent down text box because you plan to make a down payment on the loan or mortgage, the amount you borrow is lowered, as are the monthly payments.

Entering the variable-rate data

Your loan or mortgage may not have a fixed rate. Adjustable-rate mortgages (ARMs) have variable rates, and many lenders offer a low introductory rate for the first few months or years to entice you, after which they raise the rate.

Determining the cost of a variable-rate loan, also known as an adjustable-rate loan, is tricky. To figure out the costs, follow these steps after you have filled out the Loan Terms page of the Loan Planner worksheet:

1. **Click the Variable Rate tab.**

   You see the Variable Rate tab.

2. **In box 1, select Variable from the drop-down list.**

3. **Fill in the other boxes.**

   The other boxes ask when the first adjustment occurs, how much time passes between adjustments, the highest interest rate you can be charged for the loan, and how much you expect the interest rate to rise each year.

4. **After you are done filling in the Variable Rate page, click the Loan Terms tab to return to the Loan Terms page and see what the particulars of the loan look like now.**

Determining whether refinancing is worthwhile

When interest rates start to drop, homeowners get itchy. They ask themselves whether refinancing is worthwhile. *Refinancing* means to trade in one loan mortgage for another, less expensive loan or mortgage.

One way to find out whether refinancing is worthwhile is to enter the mortgage you are currently paying for in the Loan worksheet and compare it to a lower-interest mortgage.

Follow these steps to compare a mortgage you are paying to another mortgage:

1. **Open the Loan Worksheet and click the Initial Costs tab.**

2. **Click the Use My Loan button or enter the particulars of the loan or mortgage you currently have in the Loan A boxes.**

3. **Enter the particulars of the second, less expensive mortgage in the Loan B boxes, and click the Calculate button.**

Each tab offers Loan B as well as Loan A boxes. The previous sections of this chapter explain how the three tabs work. As you enter the terms of the loan in the Loan B boxes, you can do a side-by-side comparison of your present loan or mortgage with a prospective loan or mortgage.

4. **Click the Comparison tab to see a comparison of the two mortgages.**

Line 6, Break Even Point, tells you whether the savings you get from lower monthly payments cover the costs of refinancing and how long it will take to recoup refinancing costs. If line 6 shows "Never," don't refinance.

Comparing one type of loan or mortgage to another

As you must have noticed by now, the Loan worksheet includes boxes for Loan A and Loan B. Those boxes are for comparing one type of loan or mortgage to another to find out which is least expensive or which meets your needs better.

To enter the particulars of Loan B, fill in the boxes as the last handful of pages tell you to do. Each worksheet tab clearly compares the two loans, and you can also click the Comparison tab to see a summary comparison on the Comparison page. In Figure 15-6, I compared a 30-year mortgage at 7.5 percent interest (Loan A) to a 15-year mortgage at 6.25 percent (Loan B). The Comparison page tells me that I will pay $93,049.97 (144,779.45 – 51,729.48) more in interest payments on the 30-year mortgage, but that monthly payments on the 15-year mortgage will be $150.30 more (814.55 – 664.25).

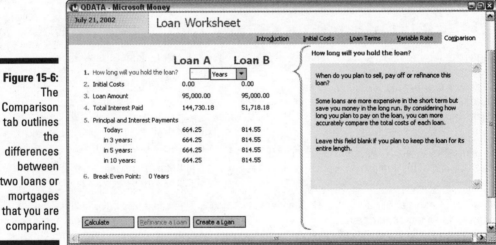

Figure 15-6: The Comparison tab outlines the differences between two loans or mortgages that you are comparing.

Finding Out What Houses Cost

Starting from House view on the Home Page, you can find out what houses cost in different parts of the United States and Canada. Click the <u>Find a Home</u> link, and, in the Houses for Sale Web page at HomeAdvisor.msn.com, declare the state and region where you are shopping for houses and how much you are prepared to pay. Then click the Go button and keep burrowing deeper and deeper until you come to real estate listings on the other side of the hill where the grass is greener.

Yahoo! offers a neat way to find out what houses cost. On Yahoo!, you can learn what houses sold for on a particular street or ZIP code. Sale prices are a pretty good indication of what houses will sell for. Go to this Web site at Yahoo! to start the search: `http://list.realestate.yahoo.com/re/ homevalues`. Then click the Comparable Home Sales link. As shown in Figure 15-7, enter information that describes where you want to look and click the Search for Home Sales button. You will see a revealing list of houses, sales dates, and sales prices.

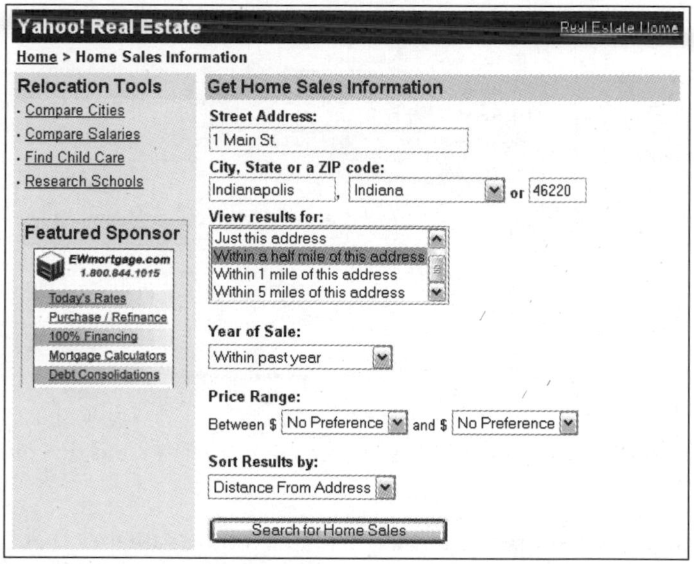

Figure 15-7: Yahoo! offers another way to check out home prices.

Cataloguing the Items in Your Household

Owners of Money 2003 Deluxe can catalog the items in their houses with the Home Inventory, a program for taking stock of what you own. Use the Home Inventory to establish the cumulative value of the things that you own or simply to make a detailed list of where all your stuff is. When you are done describing your valuable belongings, you can see how much they are worth (at least in your eyes) and how much you think it would cost to replace them.

To start the Home Inventory program, click the Start Tracking My Home Inventory button in House view on the Home Page. You see the Home Inventory window shown in Figure 15-8. The left side of the window lists categories for describing your valuable possessions. Notice the Total figures at the bottom of the window.

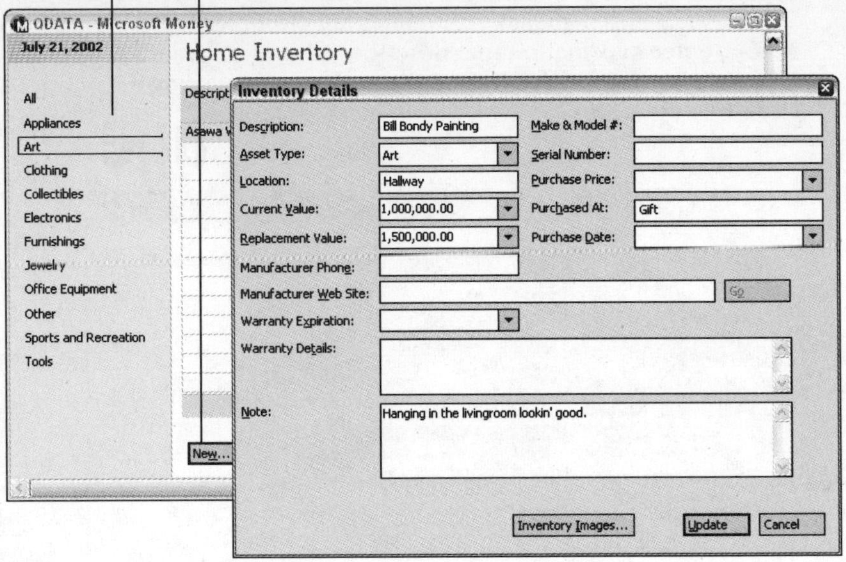

Choose All or a category.

Click New to catalogue an item.

Figure 15-8:
Click the
New button
to describe
a valuable
possession
and list it in
the Home
Inventory
window.

Follow these instructions to list the items you treasure and discover their cumulative value:

- **Catalogue a possession:** Click the name of the category that best describes your possession; then click the New button. Fill in the Inventory Details dialog box (refer to Figure 15-8) and click Update.

- **Survey your possessions:** Click a category to see the possessions listed there, or click All to survey all your possessions.

- **Update the value of an item:** Click the item and then click the Details button. In the Inventory Details dialog box, make new entries and then click the Update button.

- **Examine an item closely or find out where you stored it:** Click the item and then click the Details button. You see the Inventory Details dialog box.

- **Removing an item from the list:** Click the item and then click the Delete button.

Another way to inventory the things you own is to film them with a video camera. Go from room to room and film all the things that you have accumulated, and while you do so, describe them in intimate detail as though you were touting their merits to the audience of a TV game show.

Chapter 16

Tracking Assets, Liabilities, Loans, and Mortgages

Anything of value that you own or that adds to your net worth can be counted as an *asset* — jewelry, stock, the equity in a house, a vintage baseball card autographed by the great Willie Mays. The money in your checking and savings account is an asset. So is money that is owed to you.

A *liability,* on the other hand, counts against net worth. A debt that you owe is considered a liability. Credit card debt is a liability, as are taxes owed to the IRS, a mortgage, a student loan, and a car loan.

If you want a clear picture of your net worth or the net worth of your business, you need to identify your assets and liabilities. Fortunately, Money offers account types to track not only assets and liabilities but also loans and mortgages — two other critical elements in the net-worth equation. In this chapter, you discover how and why to set up and use these kinds of accounts. You also find out how to fine-tune them so that they track exactly what you want them to track.

Understanding How to Track Assets, Liabilities, Loans, and Mortgages with Money

If you think about it, all the accounts you can set up in Money fall either into the asset or liability category. The money in savings and checking accounts is an asset. Debt that you track in a credit card account is a liability. However, Money offers the following special account types for keeping a close tab on assets and liabilities:

- ✔ **Asset account:** For tracking the value of personal property, such as art collections, coin collections, and cars. If you use Money to track a business, you can create asset accounts for office equipment, trucks and cars, machinery, or anything else that adds to the worth of the business or can be used as collateral.

- ✔ **Car or Other Vehicle account:** For tracking the value of a car or boat. Even if you own a car, don't bother tracking its value unless you want to put it up as collateral for a loan or figure its value into your net worth.

- ✔ **Cash account:** For tracking cash on hand for business expenses. This very simple kind of account is for businesses that want to track petty-cash spending.

- ✔ **Home account:** For tracking how much equity is in a house. *Equity* is a house's market value, minus the amount that is owed on the house. For example, if $100,000 is owed on the house and its market value is $150,000, the owner has $50,000 equity in the house. Each time you make a mortgage payment, you can transfer the principal part of the payment to a house account and thereby track how much equity is in the house. A house account is a specific type of asset account.

- ✔ **Liability account:** For tracking no-interest debt, such as quarterly tax payments that you owe the IRS, property taxes, insurance premiums, or money you owe a friend. This account is for tracking business expenses.

- ✔ **Loan account:** For tracking loans on which you have to pay interest, such as student loans and car loans. Loans on which you pay interest are called *amortized loans.* With an amortized loan, part of each payment goes toward paying interest on the debt and part goes toward reducing the principal (the amount you borrowed). A loan account is a type of liability account.

- ✔ **Mortgage account:** Similar to a loan account, a mortgage account is for tracking a mortgage. A mortgage is also an amortized loan. And a mortgage counts, of course, as a liability.

Tracking the Value of a House or Other Asset

Ask most homeowners what their most valuable asset is, and they'll say their house. But ask them how much equity they have in that house, and you usually get a much less definitive answer — if you get an answer at all. And you would probably get the same response if you ask about other tangible assets, such as art collections, baseball cards, or office equipment. Money can help you peg the value of your assets.

Read on to find out how to track the equity in a house or the value of tangible assets, such as art collections, baseball cards, office equipment, and other property that you can sell.

Setting up an asset or house account

A Money house account and a Money asset account work exactly the same way. Setting them up is easy. You can find more specific instructions for setting up accounts in Chapter 2 (where I show you how to set up checking and savings accounts), but for now, follow these steps to set up a house or asset account:

1. **Go to the Account List window and click the <u>Set Up Accounts</u> link under Common Tasks.**

2. **In the Set Up Your Accounts window, click the <u>Add a New Account</u> link.**

   You see the first of several dialog boxes for setting up new accounts.

3. **Click the <u>N</u>ot Held at a Bank, Broker, or Other Financial Institution radio button and then click Next.**

   The next dialog box asks what kind of account you want to set up.

4. **Select Asset or Home and click the Next button.**

   You see the first of several dialog boxes that ask questions about the new account.

5. **Keep answering questions and clicking the Next button.**

   Only two questions may give you trouble:

   - **The asset's (or house's) current value:** When Money asks for the asset's current value, enter its value as of today if you just acquired it or if you don't want to track its growth since the time you acquired it. If you want to track how the asset (or house) has grown or shrunk in value since you acquired it, enter **0**; also, be sure to enter an appropriate date when Money asks when you acquired the asset.

- **Associate a loan with the asset (or house):** As the "Tracking Loans and Mortgages" section explains, later in this chapter, you can transfer the principal portion of a loan or mortgage payment to an asset or house account. By doing so, you can track how much the value of the asset or the equity in the house increases each time you make a loan or mortgage payment.

  To track value or equity increases this way, click the Yes radio button when Money asks whether you would like to associate a loan account with the asset or house. When you click the Next button, you see a dialog box for selecting loan accounts. From the drop-down list, select the loan account from which you will transfer the principal portion of the loan payments.

Home equity loans should be associated with a house. When you take out a home equity loan, you use your house as collateral. Even if you use the money from the loan to buy a car or boat, for example, associate the home equity loan with your house, not with the asset you purchased with money from the loan.

6. **Click the Finish button after you finish answering the questions.**

Recording changes in the value of an asset or house

After you set up the asset or house account, you can record changes in its value simply by opening the account register and entering amounts in the Decrease or Increase column. However, if you associated the asset or house account with a loan or mortgage account, changes in value are recorded automatically each time you make a loan payment. Follow these steps to record a change in value by hand:

What's your most valuable asset?

Did you know that your most valuable asset is not your car or truck, your most profitable investment, or even your house? No, your most valuable asset is you — your abilities and talents. They are the qualities employers value you for. And they can't be measured by any computer program.

1. **Open the register of the house or asset account.**

   Figure 16-1 shows an asset account for tracking the value of a Ming vase collection.

2. **Click the Update Current Value link.**

   You see the Adjust Account Balance dialog box, shown in Figure 16-1.

3. **In the New Ending Balance text box, enter what the value of the asset or home is as of the date you will enter in the next step.**

4. **Enter the date of the change in value in the As of Date text box.**

5. **Categorize the change in value in the Category for Adjustment drop-down menu.**

   For example, I suggest creating an income category called Increase Mkt Value (Increase Market Value) to record an increase in value, or a category called Decrease Mkt Value (Decrease Market Value) to record a decrease in value. Chapter 4 explains how to create new categories.

6. **Click the OK button.**

   In the Decrease or Increase columns of the account register, Money enters the amount by which the asset or home increased or decreased in value.

As you can see, the value of the Ming vase asset account in Figure 16-1 has fluctuated in the last couple of years, but the collection nevertheless is slowly increasing in value. Let's hope none of the vases gets broken.

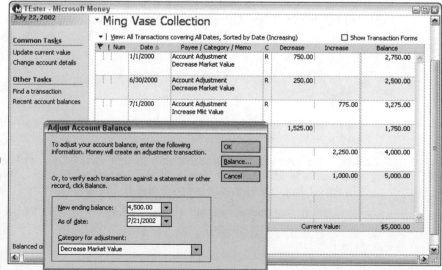

Figure 16-1:
To track the value of an asset, enter its current value.

Another way to associate an asset account with a loan account

Suppose that you set up an asset or home account but you forgot to associate it with a loan or mortgage account, and now you want to do that. Here's how:

1. **Open the asset account or house account register.**

2. **Click the Change Account Details link.**

3. **Scroll to the bottom of the Details window, and, under "Associated Loans," click the Add button.**

4. **In the Line of Credit or Mortgage Loan dialog box, choose Loan; then click Next.**

5. **In the Associate Loans dialog box, select the name of the loan or mortgage that you took out in order to pay for the asset or house.**

6. **Click OK in the Associate Loans dialog box.**

The Details window also has a Remove button. Click the button to sever the link between a loan or mortgage account and an asset or home account.

Associated Loans		
Loan	Balance	Add...
111 Main St.	33,333.00	Remove
		Go to Account
Total Outstanding Liability	$33,333.00	

Tracking Your Liabilities

Set up a liability account to track loans on which you don't have to pay interest, such as income tax payments. This is not the place for debts that fall in the credit card, line of credit, mortgage, or other interest-paying loan category, but does include anything else that counts against your net worth, such as insurance premiums.

It's hard to imagine anything easier than creating a liability account in Money. Follow these steps:

1. **Go to the Account List window, click Set Up Accounts, and click the Add a New Account button.**

2. **When Money asks for the bank or financial institution where the account is held, click the Not Held at a Bank, Broker, or Other Financial Institution radio button, and then click Next.**

   The next dialog box asks what kind of account you want to set up.

3. **Select Liability and click the Next button.**

4. **Keep answering questions and clicking the Next button.**

   The only time you may trip is when Money asks how much you owe on the account. Enter what you owe as of today if you just started owing or if you don't care to track how your liability has shrunk or grown since the time you started owing. If you want to track how the liability has grown or shrunk since the time you acquired it, enter **0**.

5. **Click the Finish button after you finish answering the questions.**

To record transactions in a liability account, click the Update Amount Owed button in the account register window. Then, in the Adjust Account Balance dialog box, enter a date and the amount you owe as of that date. Money will calculate increased or decreases for you in the register.

Tracking Loans and Mortgages

The following sections explain how to set up a loan or mortgage account for tracking amortized loan payments and mortgage payments. An *amortized loan* is a loan for which you make regular payments of the same amount. Part of each payment goes toward paying interest on the loan and part goes toward reducing the principal (the amount you borrowed).

Is creating a loan or mortgage account worthwhile?

Before you go to the considerable trouble of creating a loan or mortgage account, you should know that you may not have to create one to track mortgage or loan payments.

As long as the lender tells you how much you owe after each payment and how much you are paying in interest, you really don't need to track the loan. You can simply get the numbers from the lender and record the interest portion of the payment as a decrease in a liability account and the principal part of the payment under Loan: Loan Interest or a similar category. In other words, when you record the check you used to make a loan or mortgage payment, split the payment so that the principal portion is recorded as a transfer to the liability account and the interest portion is recorded in the Loan: Loan Interest category.

In the case of mortgages, business loans, and investment loans, the lender should send you a 1098 tax form at the end of the year that explains how much of your payments went toward interest. That is the amount you need to know for income tax purposes. To save time and heartache, you may as well let the lender do the work and get the numbers from the lender rather than track the loan yourself.

After you find out how to set up a loan account, I show you how to stand on your head and sing *Dixie*. Actually, I do no such thing. I show you how to record loan payments in loan account registers, handle irregular loan payments that involve escrow accounts, and record a payment above and beyond the amount you are expected to pay.

Setting up a loan or mortgage account

When you set up a loan or mortgage account, Money asks you all kinds of questions and uses the information to break down the loan payments into interest charges and principal reductions. With each payment you make on the loan or mortgage, Money reduces the amount you owe in the loan or mortgage register and records how much of the payment did not lower the total debt but went only toward servicing the interest in a mortgage or loan category.

Gather all the papers that pertain to the loan or mortgage and then follow these steps to set up a loan or mortgage account for tracking the payments:

1. **Go the Accounts window, click the Set Up Accounts link, and then click the Add a New Account link in the Set Up Your Accounts window.**

   You see the first of many New Account dialog boxes.

2. **Enter or select from the drop-down list the name of the financial institution that tendered you the loan or mortgage and click the Next button.**

3. **In the next dialog box, confirm that the financial institution you chose is correct, and click the Next button.**

4. **In the next dialog box, which asks what kind of account you want to set up, select Loan or Mortgage and then click the Next button.**

5. **Speed-read the "You are about to enter the Twilight Zone" message box and click the Next button.**

   No, it doesn't really say that you are about to enter the Twilight Zone. It just tells you what the dialog boxes in the New Loan Account wizard are about to ask you.

6. **Speed-read the next message, which explains the three types of general information that will be needed, and click the Next button.**

7. **You're borrowing money, and the Borrowing Money radio button is already selected, so click the Next button.**

8. **Enter a name in the Loan Name text box and choose to whom the payments will be made by entering a name in the Make Payments to box or by selecting a name from the drop-down list; then, click the Next button.**

   The name you enter will appear in the Account List window when you finish setting up the loan or mortgage account.

9. **Select Adjustable Rate Loan (ARM) or Fixed Rate Loan and click the Next button.**

   The interest rate remains the same in a fixed-rate loan or mortgage. In an adjustable-rate loan or mortgage, the rate of interest is subject to change.

   Which dialog box you see next depends on the option you choose in this step.

10. **If you selected Fixed Rate Loan in Step 9, select the Yes or No radio button to say whether payments have been made on the loan; if you selected Adjustable Rate Loan, enter the date that the first interest rate adjustment is to be made and enter the number of years or months between adjustments.**

    If you are setting up a fixed-rate loan or mortgage and you select the Yes, Payments Have Been Made option, you see an additional dialog box that asks whether to schedule all the payments made on the loan or mortgage since you began paying it. Money needs this information to create a loan payment schedule. Money can gather information for scheduling no matter how you answer this question.

    Click the Next button, of course, after you're done.

11. **Enter the due date of the first payment on the loan or mortgage.**

    Be sure to enter the due date of the first payment, not the next payment. Money needs the first due date to create the amortization schedule.

12. **Speed-read the next dialog box, which tells you how far you've come, and click the Next button.**

13. **From the Paid How Often drop-down list, select the option that describes how often payments are due (probably Monthly) and click the Next button.**

14. **Select the option that describes how the loan is calculated and click the Next button.**

    Home mortgages are usually calculated based on the date the payment is due; consumer loans (such as car loans) are based on the date the lender receives payment. However, you may have to dig into the paperwork that came with your loan or call the lender to find out how interest is calculated.

15. **In the following five dialog boxes, enter the amount of the loan, the interest rate, the loan length, the principal and interest, and the balloon payment, if there is one.**

Keep clicking the Next button after you make each entry. After you are done, your dialog box looks something like Figure 16-2. Click the Back button if you need to go back and change an entry.

Figure 16-2:
Calculating the particulars of the loan. If you leave one of the entries blank, Money calculates it for you.

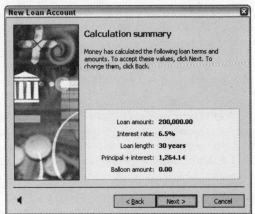

New Loan Account

Calculation summary

Money has calculated the following loan terms and amounts. To accept these values, click Next. To change them, click Back.

Loan amount:	**200,000.00**
Interest rate:	**6.5%**
Loan length:	**30 years**
Principal + interest:	**1,264.14**
Balloon amount:	**0.00**

< Back   Next >   Cancel

The Principal + Interest entry is a little confusing. What Money is really asking for is the amount of your monthly payment (or weekly payment or whatever). If you don't know the amount offhand, leave the box blank. Money can calculate payment amounts for you as long as you can provide information in the other four boxes.

When you enter the interest rate, be sure to enter the loan interest rate, not the compounded interest rate. The two are different.

16. **Speed-read the dialog box, which tells you how far you have come, and click the Next button.**

It's not as though you have any choice in the matter, is it?

17. **Type in category names or select the names from the drop-down lists; then click the Next button.**

When you make a loan or mortgage payment, the portion of the payment that goes toward interest is categorized under the category choice you make in this step. The portion that goes toward reducing the debt is recorded in the loan account register as a decrease in the amount you owe.

You can create a new category and subcategory if you want. If you enter names that Money doesn't know, you see the New Category wizard. Fill in the dialog boxes (and click the Next or Finish button) to create your new category.

18. **Click Yes or No to tell Money whether or not interest on the loan or mortgage is tax-deductible; then click the Next button.**

The interest portion of mortgages and home-equity loans is usually tax-deductible. This is an important matter. If you aren't sure whether your loan or mortgage is tax deductible, ask an accountant.

19. **If part of your payment goes toward fees such as escrow accounts, click the Other Fees button; otherwise, click the Next button.**

This dialog box asks whether you must pay fees on top of the principal and interest payments that are due. Chiefly, this dialog box is for people who pay into escrow accounts when they make their mortgage payments. An *escrow account* is an account that a mortgage company takes out on behalf of a borrower to make sure that property taxes and property insurance get paid.

If you click the Other Fees button, you see the Other Fees dialog box shown in Figure 16-3. This box works exactly like the Transaction with Multiple Categories dialog box I describe in Chapter 3. Use the Other Fees dialog box to categorize the fees you have to pay; then click the Done button.

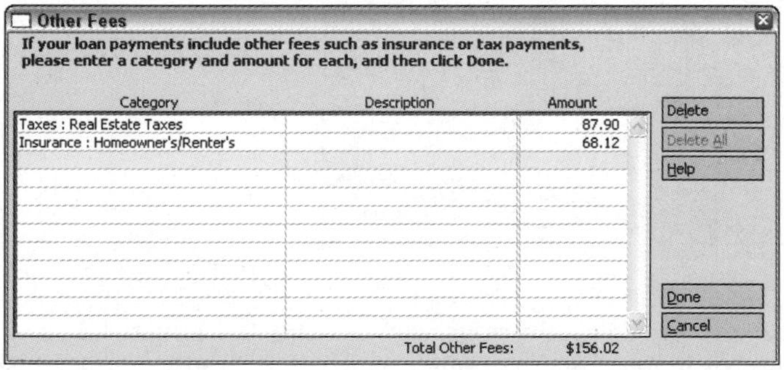

Figure 16-3:
Describing the part of a monthly payment that goes toward escrow fees.

Category	Description	Amount	
Taxes : Real Estate Taxes		87.90	Delete
Insurance : Homeowner's/Renter's		68.12	Delete All
			Help

Other Fees

If your loan payments include other fees such as insurance or tax payments, please enter a category and amount for each, and then click Done.

Done
Cancel

Total Other Fees: $156.02

20. **If you want to schedule a payment in the Bills & Deposits window so that you are reminded when payments are due, click Yes, Remind Me, fill in the dialog box, and click the Next button; otherwise, click No, Do Not Remind Me and then click the Next button.**

Chapter 11 explains how the Bills & Deposits window works. I strongly recommend scheduling the loan or mortgage payment. Lenders charge hefty fees for late payments. By scheduling your loan or mortgage payment, you increase your chances of paying it on time.

21. **Study the Summary Information dialog box and then click the Next button.**

    As shown in Figure 16-4, the next dialog box you see provides a rundown of all the information you gave Money in the last *(whew!)* 20 steps. Study this dialog box for a moment, and if anything is wrong, start clicking the Back button like crazy until you reach the dialog box where you can correct the error.

22. **If you want to associate your new mortgage or loan account with a house or asset account, click Yes, click the Next button, and select the asset or house account from the dialog box; otherwise, click No and then click the Finish button.**

    The dialog box you see if you click Yes asks whether you want to associate an asset account with this loan account. Choose the account from the drop-down menu and then click the Next button.

Figure 16-4:
The Summary Information dialog box sums up all the information you gave Money.

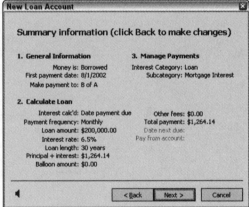

If you already created a house account for tracking the equity in a house, or if you already created an asset account for tracking the value of a car or other asset, you can associate your house or asset account with the loan account you are almost finished setting up.

You can always go back later and associate an asset or house account with your new loan account (see the sidebar "Another way to associate an asset account with a loan account," earlier in this chapter).

23. **Make sure that the I Have No Other Accounts radio button is selected; then click the Finish button.**

    Even if you had another loan account to set up, you wouldn't set it up now, would you? Who wants to suffer through this ordeal all over again?

    In the Account List window, you can find your new loan or mortgage account listed under "Loans and Liabilities."

See how much you're paying in interest

Are you curious about how much you spend in interest payments over the life of a loan? Want to know how much the total payments on a loan are?

To find out, open the account register where you track the loan or mortgage, click the Analyze Loan button, and choose View Loan Amortization Schedule. You see a Loan Amortization report.

The report shows, over time, how much of each payment is devoted to paying interest and how much is devoted to reducing the principal. Scroll to the bottom of the report and you see the total payments and total interest payments. The report in the figure shows that, on a $200,000 mortgage, $255,085.82 is devoted to servicing interest and the total payments equal $455,085.82.

Date	Payment Number	Payment Amount	Principal	Interest	Principal Balance
6/1/2031	347	1,264.14	1,172.08	92.06	15,822.95
7/1/2031	348	1,264.14	1,178.43	85.71	14,644.52
8/1/2031	349	1,264.14	1,184.82	79.32	13,459.70
9/1/2031	350	1,264.14	1,191.23	72.91	12,268.47
10/1/2031	351	1,264.14	1,197.69	66.45	11,070.78
11/1/2031	352	1,264.14	1,204.17	59.97	9,866.61
12/1/2031	353	1,264.14	1,210.70	53.44	8,655.91
1/1/2032	354	1,264.14	1,217.25	46.89	7,438.66
2/1/2032	355	1,264.14	1,223.85	40.29	6,214.81
3/1/2032	356	1,264.14	1,230.48	33.66	4,984.33
4/1/2032	357	1,264.14	1,237.14	27.00	3,747.19
5/1/2032	358	1,264.14	1,243.84	20.30	2,503.35
6/1/2032	359	1,264.14	1,250.58	13.56	1,252.77
7/1/2032	360	1,259.56	1,252.77	6.79	0.00
Grand Total		455,085.82	200,000.00	255,085.82	0.00

Fixing loan or mortgage account errors

Suppose that you make an error when you set up a loan or mortgage account. One little mistake — an incorrect due date, for example — can throw everything out of whack. To fix mistakes you made when you set up a loan or mortgage account, open the account register, click the Change Account Details link, and click the Change Loan Terms link. You can find this link in the right side of the window (you might have to scroll to find it). Money opens the Change Loan wizard. Answer the wizard's question and keep clicking the Next button until you correct your error.

Recording loan and mortgage payments

If you are not tracking the principal portion of loan or mortgage payments in a loan or mortgage account, simply write a check to the bank or lender from whom you received the loan or mortgage and be done with it. But if you linked your loan or mortgage account to a checking account so that you can track how the amount you owe decreases with each payment, follow these steps to record it:

1. **Open the loan or mortgage account register with which you track the loan or mortgage.**

2. **Click the New button in the transaction tab.**

   A dialog box asks, "What do you want to do?"

3. **Click the Make a Regular Loan Payment Radio button and click OK.**

   You see the Edit Transaction dialog box, as shown in Figure 16-5. The amount of your monthly (or weekly or yearly) payment already appears in the Amount box.

4. **In the Account drop-down menu, choose the account from which you will make the payment.**

   Your choice is probably a checking account.

   Try clicking the Split button to see how much of your payment is devoted to reducing the principal and how much is devoted to servicing interest. In Figure 16-5, part of the payment is a transfer to a House account to show how the principal of the loan is reduced; part is categorized as Loan: Mortgage Interest. At tax time, you could run a report and see in the Loan: Mortgage Interest category how much you paid for the year in tax-deductible interest payments.

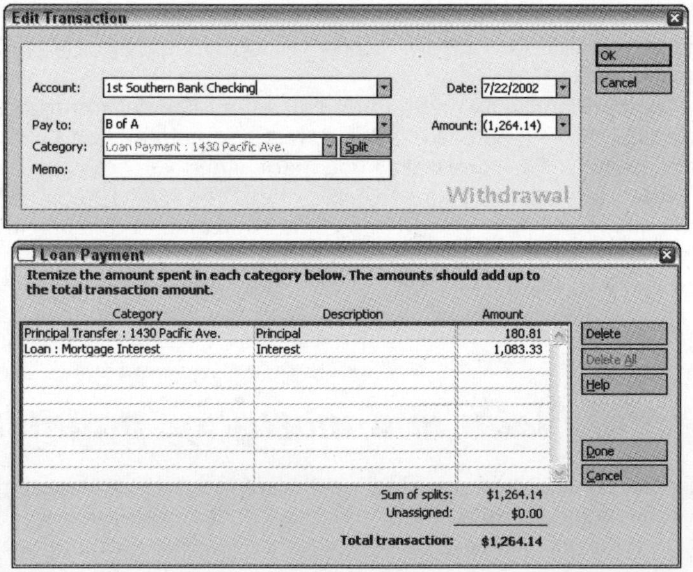

Figure 16-5: Click the Split button in the Edit transaction dialog box to see how much of a payment goes toward paying interest and reducing the principal.

5. **Enter the name of the bank or lender to whom you will write the check in the Pay To box.**

6. **Click OK.**

   In the loan account register, the balance is reduced by the amount of the payment that is devoted to reducing the principal of the loan.

The transaction is entered in both the loan or mortgage account register and the checking account register from which the payment was made. To go to the checking account in which the payment was made, right-click the transaction and choose Go to Account.

When you record a mortgage or loan payment, the payment is divided:

- The portion that goes toward reducing the principal (your debt) is recorded as a transfer to the loan or mortgage account. In the loan or mortgage account register, the balance is reduced accordingly.

- The portion that goes toward paying the interest is categorized as mortgage interest (or another category, depending on which category you selected when you set up the account).

- If you have to pay fees, the payment is divided even further.

Paying early and often

The faster you pay off an amortized loan or mortgage, the less you have to pay altogether, because much of the cost of an amortized loan goes toward paying interest. Suppose that you want to pay more than you are required to pay so that you can pay off the loan quicker and save on interest costs. How do you record a payment you've made above and beyond what the lender expects of you?

Follow these steps to record a larger-than-usual or extra loan or mortgage payment:

1. **Open the loan or mortgage account register.**

2. **Click the New button.**

   You see the dialog box that asks "What do you want to do?"

3. **Either make an extra payment or pay more on top of your usual payment:**

   - **Extra payment:** Click the Make an Extra Loan Payment radio button and click OK to go to the Edit Transaction dialog box (refer to Figure 16-5). Fill in this dialog box as you normally would, and enter the amount of the extra payment in the Amount box.

- **Larger-than-usual payment:** Click the Make a Regular Loan Payment radio button and click OK. Fill in the Edit Transaction dialog box as you normally would, and then click the Split button. In the Loan Payment dialog box (refer to Figure 16-5), increase the amount on the Principal Transfer line by the additional amount you're paying. Next, click Done. You see the Adjust Loan Payment Amount dialog box shown in Figure 16-6. Click the third radio button, Change Loan Payment Amount to Be the Sum of the Loan Split Amounts, and click OK.

Amounts you pay above and beyond what the lender expects go toward reducing the principal of the loan — they go directly toward reducing the total amount you owe. Therefore, you have to add the extra amount to the amount already shown on the Principal Transfer line.

For example, if the amount of principal you are scheduled to pay is $68.63 and you want to pay an extra $100 this time around, enter $168.63 on the Principal Transfer line.

4. **Click OK in the Edit Transaction dialog box.**

Figure 16-6:
Making a larger than usual mortgage or loan payment.

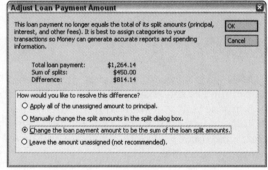

You are hereby encouraged to make extra payments on a loan or mortgage when you can afford to. Not only do you increase the amount of equity you have in the thing you borrowed money to purchase, you also dramatically lower the interest amounts you have to pay to service the debt.

Adjusting loan account balances

Money does its best to calculate interest and principal payments, but computers are only human and sometimes they make mistakes. When you receive a statement from a lender, compare the balance on the statement to the balance in your loan or mortgage account, and if the balances are out of line with each other, follow these steps:

1. **Open the mortgage or loan account register.**

2. **Click the Update Amount Owed link.**

   You'll find the button under Common Tasks. You see the Adjust Loan Balances dialog box, shown in Figure 16-7.

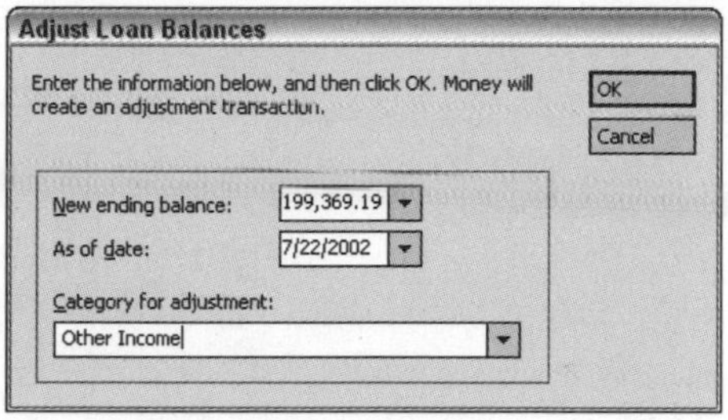

Figure 16-7:
Adjusting
the amount
you owe on
a loan.

3. **Enter the date shown on the statement in the As of Date text box.**

4. **Enter the ending balance shown on the statement in the New Ending Balance text box.**

5. **Use the Category for Adjustment box to describe the few cents' or few dollars' difference between your records and the lender's.**

   Select an expense category such as Miscellaneous if the lender's records show a higher amount than what your records show; select an income category such as Other Income if the lender's records show a lower amount.

6. **Click OK.**

   Money makes an account adjustment entry in the register and all's well that ends well, as Shakespeare used to say when he used Money version 1603.

Updating the interest rate on a loan

Suppose that the interest rate on your loan changes. If yours is an adjustable-rate mortgage (ARM), it's bound to happen sooner or later. When the interest rate changes, you have to burrow into your loan account and record the change.

To adjust the interest rate, open the loan account register and click the Change Account Details button. You land in the Update Details window. Scroll toward the bottom of the window and click the Update Interest Rate button. Money presents you with a series of dialog boxes for changing the interest rate. Keep answering the questions and clicking the Next button until, gratefully, you finish.

Chapter 17

Money for Investors

The title of this chapter is "Money for Investors." I hope you didn't come to this part of the book expecting to find 10-, 20-, and 50-dollar bills folded between the pages. No, you have to get money for your investments elsewhere. After you do, though, you can use Microsoft Money to track your investments.

In this chapter, you discover how to record the sale and purchase of mutual fund shares, stock shares, and bonds. You find out how to set up an electronic investment portfolio and examine the investments in the portfolio in different ways. You find out a lot of things, truth be told.

Your Own Electronic Portfolio

A *portfolio* is a collection of investments. This section shows you how to create an electronic portfolio for your investments like the one in Figure 17-1. After you have set up a portfolio like this one, recording investment transactions is easy. What's more, the Your Portfolio window is an excellent place to start analyzing your investments.

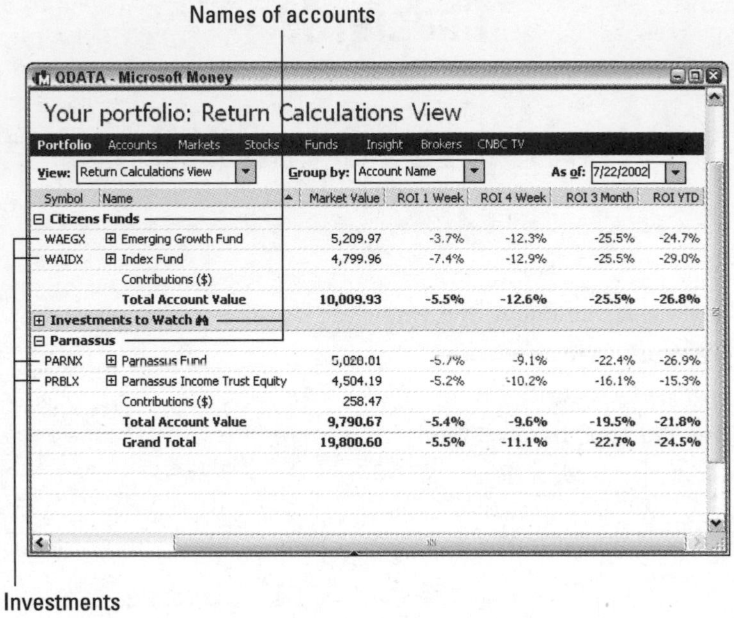

Names of accounts

Figure 17-1:
The Your
Portfolio
window
offers many
different
ways of
examining
your
investments.

Investments

Looking at Figure 17-1, you can see the following:

✔ **The names of the investment or retirement accounts.** Create one
investment or retirement account for each statement you receive from
a brokerage house, each financial institution you buy certificates of
deposit (CDs) or other investments from, and each retirement plan that
you participate in. Doing so makes keeping the records easier because
you can enter data in the account straight from the brokerage or bank
statement and even reconcile your account from the statements that
you receive in the mail.

✔ **The names of the individual investments.** After you set up the accounts,
you list the names of the securities — the stocks, bonds, mutual funds,
CDs, and so on — that belong in the account. You can then record purchases, sales, share reinvestments, capital gains, dividends, stock splits,
and so on in the register.

✔ **The grand total value of your investments.** This sum appears at the
bottom of the window, along with year-to-date capital gain and return
of your investments.

When your portfolio is complete, you can see at a glance the market value
and price of each investment. By changing views, you can see how your
investments perform, how they have changed in value, and how you have
allocated them, among other things. By clicking the Analyze My Portfolio
button, you can analyze investments in various ways.

However, before you can analyze your investments, you need to set up an investment account, retirement account, or Employee Stock Option account. Better read on.

Setting up an investment account for tracking securities

The first step in tracking investments is to create a new account for each institution, brokerage house, or retirement plan that you trade with or participate in. After you set up an investment account, you describe the securities that the account tracks. Spread the last statement from the bank or brokerage house across your desk and follow these steps to set up an investment account:

1. **Click the Account List button to go the Account List window.**

2. **Click the <u>Set Up Accounts</u> link.**

   You can find this link under Common Tasks.

3. **Click the <u>Add a New Account</u> link.**

   After you click it, the first New Account dialog box appears.

4. **Enter the name of the brokerage house or bank where you keep the account in the text box, or select a name from the drop-down list; then click the Next button.**

   If Money doesn't recognize the name you entered, you see the Confirm Your Name dialog box. Choose a name from the list of financial institutions' names and click Next.

5. **Select the Investment account type and click the Next button.**

6. **In the next dialog box, enter a name for the account.**

   The name you enter will appear on the Account List window after you finish setting up the account. For convenience' sake, you may want to enter the name of the brokerage house where you keep the account.

7. **Click the <u>T</u>axable or Tax D<u>e</u>ferred or Tax Free option button to specify whether the money you track in this account is tax deferred; then click the Next button.**

   Tax deferred means that you don't have to pay income tax on the money that the account generates until you begin withdrawing it at retirement age. Probably the option button to click is Taxable. Most tax-deferred accounts are retirement accounts (how to set up a retirement account is explained shortly).

8. **In the next dialog box, click the No, I'll Do This Later option button; then click Next.**

   A bit later in this chapter, in the section "Describing the Securities in Investment and Retirement accounts," I show you how to record security transactions in an Investment account.

9. **In the next dialog box, enter the approximate value of the account in the Investments text box, as shown in Figure 17-2.**

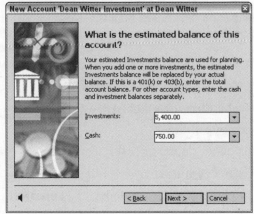

Figure 7-2:
Setting up an investment account.

   Don't worry about being accurate with these figures — they are used for planning and estimating purposes only. You can get the estimated value of the investments in the account from your most recent statement. Don't include cash in the estimated value of the account if you keep cash as well as investments in the account. If you recently sold a security or made a deposit in the account, it likely includes a bit of cash.

10. **Enter the amount of money in the account in the Cash text box.**

    As the dialog box explains, you can estimate the amount of money in the cash account if you want. The amounts you enter in the dialog box are used for planning purposes.

11. **Click the I Have No Other Accounts at This Institution option button and click Next.**

12. **Click the Finish button.**

    Uncheck the Go to Online Setup for *Your Brokerage Firm* option button and the last dialog box. That button is for setting up Money so that you can bank online with the brokerage firm. If you want to do bank online, see Chapter 7.

After you set up the investment account, go to its Details window and enter the name and phone number of your broker. You need that information in case you need to call your broker. You can enter other useful information in the Details window as well. To get to an account's Details window, right-click its name in the Account List window and choose See Account Details.

Setting up a retirement account for tracking retirement savings and investments

Follow these steps to set up an account for tracking the tax-deferred investments you have made for your retirement:

1. **Click the Account List button to go the Account List window.**

2. **Click the <u>Set Up Accounts</u> link.**

3. **Click the <u>Add a New Account</u> link.**

   You see the first New Account dialog box.

4. **Enter the name of the brokerage house or bank where the account is kept or select a name from the drop-down list; then click the Next button.**

   If Money doesn't recognize the name you entered, choose a brokerage firm from the list in the next dialog box that appears.

5. **Select the Retirement account type and click the Next button.**

6. **In the next dialog box, enter a name for the account and click the Next button.**

   The name you enter will appear on the Account List window after you finish setting up the account.

7. **In the next dialog box, as shown in Figure 17-3, click the type of retirement account you want to set up; then click the Next button.**

   If you aren't sure what kind of retirement account you are dealing with, refer to the glossary at the back of this book or click an account type and read its description in the dialog box.

8. **If you track a spouse's or partner's finances with Money, choose the name of the person whose retirement account you want to track; then click the Next button.**

   Money gets the name or names on the list from the survey you take when you install the program, but if you didn't take the survey, don't worry about it. Enter the name and then fill in the dialog boxes to describe yourself or your spouse or partner.

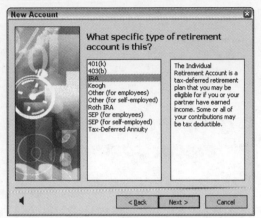

Figure 7-3:
Setting up a
retirement
account.

9. **In the next dialog box, choose the No, I'll Do This Later option button; then click Next.**

   Later in this chapter, in the section, "Describing the Securities in Investment and Retirement accounts," I show you how to record transactions in the account.

10. **In the next dialog box, enter the approximate value of the account in the Investments text box.**

    These figures are used strictly for planning and estimating purposes. You will be given ample opportunity to enter the exact numbers later on. Check your recent statement for the estimated value of the investments in the account. If cash is in the account at present, don't include it in the estimated value.

11. **Enter the amount of money in the account in the Cash text box.**

    As the dialog box explains, you can estimate the amount of money in the cash account if you want.

12. **Choose the second option button, I Have No Other Accounts at This Institution, and click Next.**

13. **Click the Finish button.**

Know the tax status of your investment

Don't confuse tax-deferred income with tax-exempt income. Income from a tax-deferred account is not taxed until you start withdrawing money from the account. In contrast, you never have to pay any tax on tax-exempt income. Most retirement accounts are tax deferred, not tax exempt.

Setting up an account to track employee stock options

If you are fortunate enough to work for a company that offers stock options to its employees, you can track the value of that stock with Money. To do so, create an investment account (see "Setting up an investment account for tracking securities," earlier in this chapter), fill in the New Account dialog boxes, and choose Employee Stock Option when you are asked what kind of account you want to set up (refer to Figure 17-3).

By now you must surely know how to set up an account in Money. Besides the usual questions, you are asked for the date you were granted the stock, how many shares you were granted, and the *strike price* — the closing price of the stock on the day it was given to you. Other than that, the only unusual screen you need to fill out is the one shown in Figure 17-4. This is where you tell Money how quickly or slowly the stock grant becomes yours.

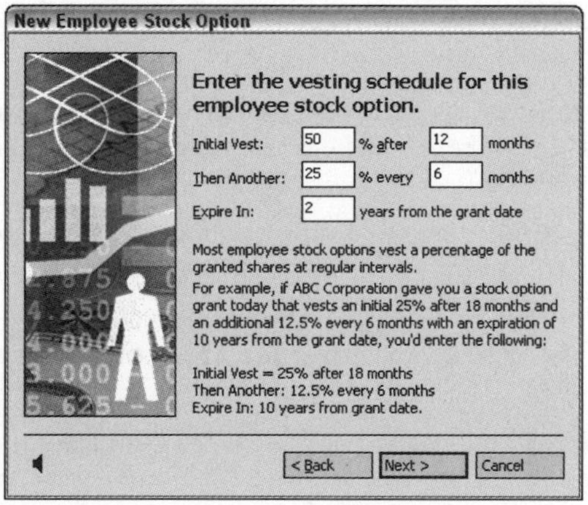

Figure 7-4:
Fill in the text boxes to describe how, slowly but surely, you become the owner of the stocks your company has granted you.

In most companies, employees are not given stocks outright. Instead, they become vested in the stocks they own over a period of time. Use the text boxes on the New Employee Stock Option dialog box to describe how your company's plan calls for you to be vested in the stock you were granted.

When you finish setting up the account, open its register. You see future entries that describe when you will receive new stock as part of the vesture. As you update the stock price in this register, it shows the stock's value.

Describing the Securities in Investment and Retirement Accounts

After you set up an investment or retirement account, you must describe each security in the account. *Securities* are the stocks, mutual funds, certificates, bonds, or other financial instruments that the account tracks. Gather the paperwork and follow these steps to describe each security that you own. If you just purchased more shares of a security that you already own, skip ahead to "Recording a purchase of more stocks or more bonds" or "Recording the sale or purchase of mutual funds."

1. **Click the Portfolio button on the Navigation bar or choose Investing⇨ Portfolio to go to the Your Portfolio window.**

   The window is the starting point for handling, managing, and analyzing investments.

2. **Click the <u>Add an Investment</u> link.**

   You'll find the link under Common Tasks on the left side of the window. After you click it, the first New Investment dialog box appears.

3. **Click the down arrow to open the Account drop-down menu, and choose the investment or retirement account where you track the security; then click Next.**

   If no account names appear on the menu, you haven't set up an investment or retirement account yet. The start of this chapter explains how to do that.

4. **In the Investment Name text box, enter the name of the security; then click Next.**

   The name you enter will appear in your portfolio. You see the Create New Investment dialog box, shown on the left side of Figure 17-5. In this dialog box, you tell Money what kind of investment you are tracking.

5. **Click an option button to describe the security and then click Next.**

   Which dialog box you see next depends on which option button you chose in Step 5. In Figure 17-5, I chose the Stock option button, so the New Stock dialog box asks me to enter the stock's symbol. Except for bonds, Money asks for your investment's ticker symbol. In the case of a bond, you will be asked for the coupon rate, interest paid, maturity date, and call date.

6. **Fill in the New dialog box or New dialog boxes and then click the Finish button.**

   If you can, enter the ticker symbol for your mutual fund, stock, CD, or money market fund in the New dialog box (refer to Figure 17-5). That way, you can update the security's price from the Internet and save a lot of time that you would otherwise spend updating the price by hand.

(Chapter 9 shows you how to update security prices from the Internet.) If you don't know the ticker symbol, look for it carefully on your brokerage statement — you can usually find it there. Or try clicking the Find Symbol button to go on the Internet and find the ticker symbol.

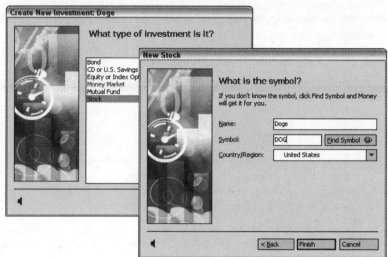

Figure 17-5:
Telling
Money
what kind
of security
you are
dealing
with.

7. **In the following dialog box, shown in Figure 17-6, enter in the Quantity text box the number of shares of the security you own.**

   For mutual funds and stocks, enter the number of shares you own. If you are describing the purchase of a single CD or bond, enter **1**. For investments such as precious metals, enter the number of ounces or other unit of measurement.

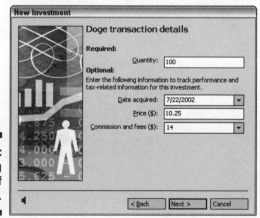

Figure 17-6:
Describing
the value of
the security.

You don't have to fill in the bottom three boxes in the New Investment dialog box, but do so if you intend to track the value of the security from the day you purchased it. By filling in these boxes, you can analyze your investment to see how it has grown or shrunk over time.

8. **In the** <u>D</u>**ate Acquired text box, enter the date that you purchased the security; enter the price per unit you paid in the** <u>P</u>**rice text box; enter the commission if you paid one in the** <u>C</u>**ommission/Fee text box; click the Next button.**

When you enter share prices of stock, you can enter fractions. For example, you can enter 50½ or 10¼. Money converts the entry to a decimal.

For bonds, enter the price of a bond as a percentage of the bond's par value (its face value). For example, if the bond's par value is $1,000 and its price is $950, enter **95** in the Price text box.

If you are tracking the value of this security from the day you bought it, be sure to enter data about your original purchase. You may have bought more shares in the security or sold shares in the past. The value may have gone up or down. You need to enter purchase data as of the date you enter back in the Date Acquired text box.

9. **Click the Finish button if you are done entering securities in the account; if other securities need listing, click the** <u>Y</u>**es button, click the Next button, and return to Step 3.**

Do not pass Go and do not collect $200.

Watch List: Tracking securities you don't own

Suppose that you want to track a stock, mutual fund, money market fund, or other security that you don't own, perhaps to decide whether you want to buy it later. You can do that by placing the security on the Watch List, a special portfolio category that Money maintains for monitoring security prices.

Getting price quotes for securities on the Watch List is a great way to find out from day to day or week to week how a potential investment performs. You can even download index prices in order to compare and contrast the securities you own to the performance of an index.

To add securities to the Watch List, click the <u>Add an Investment</u> link in the Your Portfolio window and describe the investment as you normally would, but choose Investments to Watch in the Account drop-down menu. (If you don't see Investments to Watch on the Your Portfolio window, click the See a Different View button and choose Show Watch Accounts on the submenu.)

Next time you download quotes from the Internet, you can see how the investment has performed. Watch List investments appear along with other investments in the Your Portfolio window, where you can study their performance. Right-click a security and choose See Price History to see a chart that shows how well or poorly the security has performed in the past six months.

Repeat the nine steps for each security that the account tracks, and then read on to find out how to update the prices of the securities.

Editing an Investment or Retirement Account Transaction

Suppose that you enter a transaction in an investment or retirement account incorrectly. It can happen. And when it does happen, you will be glad to know, you can edit it by using the same techniques you use to edit a transaction in a checking account or savings account — by going into the account register and making the change.

To edit an investment or retirement account transaction, open its account register. Click the Portfolio button on the Navigation bar to go to the Your Portfolio window. Then click the name of the account with the transaction that needs changing to open its account register, find the transaction, click it, and click the Edit button in the transaction form. As shown in Figure 17-7, the transaction form shows the transaction. Now you can edit it to your heart's content.

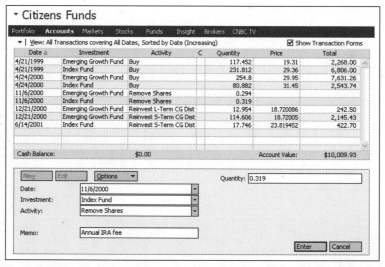

Figure 17-7: Click a transaction and then click the Edit button to change it.

A fast way to open an account register where you track retirement or investment securities is to click the <u>Work with Investments</u> link in the Your Portfolio window and click the name of the security on the submenu that appears.

Updating the Price of a Security

By tracking changes in the value of a security, you can analyze the performance of your investments and the change in the value of your portfolio over time.

By far the fastest and most accurate way to update the price of a security is to download the information from the Internet. Chapter 9 explains how.

Follow these steps to manually update the price of a security in your portfolio:

1. **Open the Your Portfolio window.**

   To get there, click the Portfolio button on the Navigation bar.

2. **Click the <u>Update Prices</u> link and choose Update Price Manually from the submenu, as shown in Figure 17-8.**

   You see the Update Price dialog box, also shown in Figure 17-8.

3. **Click the arrow to open the <u>I</u>nvestment drop-down list and select the investment whose price you want to update.**

4. **In the <u>D</u>ate box, enter the date that the price changed.**

5. **Enter the new price in the <u>P</u>rice text ($) box.**

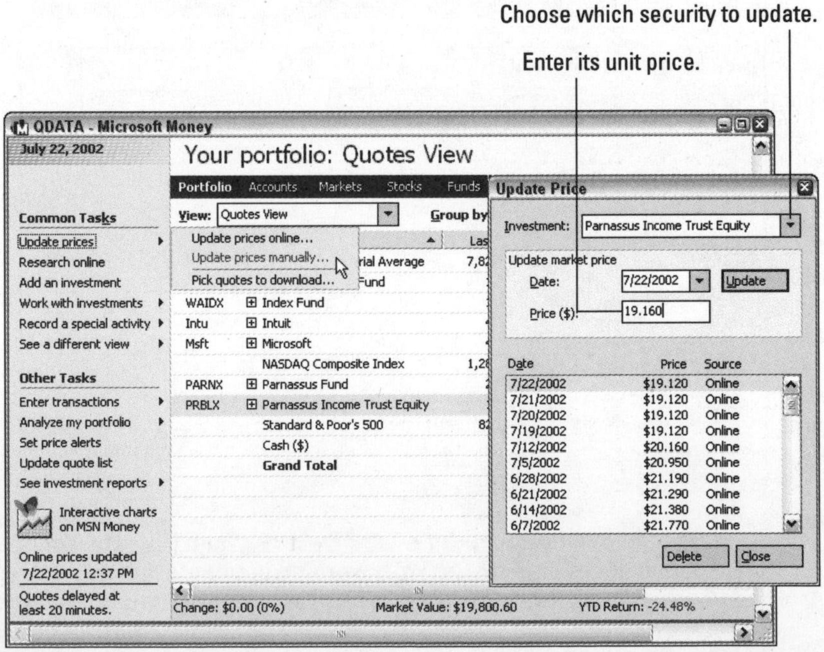

Choose which security to update.

Enter its unit price.

Figure 17-8:
Report changes in the price of a security in the Update Price dialog box.

6. **Click the Update button.**

   The new price is entered in the price history list. Note in Figure 17-6 that the Source column says "Online" next to the entries. When you enter a price yourself, the column says "Update," but it says "Online" when you get prices from the Internet.

7. **If you want to record the price history of a security, keep entering new dates and new security prices; otherwise, select a new security from the Investment drop-down list and update its price.**

8. **Click the Close button when you're done.**

Recording Payments to and Disbursements from Brokers

It might seem kind of odd, but when you write a check to a broker or make a contribution to a retirement account, you do so by transferring the money from your checking account to the account where you track your investments or retirement savings. Go ahead and make out the check as you normally would. Enter the brokerage house's name in the Pay To text box, but instead of categorizing the check, choose a Transfer option from the bottom of the Category drop-down menu, as shown in Figure 17-9.

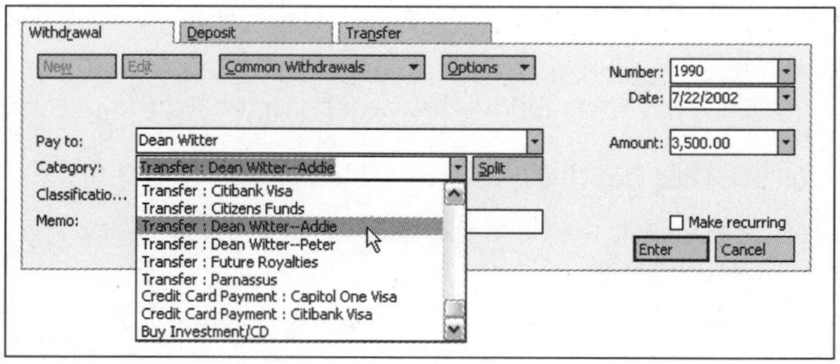

Figure 17-9: Record payments to and disbursements from brokers as money transfers.

On the other side, in the investment or retirement account, the transfer is recorded as a deposit. The cash in investment and retirement accounts is used to pay for stock, bond, and other security purchases.

Similarly, when you sell or collect interest on a security, the proceeds are recorded as a cash deposit in the Deposit column of the investment or retirement account. Suppose that you decide to take money out of an investment or retirement account. When the check comes from your broker and you deposit it in your bank account, record the transaction as a transfer from your investment or retirement account to your bank account. For example, if you sell a stock and make a $400 dollar profit, record the transaction as a $400 transfer from your investment account to the checking account where you deposit the $400.

You can click the Cash Transactions button (found on the left side of the register window) when you are looking at an investment or retirement account to see money transfers in and out of the account.

Handling Stocks and Bonds

Keeping track of stocks and bonds — especially stocks — is probably the most problematic task you will ever undertake with Money. Merely figuring out what a short sell is, not to mention a margin buy and a stock split, is hard enough to begin with. How can you record these strange events in an investment or retirement account register?

Read on, friend, and you can discover how to record everything from stock sales and purchases to short sells and margin buys.

Recording a purchase of more stocks or more bonds

When you purchase more shares of a stock you already own or more bonds of a type you already own, follow these steps to record the purchase:

1. **Go to the Your Portfolio window.**

   To get there, click the Portfolio button on the Navigation bar or choose Investing⇨Portfolio.

2. **Click the name of the security you want to work with.**

   If you want to see a miniregister with other transactions that pertain to the security, click the plus sign next to the security's name.

3. **Click the <u>Enter Transactions</u> link and choose Record a Buy on the submenu.**

   You see the Edit Transaction dialog box, as shown in Figure 17-10.

4. **Click the Ne<u>w</u> button.**

   The Edit Transaction dialog box, shown in Figure 17-10, appears.

Click to see or remove the miniregister.

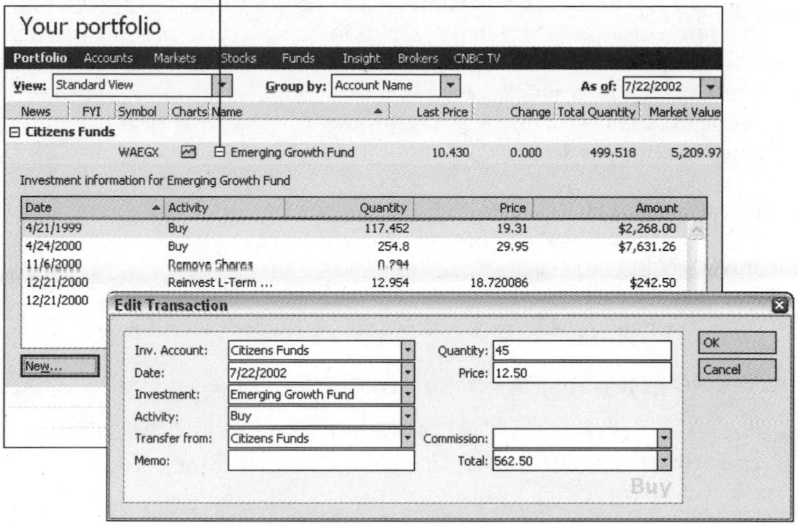

Figure 17-10:
Recording
the
purchase of
more stocks
or bonds.

5. **From the Inv. Account drop-down menu, choose the account where you track the investment, if necessary.**

   If you selected the right security in Step 2, it isn't necessary.

6. **In the Date text box on the transaction form, enter the date you purchased the stocks or bonds.**

7. **In the Investment box, click the arrow and select the security from the drop-down list.**

   Again, this isn't necessary if you selected the right security in Step 2.

8. **Select Buy from the Activity drop-down list.**

9. **Fill in the rest of the transaction form — the Quantity text box, Commission text box, Price text box, and Transfer from text box.**

   If you need help filling in these boxes, see the "Describing the Securities in Investment and Retirement Accounts" section, earlier in this chapter.

10. **Click the OK button.**

Recording the sale of stocks and bonds

Except for the problem of lots, recording the sales of stocks and bonds is pretty simple. A *lot* is a group of securities purchased at the same time for the same price (and also a nephew of Abraham whose wife got turned into a saltshaker, but that's another story). Suppose that you buy 10 shares of Burger Heaven at $10 per share in January, and then buy 10 more shares of the same company at $20 per share in February. In March, you sell 15 shares. How many shares you sell from the $10 lot and the $20 lot is important in determining how much profit you make and how much you have to pay in capital gains taxes. Fortunately, Money offers a wizard for helping you decide which shares to sell.

To see which stock lots you have purchased, click the plus sign to display the miniregister, click the More Investment Data button in the miniregister, and choose View Lots on the pop-up menu.

Follow these steps to record the sale of stocks or bonds:

1. **Go to the Your Portfolio window.**

   To get there, click the Portfolio button on the Navigation bar or choose Investing➪Portfolio.

2. **Click the name of the security you want to work with.**

3. **Click the <u>Enter Transactions</u> link and choose Record a Sell on the submenu.**

   You see the Edit Transaction dialog box (refer to Figure 17-10).

4. **Choose the investment account where you track the security, enter the date of the sale, and select the name of the security you sold from the Investment drop-down list.**

   If you selected the right security in Step 2, all you have to do is enter the date.

5. **From the Activity drop-down list, select Sell.**

6. **In the Quantity text box, enter the number of shares or bonds that you sold; enter the price in the Price text box.**

7. **If a commission was charged on the sale, enter the amount of the commission in the Commission text box.**

   Money enters the total amount of the sale in the Total text box. If the figure is incorrect, double-check the Quantity and Price text boxes to make sure that you entered the numbers correctly.

8. **Click the OK button.**

That's all there is to it — unless you purchased the shares in different lots. In that case, you see the What Shares Should I Use? dialog box after you click the OK button. Unless you tell it otherwise, Money assumes that you want to sell the shares in the lot that you purchased first. To do that, simply click the Finish button. But if you want to sell shares from different lots, follow these steps to tell Money which shares you want to sell:

1. **Click the first option, I Would Like to Specify Which Shares to Sell or Transfer, and then click the Next button.**

   You see the Allocate Lots dialog box.

   In this dialog box, you can select shares yourself from the lots, as the following steps demonstrate; you can click the Maximum Gain button to sell lots and pay the most capital gains taxes; or you can click the Minimum Gain button to sell lots.

2. **In the top of the dialog box, click one of the lots from which you sold shares.**

3. **Enter the number of shares you sold from the lot in the Enter Shares to Allocate from Lot Above text box.**

4. **Select another lot and repeat Steps 2 and 3 to tell Money how many shares you sold from it.**

   After you're done declaring which shares you sold, the Total Selected and Total to Allocate numbers in the dialog box should be the same.

5. **Click the Finish button.**

Be sure to notify your broker of which shares you want to sell. If you forget to do that, your broker may assume that you want to sell shares beginning with the first lot you purchased. Chapter 13 explains how to investigate the capital gains tax you have to pay on the sale of a security.

Recording and reinvesting dividends

Most stocks pay dividends, which means that you have to record dividends as they arrive. And some stocks and mutual funds, rather than pay dividends, give shareholders the opportunity to buy more shares with their dividends as part of a DRIP (dividend reinvestment program). The advantage of reinvesting a dividend is that you often don't have to pay a broker's commission to purchase the new stock.

To record a dividend or the reinvestment of a dividend, start from the Your Portfolio window and click the name of the security that paid a dividend. Then click the Enter Transactions button and choose Record All Details of a Sale on the submenu. You see the Edit Transaction dialog box (refer to Figure 17-10). Select Dividend or Reinvest Dividend from the Activity drop-down list and do the following:

✔ **Recording a dividend:** In the Total text box, enter the amount of the dividend. Be sure to select the account into which you deposited the dividend from the Transfer to drop-down list. Click Enter when you're done.

✔ **Recording a dividend reinvestment:** Enter the number of shares you purchased with the dividend in the Quantity text box, the price per share in the Price text box, and any commission in the Commission text box. Make sure that the total in the Total text box is correct before you click the OK button.

Recording stock splits, short sells, margin purchases, and other esoterica

The stock market, it seems, has a hundred different ways to trade stock, handle stock sales, and handle stock purchases. I suspect that the brokers like it that way because it makes them appear indispensable. Fortunately, you can use Money to record certain kinds of oddball stock trades and sales.

Stock splits

Occasionally, stock shares are split to lower the price of individual shares and make them more attractive to investors. In a 2-for-1 split, for example, investors are given twice as much stock, but the value of individual stocks is half what it was before, so the owner of 100 shares worth $2,000 now owns 200 shares worth the same amount, $2,000.

Follow these steps to record a stock split:

1. **Starting from the Your Portfolio window, click the Record a Special Activity button and then choose Record a Split from the submenu.**

   You see the Split Shares dialog box.

2. **Click the Investment down arrow and select the stock that was split from the drop-down list.**

3. **Enter the date that the stock was split in the Date text box.**

4. **In the Split the Shares text boxes, enter the ratio of new stocks to old ones.**

   For example, in a 2-for-1 split, enter 2 in the first box and 1 in the second box.

5. **Click OK.**

   In the Your Portfolio window, Money calculates and enters the number of shares you own. The total value of those shares, however, remains the same.

Short sells

A *short sell* is when you believe that a stock will fall in price and you attempt to profit by borrowing shares from a broker, selling them at a high price, and then buying shares when the price drops and using those low-priced shares to replace the ones you borrowed.

Suppose, for example, that you think that ABC Corporation's shares will fall below their current price of $20 a share. You borrow ten shares from your broker and sell those shares for $200. When the price drops to $15 a share, you buy ten shares on your own, pay $150 for them, and give the broker back his or her ten shares. By selling the shares that didn't belong to you first (for $200) and buying them later (for $150), you earn a $50 profit. Of course, if the stock rises in price, you end up paying the broker back out of your own pocket, not from the proceeds of the sale.

To record a short sell, fill in the Edit Transaction dialog box as you normally would, but select Short Sell from the Activity drop-down list. Typically, brokers charge interest for the shares you borrow. The interest is reported in the Commission text box.

Return of capital

A *return of capital* is a return of part of the price you paid for stock. Sometimes a return of capital is paid to investors in lieu of a dividend. You'll know when you have been paid a return of capital because your statement tells you so. To record a return of capital, select Return of Capital from the Activity drop-down list on the Edit Transaction dialog box. Enter the amount of the return in the Total text box and select the account where you will stash it from the Transfer to drop-down list.

Margin purchases

Brokers gladly lend money to buy stocks and bonds. Buying a stock or bond with money you borrowed from a broker is called *buying on the margin*.

To record stocks or a bond you purchased on the margin, record it as you would a buy, but select Other Expense from the Activity drop-down list. When you select Other Expense, a category box appears on the transaction form so that you can categorize the expense. Select an expense category from the category drop-down list to describe the interest you had to pay your broker for the loan.

Corporate mergers

When one corporation merges with another and the two swap stocks, you need to record how many shares are being issued for each share of the parent company and the share price that the parent company has to pay for each share of the company that it has swallowed.

How to record brokerage account fees

Brokers charge fees. Not a few of them have been known to nickel-and-dime their customers to death. How do you record brokerage fees in Money? The answer: You record transactions in the investment or retirement account register and select Other Expense from the Activity drop-down list on the transaction tab.

When you select Other Expense, the Category drop-down list appears so that you can categorize the brokerage fee. If the expense is associated with a particular security, select the security from the Investment drop-down list; otherwise, leave the Investment box blank. And make sure that the account from which you paid the fee appears in the Transfer from box.

When you own stock that is involved in a swap, go to the Your Portfolio window, click the Record a Special Activity button, choose Record a Merger, and fill in the Record a Merger dialog boxes.

Corporate securities spin-off

When a corporation spins off, drops off, or lops off part of itself and you own shares in the corporation, you need to record how many new shares the corporation is issuing for each old share. To do that, go to the Your Portfolio window, click the Record a Special Activity button, and choose Record a Spin-Off. Then fill in the Record a Spin-Off dialog boxes.

Handling Mutual Funds

Mutual funds seem to be everybody's favorite investment. A *mutual fund* is an investment company that raises money from shareholders and invests the money in a variety of places, including stocks, bonds, and money market securities. With a mutual fund, you let experts do the work of deciding what to invest in. All you have to do is collect the profits, count them, and hide them under your mattress.

Recording the sale or purchase of mutual funds

You record the sale or purchase of a mutual fund the same way as you record the sale or purchase of stocks and bonds. Earlier in this chapter, the sections "Recording a purchase of more stocks or more bonds" and "Recording the sale of stocks and bonds" explain how.

When you buy shares in the fund, select Buy from the Activity drop-down list; when you sell shares, select (duh) Sell. Be sure to accurately describe the number of shares you purchased or sold in the Quantity text box. And don't forget to enter the price per share correctly in the Price text box, either.

Recording dividends and distributions

From time to time, mutual fund managers send dividend distributions. More than likely, however, dividends are paid in the form of *reinvestments*. Instead of profits that your shares have made coming to you in a check, the profits are used to purchase more shares in the fund. Following are instructions for recording a dividend payment and for recording a mutual fund distribution.

Mutual fund dividend distributions

Follow these steps to record the receipt of mutual fund dividend distributions:

1. **Go to the Your Portfolio window and click the name of the fund from which you received a dividend distribution.**

2. **Click the Enter Transactions button and choose Record All Details of a Trade on the submenu.**

   You see the Edit Transaction dialog box.

3. **Enter the date that the dividend was disbursed in the Date text box.**

4. **From the Activity drop-down list, select the option that describes the dividend distribution.**

   Look on your mutual fund statement to find out which option to select:

   - **Interest:** An interest distribution

   - **Dividend:** A dividend distribution

   - **S-Term Cap Gains Dist:** A short-term capital gains distribution

   - **Mid-Term Cap Gains Dist:** A mid-term capital gains distribution

   - **L-Term Cap Gains Dist:** A long-term capital gains distribution

5. **Enter the amount of the dividend in the Total text box.**

   The Edit Transaction dialog should look something like the one in Figure 17-11. Make sure that the account into which you deposited the distribution appears in the Transfer to box.

6. **Click the OK button.**

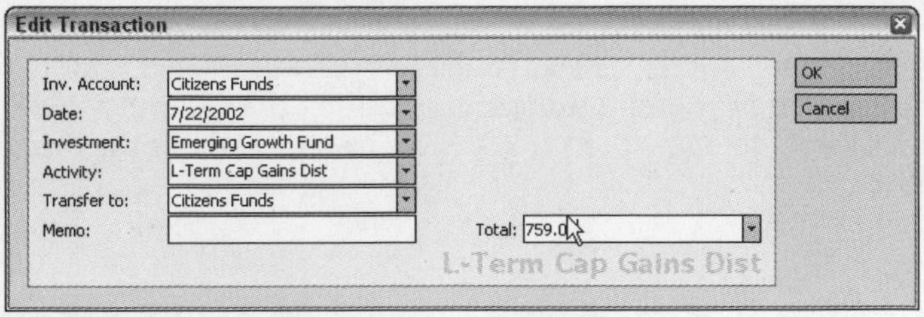

Figure 17-11:
Recording a
mutual fund
dividend
distribution.

Edit Transaction

Inv. Account:	Citizens Funds		OK	
Date:	7/22/2002		Cancel	
Investment:	Emerging Growth Fund			
Activity:	L-Term Cap Gains Dist			
Transfer to:	Citizens Funds			
Memo:		Total: 759.0		

L-Term Cap Gains Dist

Mutual fund reinvestment distributions

Follow these steps when the profits from a mutual fund are used to purchase more shares in the fund:

1. **In the Your Portfolio window, click the name of the mutual fund.**

2. **Click the Enter Transactions button and choose Record All Details of a Trade on the submenu to open the Edit Transaction dialog box.**

3. **Enter the date of the reinvestment in the Date text box.**

4. **From the Activity drop-down list, select the option that describes how the profits were reinvested.**

   Your mutual fund statement tells you which of these options to select:

   • **Reinvest Interest:** A reinvested interest distribution

   • **Reinvest Dividend:** A reinvested dividend distribution

   • **Reinvest S-Term CG Dist:** A reinvested short-term capital gains distribution

   • **Reinvest Mid-Term CG Dist:** A reinvested mid-term capital gains distribution

   • **Reinvest L-Term CG Dist:** A reinvested long-term capital gains distribution

5. **In the Quantity text box, enter the number of shares that the reinvestment purchased.**

6. **In the Price text box, enter the price of shares in the mutual fund.**

7. **If necessary, enter a commission you had to pay in the Commission text box.**

   One of the advantages of reinvesting mutual fund profits is *not* having to pay a commission to purchase the shares. Most funds do not require you to pay a commission when you reinvest. If your fund makes you pay a commission, complain about it to the fund manager.

8. **Click the OK button.**

Other Kinds of Investments

The tail end of this chapter is for investors who believe in precious metals and certificates of deposit. How do you handle those types of investment with Money? Read on.

Precious metals

To track precious metals in an investment account, treat the metal as you would stock shares and describe the investment by units of measurement. For example, to describe the purchase of two ounces of gold, record the purchase as you would a purchase of two stock shares.

You can use the same method to track commodities. For example, if you are the proud purchaser of five bushels of wheat, record the purchase as you would a stock purchase and count the five bushels as five shares.

Certificates of deposit

You can track the value of a certificate of deposit (CD) in an investment or retirement account by selecting Certificates of Deposit in the Create New Investment dialog box (refer to Figure 17-3). As the CD accumulates interest, record the interest payments by selecting Interest from the Activity drop-down list.

Analyzing and Comparing Investments

The fun begins after you enter the securities and list their prices. Now, starting from the Your Portfolio window, you can examine your investments in different ways. Like peering into the different windows of a house (with the occupants' permission, of course), you can stare into your investments from different angles and see whether you gain any insights that way. (Be sure to check out Chapter 9 as well — it offers techniques for going online and researching investments.)

 To get to the Your Portfolio window, click the Portfolio button on the Navigation bar or choose Investing⇨Portfolio. Next, choose an option from the View menu. Table 17-1 describes the nine different options from which you can choose. Test them all and see whether you can gain any insights and be a better investor.

Table 17-1	Ways of Examining Investments on the Your Portfolio Window
View Option	*What You See*
Standard View	Securities arranged by account. Choose this view to see in which accounts you keep securities.
Asset Allocation View	Securities arranged by type — stocks first, then mutual funds, CDs, bonds, and so on. Choose this view to see whether you incorrectly placed all your investment eggs in the same basket.
Performance View	Performance data, including how much you have profited or lost on each investment, the gain or loss by percentage, and the annual return by percentage.
Return Calculations View	Return on investment projections for the coming week, four weeks, year, and three-year period. Money makes these calculations based on investment type. Choose this view to see how the wizards at Microsoft think your investments will grow.
Valuation View	Value information about your securities, including their cost bases, appreciation, and increase in value.
Quotes View	Market data on each investment, including its latest price, latest change in price, and daily and yearly high and low.
Holdings View	The latest price, number of units you own, and market value of your investment holdings.
Fundamental Data View	Historical price information, including 52-week high and low prices and P/E ratios.

Choose Investing⇨Portfolio Analysis to get a very useful report about your investments and how they stand. The report tells you how your investments are allocated, which are performing best and worst, and your risk profile, among other things. You can also choose Investing⇨Investment Reports to generate an investment report. These reports are explained in Chapter 14.

Charting the Performance of an Investment

If you want to press your nose to the glass and get a very, very close look at an investment, double-click its name in the Your Portfolio window. That action takes you to the Price History window, where a chart shows you precisely how well the security is performing, as shown in Figure 17-12.

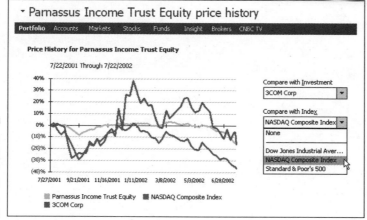

Figure 17-12: Charting the performance of an investment.

In the Price History window, make selections from the drop-down lists to compare an investment's performance with another investment or with an index. This chart compares the performances of two different stocks and the NASDAQ Composite Index over a one-year period.

Part V
The Part of Tens

The 5th Wave — By Rich Tennant

"I'm not sure — I like the mutual funds with rotating dollar signs although the dancing stocks and bonds look good too."

In this part . . .

Each chapter in Part V offers ten tidbits of good, rock-solid advice. With four chapters in this part, that makes 40 — count 'em — 40 tidbits in all.

You'll find suggestions for staying on top of your finances, improving your financial health, using Money when you are self-employed, and converting from Quicken to Money.

Chapter 18

Ten Things You Should Do Periodically

● ●

In This Chapter

▶ Back up your data file

▶ Update your savings and checking account registers

▶ Balance your bank statements

▶ Balance your credit card accounts

▶ Personalize the Home Page

▶ Generate an "income versus spending" report

▶ Print your account registers

▶ Make an archive file and put it away

▶ Prune your Payee list

▶ Stop and smell the roses

● ●

*T*his little chapter explains ten things you should do from time to time with Money. Do these ten things and you will live happily ever after.

Back Up Your Data File

Whenever you shut down Money, the Back Up dialog box appears, and you get an opportunity to back up your data file. Seize this opportunity! Grab it by both ears and shout, "Yes, I want to back up my data file." If you don't back up your file and something bad happens to your computer, you may lose all the financial data you so carefully assembled.

Chapter 10 explains how to back up a file — and how to restore a file from its backup copy. Be sure to back up your file to a floppy disk. The data needs to be outside your computer, preferably in a hidden place that is safe from hurricanes, tornadoes, and earthquakes.

Update Your Savings and Checking Account Registers

Breaking up may be hard to do, but falling behind is easy — especially when it comes to entering the checks you've written in a checking account and the transactions you've made in a savings account.

If you procrastinate, you fall further and further behind. Soon, updating your savings and checking accounts seems overwhelming. You stop updating your accounts, and not long after that, you stop using Money.

Set aside 10 minutes in the middle of the month and 10 minutes at the end of the month to update your account registers. Twenty minutes a month isn't that bad, is it? Okay, you may miss a third of an "I Love Lucy" rerun each time, and that could be the death of you, but life isn't exciting unless you take a few risks.

Balance Your Accounts

Balance your bank accounts each month when the statements arrive. Balancing, also known as reconciling, is easy to put off until tomorrow. However, if you keep putting it off, you end up with a stack of unreconciled bank statements and a bad case of the blues.

In Chapter 5, I explain a few tricks for recognizing and fixing reconciliation problems. After a while, you get good at balancing your records with the bank's. Not that you enjoy it, but you do start to understand it. Eventually, a minute or two is all you need to reconcile. No kidding.

Balance Your Credit Card Accounts

Not only do you have to record credit card purchases from the statement if you don't record purchases throughout the month, but you also have to balance your credit card account when the statement arrives. Balancing a credit card statement, as with balancing a bank statement, is one of those monthly jobs that's easy to put off until next month. Try to do it each month. If you don't, you get behind, become discouraged, fall into a state of despair, stop grooming yourself, stare at the ground a lot, and wear a permanent grimace on your face.

Personalize the Home Page

The Home Page is the first thing you see when you start Money. It is supposed to give you a quick overview of your finances — your changing finances, I should say. As your financial picture changes, as you buy and sell investments, or take on new debt, or win the lottery, or donate all you own to a worthy cause, periodically change what is shown on the Home Page so that you see precisely where you stand financially.

To change the Home Page, start by clicking the Customize button. Chapter 1 explains the Home Page in detail.

Generate a "Monthly Income and Expenses" Report

One of my favorite Money reports, and certainly one of the most revealing, is the Monthly Income and Expenses report. It shows in no uncertain terms where you spent all that money, how you earned it, and whether you earned more than you spent.

Chapter 14 explains how to generate and customize reports and charts. The Monthly Income and Expenses report shows spending and income in the past month, but you can customize the report to show what you did financially in the past year or the past six months, for example.

Print Your Account Registers

When you file your income tax return in April, print a copy of your account registers and put them away with the rest of your income tax stuff — copies of your returns, receipts, and bank statements. To print a year's worth of transactions, go to the Income and Expenses category of the Pick a Report or Chart window, generate an Account Transactions report, customize the report, and choose Previous Year as the date range. I explain how to generate reports in Chapter 14.

By printing the past year's transactions, you leave behind a wide, easy-to-follow paper trail that the IRS posse can follow if it audits you.

Make an Archive File and Put It Away

Besides filing away a printed copy of your registers, make an *archive file* and put it away, too. An archive file is a file in which you store transactions from a certain time period. Make an archive file of transactions from the past year and file it away with copies of your tax returns and other important tax records. That way, you have a file of one year's records that auditors can examine at their leisure. Chapter 12 explains how to generate an archive file.

Prune Your Payee List

Once in a blue moon, go into the Payee list and remove the names of payees you no longer write checks to or receive money from. Money enters payee names automatically in the Payee box on transaction forms. Type the first few letters, and Money immediately enters a name for you.

When the Payee list gets too long, however, Money throws outdated names in the Payee box. To keep from seeing the names of people and companies you haven't dealt with for months, prune the Payee list. Chapter 10 explains how to do it.

Stop and Smell the Roses

I'm going to propose a radical idea: Computers aren't as wonderful as many people make them out to be. Even when you're surfing the Internet or exploring new cyberspace worlds, all you're really doing is staring into the glare of a monitor.

You can easily get carried away with all the features that Money has to offer. If you own stocks and track them with Money, you may be tempted to download stock quotes each day from the Internet. If you've read Chapter 12 of this book, you know how to forecast your future income, and you may be tempted to find out, for example, how rich you'll be in the year 2013.

Money is simply a tool to help keep your financial house in order. It simplifies the task of tracking your finances so that you can devote time to other things. So do those other things! Stop and smell the roses. Money shouldn't be another computer toy that distracts you from the rich and intriguing real world, the one that begins just outside your computer screen.

Chapter 19

Ten Ways to Good Health — Financially Speaking, That Is

● ●

In This Chapter

▶ Record credit card transactions as you make them

▶ Pay off all your credit cards

▶ Leave your plastic at home

▶ Create a Spending by Category chart

▶ Create a Monthly Income and Expenses report

▶ Create a budget

▶ Plan ahead for your retirement

▶ Set aside money for a rainy day

▶ Make like a new dog — learn new tricks

▶ Take the day off

● ●

*W*arning: The Surgeon General has determined that not being in good financial health causes undue stress and worry and can lead to other health complications. The 10 tidbits of advice in this chapter are meant to improve your financial health.

Record Credit Card Transactions as You Make Them

You can very, very easily run up a credit card debt. A purchase here and a purchase there, and pretty soon you owe $3,000, $4,000, or $5,000. Ouch!

To keep from spending so much with a credit card, record the transactions as you make them. After you buy the expensive piece of stereo equipment or the designer-label jacket, carry the credit card receipt home, lay it flat on your desk, and record the purchase in a credit card register. Watching the amount that you owe climb higher may discourage you from buying so many things with your credit card.

Pay Off All Your Credit Card Debt

Paying down or paying off a large credit card debt isn't easy, but it's worth it because credit card companies charge outrageous interest rates on credit card debt. Unless you pay off your credit card each month, you're paying extra for everything you buy with your credit card.

Look at it this way: If your credit card company charges 18 percent interest (the common rate in the United States) and you don't pay off your credit card debt over the course of a year, you pay an extra 18 percent with every purchase you make. The fancy handbag on sale for $180 doesn't really cost $180; it costs $212.40 after you add the 18 percent. The two tires don't really cost $112; they cost $132.16.

Leave Your Plastic at Home

Do you notice a theme developing in this chapter? Sorry for harping on credit card debt, but it is the single most daunting obstacle that comes between people and their financial well-being. If you have trouble keeping credit card spending in check, try leaving your credit card at home. Studies show that people are far more apt to spend with a credit card than they are to spend cash.

Create a Spending by Category Chart

I can't get enough of Money's Spending by Category chart. It's easy to generate, and it shows so plainly and nakedly where you spend money. The first time I saw the chart was a revelation. "Eureka!" I shouted. "So that's where all the money went — to ice cream!" Actually, my two biggest spending categories were Taxes and Home: Mortgage, which wasn't a very big surprise. It was surprising, however, to discover what a large chunk of my income I spent in those two categories.

Chapter 14 explains how to generate a Spending by Category chart. Money can generate 28 different and revealing charts in all.

Create a Monthly Income and Expenses Report

Another way to get a good look at your finances is to create a Monthly Income and Expenses report. The report shows how much you earned in the last six months and how you earned it. It also shows how much you spent in each category and subcategory. Chapter 14 explains how to generate reports.

Reading down the Expenses list, you may find a few surprises. You may discover one or two categories in which you spent much more than you thought. Next time you consider buying an item that falls into one of those categories, think twice.

Create a Budget

Chapter 11 explains how to formulate a budget with Money. Formulating a budget takes an entire evening, but if you have trouble keeping your spending in check, it is an evening well spent. Also, Money makes it very easy to find out whether you met your budget.

Plan Ahead for Your Retirement

For some people, retirement is a dirty word. They don't want to think that far ahead. But you really ought to plan for your retirement for two reasons. First, to spend your golden years comfortably, you have to start saving now. Second, setting aside money for retirement is the best way to lower your tax bill. With 401(k) plans, SEPs, and other tax-deferred investment plans, the federal government has made saving for retirement very practical.

Chapters 12 and 17 describe how to use Money to help you lay the foundation for your retirement.

Set Aside Money for a Rainy Day

One of the first things that you realize when you read most financial self-help books is how important "rainy day" money is. Most authors recommend setting aside two month's income, the idea being that it usually takes two months to find a new job if you're bounced out of your present job.

Make Like a New Dog — Learn New Tricks

In Chapter 16, which describes how to set up an asset account, I explain that assets are things that add to your net worth — the money in savings and checking accounts, an object of value that you own, the equity in a house. However, you can't record your most important asset in an account register: Your most important asset is *you*.

Your talents, your abilities, and your know-how are your most important assets. As such, you can make like a new dog and learn new tricks. Go back to school and acquire a few new skills. Or volunteer somewhere, learn new skills, and acquire new experiences. Doing so can make you a more valuable employee to others.

Take the Day Off

To use one of those man-as-machine metaphors, sometimes you have to relax and recharge your batteries. Take the day off. In fact (I'm writing this chapter late Friday afternoon), take the rest of the week off! You deserve it. The object of using Money is to get more free time to enjoy yourself.

Chapter 20

Ten Things to Do If You Are Self-Employed

As of the year 2003, I will have been self-employed for 13 years. Not bad for a country boy from Idyllwild, California!

Being self-employed isn't for everyone. You need the right temperament, and you have to be willing to suffer the risks as well as reap the rewards. The following pages offer a few suggestions for self-employed people who use Money.

Diligently Record Your Financial Activity

One of the difficulties of being self-employed is that you have to account for all the money you spend. At tax time, you use your records, not those of an employer, to calculate how much income tax you owe. And because you can deduct certain expenses from your gross income on your income tax report, you have to record expenses as carefully as income.

Money, of course, makes recording income and expenses an easy task. But you have to stay on top of it. Don't let several weeks or months pass before you update your savings and checking account registers. Be sure to reconcile your account on a monthly basis, too. Falling behind is too easy.

Make Sure That All Tax-Related Expenses Are Marked As Such

Being self-employed, you can deduct certain expenses from your gross income when you file an income tax report. Office expenses, rent payments (if you rent an office), and any payment you make on behalf of your business is tax deductible.

To mark an expense as tax deductible, you assign it to a category or subcategory that has tax-related status. Chapter 4 explains how to give categories and subcategories tax-related status. Give all categories and subcategories that have anything whatsoever to do with taxes a tax-related status.

Print a Tax-Related Transactions Report for Your Accountant

Transactions that are assigned to a tax-related category appear on the Tax-Related Transactions report. Under the name of each tax-related category and subcategory, the report lists transactions and gives the total amount that was spent. For example, the report lists each transaction assigned to the Charitable Donations category. At the bottom of the list is the total amount you spent on charitable donations.

Charitable donations are tax deductible. An accountant who examines the Tax-Related Transactions report knows right away how much you can deduct for charitable donations. You don't have to pay the accountant to study your account registers and find charitable donations, because the numbers are right there on the Tax-Related Transactions report.

Chapter 14 explains how to generate reports. You can save a great deal of money on accounting fees by generating a Tax-Related Transactions report for your accountant.

Use the Memo Box Early and Often

As a self-employed individual, you have to track your own finances — your income, expenses, and so on. In account registers, you have to describe the money you spend and the money you take in. Usually, the Category boxes on transaction forms are adequate for describing your income and expenses, but consider using the Memo text box as well. When you record an odd expense, describe it in the Memo box in case you have to explain it to an accountant months from now, when you will have forgotten what it was.

Set Aside a Tenth of Your Income in a Savings Account

Being self-employed takes discipline. Employers deduct income taxes, Social Security payments, and Medicare payments from the paychecks of wage earners and salaried employees. Not so with self-employed individuals. The self-employed are responsible for paying their own taxes and Social Security.

You have to make the payments four times a year: on April 15, June 15, September 15, and January 15. More important, you have to be ready to make these payments, which means setting aside some of your income throughout the year to meet your tax obligations.

I suggest stashing a tenth of your income in a savings account. If you're making more money than the previous year, set aside more than a tenth, because you'll owe extra when April rolls around.

Schedule Your Quarterly Tax Payments

Missing or being late with a quarterly tax payment is catastrophic. Heads roll. There is much sorrow and gnashing of teeth. To make sure that you make the quarterly payments on time, schedule them. Chapter 11 explains how to use Money to schedule a payment. Depending on how you set up your Home page (see Chapter 1), you can make scheduled bills appear very prominently on the Home Page under Bills & Deposits.

Use Classifications to Track Business Expenses

One of the dilemmas of being self-employed is keeping your personal expenses separate from your business expenses. One way to keep them separate is to create a classification called Business and assign transactions that pertain to your business to the Business classification. See Chapter 4 for more about classifications.

Open a Checking Account for Business Transactions

Another way to keep business expenses and personal expenses separate is to open a checking account for business transactions. I got this idea from my accountant, who told me — mysteriously I thought — that I had "some ambiguity" between my personal and business expenses, but I could "resolve these ambiguities" by opening a business checking account.

Now, I deposit all incoming checks in my business checking account. When I need money for my family's personal finances, I transfer it into the family checking account. Expenses for office supplies and such that fall in the business category are all paid out of my business checking account. I'm unambiguous. I'm as cut-and-dried as a salami sandwich.

Write a Check to Yourself Periodically

My accountant also told me that I need to spend more money on my business. "Why should I spend more money?" I asked. "I'm trying to save money." He said that my overhead was extremely low and that I should "beef it up." To do so, he suggested writing down all the piddley cash payments I make — for pencils, bus fare, and so on — in a book, and when the total expenses reach $100 or so, to write myself a check for that amount. By doing this, I can spend more money on my business and lower my tax bill.

I was surprised by how much the little expenses added up. Personally, I don't like having to write down payments in a book, but I do like saving money on taxes.

Keep Your Irons on the Fire

In the days before the electric iron, when people used irons that were made out of, well, iron to smooth the wrinkles from their clothes, the person whose job it was to iron clothes had to keep more than one iron on the fire. While one iron was in use, a second and third iron lay on the fire. That way, the person who ironed clothes never lacked a warm iron.

If you are self-employed, you also have to keep more than one iron on the fire. You need to devote an afternoon every other week to looking for work. Looking for work means sending out your résumé, making phone calls, and maybe going to lunch. Looking for work does not pay well. In fact, the hourly wage for looking for work is zip. But looking for work is something you have to do if you expect to stay self-employed.

Chapter 21

Ten Things Ex-Quicken Users Should Know about Money

About six years ago, on the idea that "if you can't beat 'em, buy 'em," the mighty Microsoft Corporation made a bold attempt to purchase Intuit, the company that makes Quicken, Money's rival. Everyone shook hands and the deal appeared completed until the Federal Trade Commission stepped in. The FTC insisted that the deal created a monopoly and constituted unfair business practices.

After being rebuffed by the federal government, Microsoft redoubled its efforts to make a financial management application as good as or better than Quicken. I believe Microsoft has succeeded in doing that. As one who has written books about Quicken and Money, I know both products very well, and Money is the better of the two. It offers more features and it is better integrated with the Internet. I think the interface is easier to use, too.

This brief chapter is for people who have made the switch from Quicken to Money. I describe the chief differences between the programs and tell ex-Quicken users what to watch out for as they use Money.

You Can Use Your Old Quicken File in Money

Money offers a wizard that you can use to convert a Quicken data file to a Money file. Actually, the wizard doesn't convert the file. It makes a copy of the Quicken data file, converts the copy, and leaves the original data file intact. So if you decide after all that you like Quicken better than Money, you can go back to Quicken and continue using the data file as if nothing happened. After you convert a Quicken file, a new file called Qdata.mny opens on the Money screen. The file extension of Money files is .mny.

Before you convert your Quicken file, open the Quicken file and do the following to make the conversion go smoothly:

✔ **Back up your Quicken file so that the backup copy is completely up-to-date.**

✔ **Validate the file.** To do so, choose File➪File Operations➪Validate.

✔ **If you formulated more than one budget, open the one you want to keep.** Sorry, only one budget can make the trip from Quicken to Money.

Follow these steps to convert a Quicken data file to Money:

1. **Close Quicken if the program is running and open the Money program.**

2. **Choose File➪Convert Quicken File.**

   You see the Convert Quicken File dialog box.

3. **Find and select your Quicken data file.**

   Unless you tinkered with Quicken's default settings, the Quicken data file is called Adata.QDG, Quicken.QDF, or Quicken.QDT, and it is located in the C:\Quickenw folder.

4. **Click the Convert button.**

5. **In the Back Up dialog boxes, click the Back Up button to back up whatever data file is currently open in Money.**

   You land in the Quicken File Conversion window.

6. **Click the Next button and follow the on-screen directions.**

   When Money asks where you want to store your new Qdata.mny file, be sure to choose a folder whose name and location you will remember.

After the conversion is complete, a Summary of the Conversion window appears. It lists account balances in Quicken and account balances in Money. Compare the two to make sure that the Quicken data was converted successfully.

Some Things Are Lost in the Conversion

The following elements are not converted from Quicken files because Money does not offer similar features:

- ✔ Memorized charts
- ✔ Transaction passwords
- ✔ Category groups
- ✔ Savings goals

Some Quicken Features Have No Equivalent in Money

Besides savings goals, converts and forced converts to the Money 2003 standard edition will not find equivalents to Quicken alerts and the financial planners. You have to own Money 2003 Deluxe if you want to plan ahead.

You Can Find Out Exactly How Quicken and Money Differ

The Help program in Money has a page that tells you in excruciating detail what happens when a Quicken data file is changed into a Money data file. To read the page, choose Help⇨Help for Quicken Users. In the Help box, click Learn about Converting a Quicken File.

In Money, Transactions Are Entered on Forms

In my opinion, the biggest difference between Quicken and Money is that, in Money, you enter transactions on forms at the bottom of the account register. In Quicken, you enter a transaction by typing it directly into the register. True, you can choose View⇨Enter Transactions Directly into the Register in an account register window and enter transactions that way, but the people who designed Money make that hard to do. The drop-down lists are unwieldy and hard to use.

The transaction forms in Money take a bit of getting used to. Chapter 3 explains how forms work and how to record a transaction on a form.

You Get from Place to Place Differently in Money

In Quicken, you get from window to window by clicking buttons on the icon bar, by clicking Quick Tabs on the right side of the screen, and by clicking account buttons and activity buttons.

In Money, the chief means of getting from place to place are the buttons on the Navigation bar. Click one and you move to a different window. You can also get from place to place by choosing commands on menus.

You can use the old Quicken keyboard shortcuts to get around in Money. To do so, choose Tools⇨Options, click the Editing tab in the Options dialog box, and click the Keyboard Shortcuts for Quicken Users check box.

Your Quicken Checks Are Good in Money

Money puts Quicken check options in the Check Setup dialog box so that users who switch from Quicken to Money can use their Quicken checks. As long as you printed checks with Quicken, you can find the following options in the Check Setup dialog box:

- ✔ Laser Standard (Quicken)
- ✔ Laser Voucher (Quicken)
- ✔ Laser Wallet (Quicken)

Chapter 6 explains how to reach the Check Setup dialog box and select a check option.

If the Quicken check options do not appear in the Check Setup dialog box, choose Tools⇨Options and click the Print Checks tab. Under Printing Checks, click the Use My Existing Checks form Quicken check box.

Quicken's Online Banking Services Are No Good with Money

If you bank or pay bills online with Quicken, you can't pick up where you left off after you switch to Money. Sorry. You have to cancel the online services you use with Quicken, reapply for the services, tell you bank that you use Money now, and start all over again. Chapter 7 explains how to set up the online banking services in Money.

Your Payee List Is Way, Way Too Long

Quicken has a very nice feature whereby payees whose names haven't been entered in account registers for a certain amount of time are dropped from the Payees list. Unfortunately, Money has no such feature. When you import a large Quicken file, you may end up with a Payees list as long as a brontosaurus's tail.

The only way to delete payees is to visit the Categories & Payees list and delete them one at a time. Chapter 10 explains how.

Money Offers Help for Quicken Users

So anxious is Microsoft to woo Quicken users to Money, the program offers special help features for converts from Quicken. Choose Help⇨Help for Quicken Users if you've recently made the switch to Money. In the Help window, you will see different topics to help you leap the chasm to become a better user of Money 2003.

Appendix

Installing Microsoft Money 2003

• •

*T*his appendix explains how to install Microsoft Money 2003 on your computer. I'm happy to report that installing and reinstalling the program is as easy as falling off a turnip truck.

Before you install, Microsoft recommends closing all open applications that are currently running and making a backup copy of your old Money files (if you have old Money files). In the course of installing the software, Money asks for your CD-Key (you can find it on the CD case). Be prepared to type in these numbers.

Installing (Or Reinstalling) the Program

If you have already installed a computer program in Windows, you probably don't have to read the following step-by-step instructions because you already know how to install new software. All you have to do is click the Add/Remove Programs icon on the Windows Control Panel and proceed from there. Installing a brand-new copy of Money takes five to 10 minutes, depending on the speed of your computer. In fact, you hardly have to do anything at all if your computer is capable of "auto-running" CDs. If it is, you just put the CD in the computer and twiddle your thumbs while the program installs itself.

Some anti-virus software interferes with the installation of Money. Turn off anti-virus software on your computer before installing the program.

Follow these steps to install Money 2003 or Money 2003 Deluxe:

1. **Go to the Windows Control Panel.**

   In versions of Windows prior to XP, you can get there by clicking the Start button and choosing Settings⇨ Control Panel. On XP, click the Start button and choose Control Panel.

2. **In the Control Panel window, double-click the Add/Remove Programs icon.**

3. **Click the Install button in the Add/Remove Programs Properties dialog box**.

   The next dialog box asks you to insert a floppy disk or CD-ROM in your computer.

4. **Insert the Money 2003 CD-ROM in your computer and click the Next button.**

   You see the Run Installation Program dialog box, and the installation process begins.

   If a dialog box tells you that Windows was unable to locate the installation program, click the Browse button, go to the drive where your CD-ROM is located, find the `setup.exe` file on the CD-ROM, and double-click it.

5. **From this point forward, follow the on-screen instructions to install Money.**

   The Installation program asks you for your name, the CD-Key or Setup number that identifies your copy of the program, and the location where you want to install the program on your computer.

   Unless you are competent enough or have a good reason to install the program elsewhere, be sure to install the program in the default folder that Microsoft recommends, `C:\Program Files\Microsoft Money`. By installing the program in the default folder, you make sure that the program files that you install all work together.

   Twiddle your thumbs while your computer restarts. That wasn't so bad, was it?

The first time you run Money, you see the Microsoft Money Setup Assistant. The Assistant wants to help you set up bank accounts and do the other groundwork so that you can get going with Money 2003. However, you can click the Skip the Setup Assistant and Start Using Money Now link to get going right away. Chapter 1 of this book explains how to get around in Money, and Chapter 2 explains how to set up accounts.

Glossary of Financial Terms

401(k) plan: A tax-deferred retirement plan by which a portion of an employee's pay is deducted from each paycheck and invested. Employees do not have to pay taxes on income from the plan until they start withdrawing it at retirement age.

403(b) plan: A 401(k) plan for public school teachers and employees. See *401(k) plan.*

adjustable-rate mortgage (ARM): A mortgage whose interest rate is changed periodically. Usually, ARMs are tied to a money index such as the prime lending rate.

amortized loan: A loan for which you make regular payments of equal size. With each payment, some money goes toward paying interest on the loan and some goes toward reducing the principal (the amount you borrowed). See *interest* and *principal.*

asset: Something of value that you own, such as a house, stocks, or jewelry. Money that is owed to you is also an asset, as is the money in savings and checking accounts. See also *liability* and *net worth.*

balance: The amount of money in a bank account; also, the amount left to pay off on a debt. In the case of an asset account or investment account, the balance is the worth of the account. The balance on a liability is what you owe.

bond: A paper promise to pay back a debt with interest by a certain date. Governments issue bonds, as do companies. With a standard bond, regular interest payments are made to investors. With a discount bond, the buyer pays less than the face value (also known as the par value) of the bond. When the bond is redeemed, the owner receives the face value or more than the face value if the bond has increased in value. Discount bonds are also known as zero-coupon bonds.

CD (certificate of deposit): A bank deposit in which the depositor agrees to leave the money in the bank for a certain period of time. Banks guarantee a fixed rate of interest on CDs that is higher than the interest rate paid on savings accounts, for example.

closing costs: The appraisal fees, sales commissions, and other fees that are charged when you take out a loan or mortgage. The costs, sometimes called points, are expressed as a percentage of the loan.

cost basis: The total cost of purchasing a security, including commissions, fees, and mutual fund loads.

dividend: From the word *divide,* a portion of a company's earnings that is distributed to the holders of stock in the company. Usually, dividends are paid quarterly.

equity: A house's market value less the amount that is owed on the house. For example, if $100,000 is owed on the house and its market value is $150,000, the owner has $50,000 equity in the house.

escrow account: An account that a mortgage lender takes out on behalf of a borrower to make sure that property taxes, property insurance, and other such fees are paid.

index fund: A mutual fund that invests in all the companies listed in an index such as the S&P 500. Index funds provide returns similar to that by which the index grows or declines.

interest: The cost, expressed as a percentage of the loan amount, for borrowing money. Also, money paid to a lender or bank patron for the use of his or her money. See also *principal.*

IRA (individual retirement account): A tax-deferred retirement plan for employees. The maximum contribution is $3,000 per year. You do not have to pay taxes on income from an IRA until you start withdrawing income from it at retirement age. See also *Roth IRA.*

Keogh plan: A tax-deferred retirement plan for self-employed individuals. Money invested in Keogh plans is tax deductible. Withdrawals are taxed.

liability: A debt that you owe. Credit card debt is an example of a liability, as are taxes owed to the IRS. See also *asset* and *net worth.*

lot: A group of securities purchased simultaneously at the same price. Also a nephew of Abraham whose wife got turned into a saltshaker.

money market fund: An interest-earning mutual fund that invests in Treasury bills and other short-term securities.

mutual fund: An investment company that raises money from shareholders and invests the money in a variety of places, including stocks, bonds, and money market securities.

net worth: What you are worth, not as a human being but as a financial entity. Assets add to net worth; liabilities count against it. See also *asset* and *liability.*

P/E ratio: The price of a stock divided by its per-share earnings. If the price-to-earnings ratio is high, the stock is being traded for its future value, not for its present value, which indicates that the investors are expecting high earnings on the stock.

points: The amount, expressed as a percentage of a loan, that you have to pay to a loan broker or bank to take out a loan. Also called *discount points.*

portfolio: The securities owned by an individual or investment firm.

principal: The actual amount of money borrowed on a loan. The principal is different from the interest, which is the price — expressed as a percentage of the loan amount — that you pay for borrowing the money. See also *interest.*

rollover: When you transfer funds from one investment or retirement account to another. Also, what Beethoven did in an old Chuck Berry song.

Roth IRA: An IRA to which investors can make after-tax contributions. Unlike an IRA, withdrawals from a Roth IRA are tax free because taxes on Roth IRA contributions are paid before the money is contributed. See also *IRA.*

securities: Bonds, stock certificates, and other financial instruments that can be traded and whose value fluctuates.

SEP (Simplified Employee Pension): A retirement plan, similar to an IRA, for the self-employed and small businesses. Money invested in SEPs is tax deductible. Earnings from SEPs are tax deferred.

stock: Shares of ownership in a company. Stocks pay dividends and can be bought and sold. See also *dividend.*

tax deductible: In income tax reporting, expenses that can be deducted from total income.

tax deferred: Refers to income for retirement on which you don't have to pay taxes until you begin withdrawing it at retirement age.

tax-deferred annuity: An annuity for employees of nonprofit and education organizations whereby a part of the employees' income is excluded from taxes and is invested in securities. Tax on income from the annuity is paid when employees withdraw money from the plan.

Index

 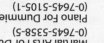

   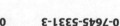        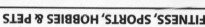

TRAVEL

0-7645-5453-0

0-7645-5438-7

0-7645-5444-1

Italy

Hawaii

Walt Disney World & Orlando

Also available:

France For Dummies (0-7645-6292-4)
Las Vegas For Dummies (0-7645-5448-4)
London For Dummies (0-7645-5416-6)
Mexico's Beach Resorts For Dummies (0-7645-6262-2)
Paris For Dummies (0-7645-5494-8)
RV Vacations For Dummies (0-7645-5443-3)

America's National Parks For Dummies (0-7645-6204-5)
Caribbean For Dummies (0-7645-5445-X)
Cruise Vacations For Dummies 2003 (0-7645-5459-X)
Europe For Dummies (0-7645-5456-5)
Ireland For Dummies (0-7645-6199-5)

EDUCATION & TEST PREPARATION

0-7645-5194-9

0-7645-5325-9

0-7645-5249-X

Spanish

Algebra

U.S. History

Also available:

The ACT For Dummies (0-7645-5210-4)
Chemistry For Dummies (0-7645-5430-1)
English Grammar For Dummies (0-7645-5322-4)
French For Dummies (0-7645-5193-0)
GMAT For Dummies (0-7645-5251-1)
Inglés Para Dummies (0-7645-5427-1)

Italian For Dummies (0-7645-5196-5)
Research Papers For Dummies (0-7645-5426-3)
SAT I For Dummies (0-7645-5472-7)
U.S. History For Dummies (0-7645-5249-X)
World History For Dummies (0-7645-5242-2)

HEALTH, SELF-HELP & SPIRITUALITY

0-7645-5154-X

0-7645-5302-X

0-7645-5418-2

Diabetes

Sex

Parenting

Also available:

The Bible For Dummies (0-7645-5296-1)
Controlling Cholesterol For Dummies (0-7645-5440-9)
Dating For Dummies (0-7645-5072-1)
Dieting For Dummies (0-7645-5126-4)
High Blood Pressure For Dummies (0-7645-5424-7)
Judaism For Dummies (0-7645-5299-6)

Menopause For Dummies (0-7645-5458-1)
Nutrition For Dummies (0-7645-5180-9)
Potty Training For Dummies (0-7645-5417-4)
Pregnancy For Dummies (0-7645-5074-8)
Rekindling Romance For Dummies (0-7645-5303-8)
Religion For Dummies (0-7645-5264-3)